URBAN
LIBERALISM
and
PROGRESSIVE
REFORM

URBAN LIBERALISM and PROGRESSIVE REFORM

JOHN D. BUENKER

The Norton Library
W · W · NORTON & COMPANY · INC ·
NEW YORK

*For Lee, Jeannie, Cathy, Eileen,
Tommy, and Joey, with love*

First published in the Norton Library 1978.

Books That Live

The Norton imprint on a book means that in the publisher's
estimation it is a book not for a single season but for the years.
W. W. Norton & Company, Inc.

Library of Congress Cataloging in Publication Data
Buenker, John D
    Urban liberalism and progressive reform.
    Bibliography: p.
    Includes index.
    1. United States—Politics and government—20th
century. 2. Progressivism (United States politics)
3. Liberalism—United States. I. Title.
E743.B83   1978   320.5'13'0973   77-17267
ISBN 0-393-00880-0

1 2 3 4 5 6 7 8 9 0

TABLE OF CONTENTS

Illustrations between pages 142 and 143

Preface   vii

Chapter 1   The Emergence of Urban Liberalism   1

Chapter 2   Bread and Butter Liberalism: Launching the Welfare State   42

Chapter 3   The Politics of Amelioration: Unions, Business Regulation, and Taxation   80

Chapter 4   Revamping the Political System   118

Chapter 5   An American Kulturkampf: The Birth Pangs of Cultural Pluralism   163

Chapter 6   The Dimensions of Urban Liberalism   198

Notes   240

Bibliography   278

Index   292

PREFACE

The subject of this book is the relationship between two very controversial entities: the Progressive Era and the urban political machine. Both are extremely complex, and the very terms are charged with value judgments. Since there are so many definitions of each, it seems necessary at the outset to clarify the meanings they will have in this study.

The Progressive Era was a period of time beginning in the late nineteenth century and running roughly up until U.S. entry into World War I. It was characterized by so many efforts to cope with the nation's political, social, and economic problems, and to promote "progress," that contemporaries and scholars alike have generally dubbed it "progressive." Fifty years of intensive investigation have failed to establish any consensus on the precise meaning of that elusive word. Even the participants disagreed vociferously about the "progressiveness" of specific pieces of legislation, such as Prohibition, immigration restriction, or the disfranchisement and segregation of southern blacks; nor has anyone agreed on what set of attitudes or positions made a particular individual a "progressive," since the term has been applied to many men holding opposite views on important issues. Even the cumulative effect of the period's reformist efforts has been called into question, with several scholars suggesting that the term "progressive" is really a misnomer. Until someone suggests a more descriptive designation, the solution lies in using the term as infrequently as possible and in the most limited sense. As a general rule, this study refrains from using "progressive" as a description either of an individual political leader or a piece of legislation unless the context is spelled out. "Progressive" is capitalized only when referring either to the Progressive party or the Progressive Era, since the latter is an agreed-upon time span like the Gilded Age or the Roaring Twenties. If used with a small *p*, "progressivism" refers to the reformist surge of the era, irrespective of the group or issue involved. The last chapter is a fairly extensive attempt to provide an interpretation that will account for all the diversity of the era and establish some measure of unity. A complete discussion is a task that requires another book-length study, a project for the future.

The same caveat applies to the terms "liberal" and "urban liberal." Again I have generally tried to avoid using the former in any generic sense, but instead concentrate on attitudes toward specific pieces of legislation. This book's major contention, however, is that "urban liberalism" is a reasonably precise description of the complex of social, economic, and political positions taken by urban new stock lawmakers in the seven states considered over a lengthy time span. These positions were the result of their geographic, socioeconomic, and ethnoreligious backgrounds and consequently distinguished them fairly effectively from others who desired social change. On many issues "urban liberalism" may have been compatible with other brands of "liberalism," but they were not coextensive. In the main, "urban liberalism" included a desire for government intervention in the economy to protect the less fortunate, the welfare state, a tax policy based primarily upon the ability to pay, a "one man, one vote" political philosophy, and a determined opposition to legislated morality. The specifics of those positions constitute the bulk of this work.

Until recently the term "urban political machine" had an almost universally pejorative connotation. The words "boss" and "machine" still conjure images of vote buying, bribery, electoral frauds, and the manipulation of ignorant foreign stock voters by unscrupulous politicians. Without denying in any way the truth of those assertions, many scholars have revealed the picture as a seriously deficient, one-dimensional one. Their views are considered in the text in some detail, so it suffices here to note that the machine emerges not as a diabolical conspiracy of evil men, but as an institutional outgrowth of the urban environment performing many vital functions that might otherwise have been left undone. Some authorities have even concluded that bosses and machines were more socially beneficial in such areas as welfare, race and ethnic relations, and personalized government than the so-called reform administrations.

The present study seeks to shed light on another aspect of machine politics, the attitude of the boss and his followers toward reform legislation. Prevailing opinion has usually characterized machine politicians as unabashed conservatives, in league with business interests and opposed to any forward-looking legislation. Yet even a casual observer of politics understands that, at least since the days of the New Deal, urban politicians and voters have been the mainstay of liberal causes. It seems that at least some inklings of those trends might have been manifested in the earlier reform era as well. In 1962 J. Joseph Huthmacher produced a pathfinding essay that sought to resolve that dilemma by arguing that machine politicians did indeed make valuable contributions to reform efforts before the First World War. Since then other scholars have discovered evidence of that contention in such far-flung places as New York, California, Baltimore, and Detroit, to name but a few. This book is an attempt to demonstrate that these were not aberrations or isolated instances, but rather parts of a general pattern that Huthmacher dubbed "urban liberalism." Together with the excellent studies that have appeared on the nature and function of the urban political machine, it may serve to correct the simplistically negative attitude that has often barred intelligent discussion of the role of the boss and the machine. To write off a tradition that produced men of such national stature as Al Smith, both Robert Wagners, the three Kennedys, David I. Walsh, and Justice Frank Murphy, among others, is to ignore a very vital source of present-day liberalism.

In the course of more than seven years of investigating urban liberalism, I was fortunate to produce a number of articles dealing with various aspects of the question. I am grateful to the editors of the following journals for permission to incorporate the ideas, information, and, in some cases, the language of those articles into this manuscript: *The Journal of American History, Mid-America, The Historian, New England Quarterly, Ohio History, New Jersey History, New York Historical Society Quarterly, Rhode Island History, Journal of the Illinois State Historical Society*, and *The Connecticut Historical Society Bulletin.* The full citations appear in the appropriate notes and in the bibliography.

The research was partly funded by grants from the Eastern Illinois University Council on Faculty Research and the Wisconsin Alumni Research Foundation. Most of the work was done in the libraries of the University of Illinois, Eastern Illinois University, and the University of Wisconsin-Parkside, and I would like to acknowledge the assistance of their very capable staffs, especially Alice Cooper and Betty Hartbank of E.I.U. and Judith Hamilton of U.W.P. My thanks also to Joyce Maurer, Karen Gombar, Grace Zdanowicz, Sue Gursky, and Hari Barker, who typed the manuscript at various stages of its evolution. A special acknowledgment is due to Elisabeth Krabisch, Elsie Kearns, and Barbara Wood of Charles Scribner's Sons for their enthusiasm for the project and the efficiency with which they facilitated its publication.

Over the years I have benefited from the work of countless scholars, and my indebtedness is partly reflected in my notes. Many of the concepts were sharpened by discussions with my E.I.U. and U.W.P. colleagues, especially Professors Donald Tingley, John Keiser, David Maurer, Leonard Wood, Bill Murin, Mike Holmes, Paul Toews, and Thomas Reeves. My greatest intellectual debt is to my teacher and mentor, Professor J. Joseph Huthmacher of the University of Delaware, who pioneered in this field and taught me to look at the Progressive Era and all of U.S. history from a much different perspective. It is my fervent hope that this book justifies in some small measure the faith he has always expressed in his "uppity graduate student."

Finally there are the debts I owe to my various families

which can never be repaid in any coin but love and appreciation. My parents and my brother, Professor Robert Buenker of the University of Nebraska, nurtured and sustained me in my formative years, and instilled in me the essentials of urban liberalism by their own experience; years of study may have refined these convictions, but they have not altered them. My in-laws, Tom and Ruth O'Leary, encouraged me along the way, and my major regret is that Tom, journalist *extraordinaire,* did not live to read the final result. My wife Lee provided stimulating discussion, sympathy, love, and the nucleus of our own political machine—Jeannie, Cathy, Eileen, Tommy, and Joey.

JOHN D. BUENKER

CHAPTER 1

The Emergence of
Urban Liberalism

Urban new stock lawmakers, acting primarily through the medium of the Democratic party, emerged as the major progressive force in several industrial states. Although this phenomenon could be traced to developments before the Civil War, the full impact was not felt nationally until the New Deal years. However, in New York, New Jersey, Connecticut, Rhode Island, Massachusetts, Ohio, and Illinois, the implications were already clear by the second decade of the twentieth century.

English Protestants had first settled these states; they developed the resources and gained control of the means of production. They also established each state's political framework and set its cultural tone, based largely upon the ethos of Calvinist Protestantism. From 1830 on, successive waves of immigrants challenged the security of the English Protestant descendants. Between 1815 and 1914 an estimated thirty-five million newcomers entered the United States, the great bulk of them settling in the Northeast. By 1910 only 16.3 percent of the nation's population was foreign-born, and 23.1 percent was second-generation American; but in New England the respective figures were 28 and 31.7 percent, and in the Middle Atlantic region, 25.6 and 29.6 percent. The so-called Old Immigrants, from Britain, Ireland, Germany, and Scandinavia, predominated from 1830 to 1885. Many of these readily assimilated the native culture or moved to the frontier where their presence seemed less alarming.

The Irish poured into the cities of the East and Midwest where they evoked a virulent nativist reaction in the 1850s. The 1880s brought a steady shift in the origins of immigration to southern and eastern Europe and French Canada, to peoples who differed significantly from both natives and Old Immigrants and who seemed to pose a severe threat to the relative well-being of both.[1] The most striking demographic fact about the New Immigrants, like the Old Immigrant Irish, was their tendency to settle in urban areas. Although generally peasants in their homeland, most of the new arrivals lacked either the resources or the desire to resume agrarian life. Arriving at a time when available land was scarce and agriculture mechanized, most sought work as unskilled laborers in the burgeoning industrial metropolises. Their natural desire to band together and preserve Old World traditions and religious practices also kept them from becoming too widely dispersed. By 1910 only 22.1 percent of the nation's population lived in cities of over 100,000 population, but 43.6 percent of its foreign-born residents did. In the New England and Middle Atlantic states over 45 percent of the foreign-born lived in cities of over a quarter of a million people, and 30 percent resided in urban centers having half a million residents or more.

Immigrants and their children comprised upwards of two-thirds of the population of most major northeastern cities and more than three-fourths of the population of New York, Boston, and Chicago. In New Bedford and Fall River, Massachusetts, the figures were a near staggering 87 and 83 percent, respectively. The 1910 census showed that most new stock groups were at least 70 percent urban, the Irish and Russian Jews topping the list at well over 80 percent.[2]

For the most part these urban arrivals, whether of the Old or New Immigration, shared a common experience and met similar hostilities. Lacking skills and feared by native laborers as threats to their employment, male immigrants were usually the "last hired and first fired." The work they could find was frequently dangerous, monotonous, and poorly compensated, circumstances that repeatedly compelled the women and children to seek employment as well. If he was ill, injured, or laid off, the new stock worker found himself without adequate income.

The new arrivals were forced into substandard housing in sections of the city seemingly reserved for their own ethnic group. Higher education and advancement into the white-collar world was extremely difficult because of the need for youthful employment and the social discrimination exercised by professional and business elites. The urban immigrant also found his customs and religious beliefs subjected to stringent attack from many quarters of the native population, ranging from those who wished to ostracize him completely from polite society to those who sought to remake him in the image of English Protestantism.[3]

Beset by hostility and discrimination on virtually all sides, the immigrant gradually found that he possessed at least one commodity that some native Americans coveted: his vote. The phenomenal expansion of the city emphasized the need for a wide variety of services, a need that a plethora of entrepreneurs were willing to fill—for a price. The archaic governmental structure and the almost total control exercised by the state legislatures made it virtually impossible for most cities to perform these services. A new breed of professional politicians arose to act as brokers among the economic groups, and to "get things done" in spite of the archaic political structure. Often these politicians united the elements in a divided society in "the only manner in which they could be united: by paying them off." The development of universal male suffrage required broad popular support and the large mass of pliable foreign stock voters admirably filled the bill. The native politicians soon found that by performing basic services for the immigrants they could secure their political allegiance. The natural leaders of the immigrants quickly discovered that they could exchange a bloc of votes for considerations that the existing social and economic order otherwise failed or refused to provide. This dependence formed the cement for what was popularly known as the urban political machine, and what the late Richard Hofstadter termed the "boss-machine-immigrant complex." [4]

The machine performed various functions for the immigrant. Employment was his most pressing need and the most common political arrangement was the exchange of votes for jobs both in government and with private businesses holding city contracts. In addition, the machine's minions also became "pioneers in social work" at a time when public assistance was unheard-of and private charity wholly inadequate to the task. The ideal, according to Martin Lomasney of Boston, probably the most famous ward leader in the nation, was that there should be "in every ward a guy that any bloke can go to when he's in trouble and get help—not justice and the law, but help." A bucket of coal, a basket of food, a rent payment, funeral expenses, clothing, and other material benefits were made available to those in need, as were interventions with the law such as providing bail, cutting the red tape to receive a license or permit, or getting charges dismissed.[5]

Beyond this the machine provided a career ladder for many immigrants and their children. Politics, whatever its status in the days of the founding fathers, had become a profession held in low repute by more advantaged peoples. It was also one in which performance—the ability to deliver votes—counted much more than background or preparation. Like show business, professional athletics, and the rackets, politics enabled ambitious immigrants to rise to positions of wealth, power, and security when more respectable avenues were blocked. In the beginning, most ethnic groups had to deal with "outside politicians," natives who held power and bargained for immigrant votes. In time the immigrants themselves supplanted the natives in the hierarchy of both party and government. By the time the political scientist Harold Zink finished his well-known study on twenty prominent city bosses in 1931, he found that five of them were immigrants and ten others were second-generation Americans, and that "there seems to be some relationship between the racial stock of municipal bosses and the dominant racial group of foreign origin in their cities." The contacts made in politics opened the doors to business and social opportunities for themselves and their children that would otherwise have been closed. In a larger sense, also, the advancement of an ethnic politician bred "a kind of group patronage," giving his compatriots greater visibility, enhanced prestige, renewed self-respect, and an influential friend at court. The astute urban politician cultivated the immigrant's ethnic pride by defending him against nativist attack, observing his customs, and concerning himself with conditions in the homeland. Mostly, the machine played "the politics of recognition," granting political office and party positions to representatives of any ethnic group large enough to merit consideration.[6]

The political machine performed functions for the immigrant that were more subtle but no less real. Old-fashioned ward politicians made it their business to know their constituents as individuals and at least to give the impression that government was responsive to people's needs. Lomasney personally worked an eighteen-hour day, while the Pendergast machine in Kansas City "had its captains and lieutenants running down to every block," and Tammany Hall had one committeeman for every fifteen voters. "Votes like babies, require both time and labor to produce," a Philadelphia ward leader once philosophized. "Neither are dropped down chimneys by storks." In the strange, impersonal world of machines and concrete, the ward politician was one of the few people who provided "humanization of the often difficult process of settlement." The political clubhouse, often located over, behind, or next door to a saloon, was one of the social centers of immigrant life, while the picnics and outings provided high spots of the "social" year in most wards. Since the nation was seemingly content to trust the assimilation and civic training of the immigrant to the same winds of chance that it assigned his physical well-being, the machine again took up the slack. Naturalization and voter registration were primarily accomplished by the politicians, even though the more respectable elements in society often railed at the results. Despite important shortcomings, the urban political machine was one of the major institutions providing political and social integration for millions of immigrants. Over sixty years ago Henry Jones Ford judged the ward politician "probably the secret of the powerful solvent influence which American civilization exerts upon the enormous deposits of alien populations thrown upon this country by the torrent of emigration." [7]

All told, the political system provided ethnic minorities with vital benefits that the economic and social order often denied them. None achieved more success by this route than the Irish. The cause of their outstanding political aptitude was a combination of the experiences of the Old World and the New. They spoke the language, thanks to the British substitution of English for Gaelic in their schools. They possessed political experience, since the forty-shilling free-holder voting system in Ireland (before it was repealed in 1829) permitted landlords to lead their tenants to the polls and oversee their votes. This practice of bargaining with overlords who despised their religion and traditions equipped the Irish for a similar situation in the United States, and their occasional victories in the old country, such as Catholic emancipation, awakened them to the possibilities inherent in politics. Old World experience also taught that informal government arrangements were often more important than the formal structure, a lesson well learned in the heyday of machine politics. Moreover, the Irish arrived in great numbers within a short span of time and settled en masse in the largest cities, thus giving their vote maximum effect. The sense of discipline and camaraderie engendered both by religious practice and the struggle against Britain stood them in good stead, as did their gregarious personality traits. In sum, the Irish excelled in politics because "no other group has shown the flair and skill and group cohesiveness." [8]

Existing conditions also caused the Irish to become rabid partisans of the Democratic party. Their association of government with British oppression inclined them to seek membership in the party that professed to believe in decentralization. The proportionately high number of nativists within the Whig and Republican parties reinforced this conviction, as did the determined wooing of Democratic leaders on the local level. Not even the issues of abolition and disunion seriously dented the immigrants' Democratic affiliation, for Republican reformers often embraced such other issues as Sunday observance, temperance, and immigration restriction, while free black labor was held to be a threat to the tenuous Irish hold on the bottom rung of the socioeconomic ladder. The association of the Democratic party with secession led to the defection of many old stock Americans, thus facilitating the progress of Irishmen to positions of leadership. The three-time candidacy of the agrarian William Jennings Bryan and the GOP's success in establishing itself as the spokesman for industrial Americans added to the depletion of Yankee Democratic ranks in the urban centers of the nation. In Providence the percentage of Irish-Americans on the Democratic ward committees jumped from 35 to 73 in the decade of the 1890s. In many major cities the Democratic hierarchy "read like the Limerick telephone directory" by the Progressive years, and Irish candidates predominated on state and local tickets. Irish-American bosses ran the Democratic party in most major cities and many of their number became influential in national party politics as well, such as Roger Sullivan of Illinois, Thomas Taggart of Indiana, Charles F. Murphy of New York, "Big Jim" Smith of New Jersey, and Martin Lomasney and John F. Fitzgerald of Massachusetts. By 1910 the term "Democrat" had become almost as synonymous with "Irish" as the term "Catholic" was.[9]

The other components of the Old Immigration are more difficult to categorize. Many apparently leaned toward the Democratic party during the Know-Nothing hysteria of the 1850s, but the British immigrants especially were generally

accepted by the nativists and joined in the latter's denuncia-
tions of the despised Irish. Since much of the thrust of the
pre–Civil War anti-immigrant feeling was anti-Catholic, the
German communicants of that faith were often compelled to
side with their Irish coreligionists. The free soil issue, along
with antipathy toward the Irish, apparently attracted most
British, Scandinavian, and German Protestants to the GOP,
where they tended to remain for many decades to come.
Recent studies have demonstrated that religious differences
along the lines of "ritualism" and "pietism" also had a
marked effect on political affiliation. The adherents of the
ritualistic religions, such as Catholics and many German
Lutherans, were inclined to accept the world as they found it,
eschewing attempts to uplift or reform it through moral
crusades like abolitionism, Prohibitionism, and Sabbatarianism. The pietistic religions, on the other hand, were generally
attracted to such movements because of their more activist
orientation. Consequently the ritualists tended to favor the
Democratic party with its traditional antigovernment position, while the pietists were much more likely to join the
more activist Republican party. Although many members of
the Old Immigration rose to positions of prominence in the
Republican party in the late nineteenth century, the leadership of the organization remained largely in Yankee hands.[10]

The onset of the so-called New Immigration in the 1880s
set off a vigorous competition between the two major parties
in the industrial states for the loyalty of the latest arrivals. In
this struggle, which lasted until the late 1920s, the predominantly old stock leadership of the Republican party had
certain undeniable advantages. The GOP's staunch alliance
with big business and its association of a high tariff and other
proindustry policies with jobs and a full dinner pail proved
very persuasive to people whose economic existence was
precarious. This was especially true in those mill towns of
New England where the entire local economy depended
upon a few industries; French-Canadian and eastern European employees were almost literally "under the thumb of
Yankee mill owners." Moreover, the old stock Republican

leaders did not need either the status or the income yielded by their political positions nearly as much as the Irish because of their socioeconomic standing in the private sector; they therefore often proved more willing to slate minority group candidates for public office. The Irish unwittingly aided the Republican cause by their attitude toward the later arrivals. Feeling threatened from below at a time when they were still despised from above, the Irish often vented their frustrations on the people beneath them in the social scale. Many Irish politicians were unwilling to share the prestige and spoils of office with the New Immigrants, while Irish bishops and priests imposed their peculiar brand of Catholicism upon peoples whose own religious traditions were often much different. Non-Catholics among the New Immigrants, such as the Bohemians, often brought their Old World antipathy to the Roman church with them and transferred it to that Irish-dominated institution in the United States.[11]

There were also Republican organizations that made special efforts to gain the support of the New Immigrants. In Pennsylvania, state GOP leaders Matthew Quay and Boies Penrose financed the American Association of Foreign Language Newspapers which awarded lucrative advertising contracts to the immigrant press in return for editorial support. The Pennsylvania organization's urban adjutants, William S. Flinn and Christopher Lyman Magee in Pittsburgh and the Vare brothers in Philadelphia, were so successful in wooing new stock voters that they even co-opted many Irish politicians and made the Democratic party a subsidiary of the dominant GOP. In San Francisco, Abe Ruef, the notorious "Curly Boss," helped create the Union Labor party as an adjunct of the Republican organization, thereby gaining the allegiance of the majority of the city's workers, including many Irish-Americans. Hazen Pingree, four-time mayor of Detroit, detached the city's Germans and eastern Europeans from their Democratic moorings by his patronage and recognition policies, as well as by his social and economic programs. In New Haven the

Ullman brothers, of German Jewish descent, labored judi-
ciously among the city's Italians and played skillfully upon
their resentment of the Irish who controlled the Democratic
party. In Rhode Island the GOP leadership openly courted
the support of the state's sizable French-Canadian population by running gubernatorial candidates Emery San Souci
and Aram Pothier in the early twentieth century. In the
Massachusetts mill towns, the so-called "labor legislators,"
old stock and Old Immigrant union officials who were
Republicans, gained the following of their New Immigrant
constituents by defending them against discrimination and
sponsoring socioeconomic legislation in their behalf.[12]

The Irish Democrats also possessed important assets in
attracting New Immigrant votes. They most resembled the
New Immigrants in their patterns of settlement and in their
distribution in the work force. They had suffered the same
kinds of discrimination and deprivation; this gave them a
certain empathy with the plight of the more recent arrivals,
even if it did not always develop into sympathy. Their shared
religious ties, while productive of many intrafaith disputes,
were in the long run a bond, giving both a similar outlook on
a wide variety of questions. Attacks on the church's doctrines
or practices tended to draw the Irish and the Catholic New
Immigrants closer together. Perhaps most importantly, the
Irish were the strategic middlemen in American society,
occupying so many positions that almost automatically gave
them political influence with the foreign-born: factory fore-
men, construction bosses, labor organizers, civil servants,
priests, policemen, firemen, and political functionaries. In
these positions day-to-day contacts occasioned resentments
that reverberated to the advantage of their political opponents if done badly, but, if properly handled, gave the Irish
tremendous electoral leverage. Not all those newer immigrant groups who resented Irish domination of the Democratic party reacted by becoming Republicans, either. The
Bohemians in Chicago, for example, were militantly anti-
Irish but they remained heavily Democratic in their loyalties,
and united behind Anton Cermak to try to wrest control of

the party from their antagonists. The Jews and Italians in New York City seem to have leaned to the Democratic side despite their disagreement with the Irish, while most of Chicago's ethnic groups, with the exception of Germans, Scandinavians, and Negroes, inclined that way also.[13]

Indeed, certain Irish political leaders displayed a great talent for winning the loyalty of the New Immigrants. Johnny Powers, the notorious Chicago ward leader, adjusted to the Italian influx in his neighborhood so well that he became known as "Johnny De Pow" and "Gianni Pauli," and was able to hold power until well into the twenties. Mayor Edward F. Dunne vigorously championed Chicago's recent immigrants in his speeches and writings. Martin Lomasney enjoyed phenomenal support from the Jews, Italians, and Negroes in his Boston ward and was very careful to slate members of each group for public office. His contemporary, John F. Fitzgerald, earned a reputation as a staunch defender of the same groups against discrimination and slander, and James Michael Curley became a favorite of Boston's Italian and Jewish newcomers. In New York Charles F. Murphy took on German and Jewish advisers, while Al Smith enjoyed very cordial relations with several ethnic minorities, especially Jews. Since machines were organized territorially, they "collapsed if they failed to adjust as the drift of population altered the character of the neighborhoods." Irish Democrats controlled certain cities, notably New York and Boston, so completely that there was little or no choice for the New Immigrants. The Republican party had become simply a gentlemen's club with memberships limited largely to the silk stocking districts and the Back Bay. Since it rarely achieved local power, the GOP in such places had little to offer the city's disadvantaged minorities.[14]

The Democrats generally won the struggle for the allegiance of the New Immigrant, and the victory gave them electoral supremacy in the major industrial states for decades to come. That accomplishment, however, was largely the result of the bitter ethnoreligious struggles of the 1920s, the candidacy of Al Smith, the Great Depression, and the New Deal, all of which lay well in the future. During the Progressive Era the issue was still very much in doubt, but in retrospect it seems that the basic composition of the Republican party severely limited its potential as an instrument for the advancement of the urban new stock working class.

Despite the efforts of men like Pingree, the Vares, the Ullmans, and the Massachusetts labor legislators, the GOP in the major industrial states was essentially a coalition of those segments of society most inimical to immigrant progress: the business interests and the old stock Americans inhabiting the small towns and the better residential sections of the cities. Businessmen generally looked to the Republican party as their main line of defense against taxation, regulation, and welfare measures. Even more adamantly, they relied upon the GOP to blunt the drive for recognition by organized labor. Since any significant accretion in the political power of the urban working class might facilitate these developments, business leaders were more inclined to rely upon rural and small town legislators who were under little pressure from their constituents to alter the economic status quo. These legislators also feared the rise of urban, immigrant America because they saw in it a powerful threat to their own political and cultural hegemony. Accordingly, they looked to the Republican party to fend off any measures augmenting urban political leverage and to combat the pernicious influence of alien customs and beliefs. This mutual fear of the urban new stock working class, then, generally welded the Republican party in the populous industrial states into a union of "business interests and rural Yankees" who came together for "cultural-religious, as well as political, and perhaps at times economic, self-protection." [15]

There were a few issues that threatened this marriage of convenience from time to time, but they were generally resolved in favor of the proclivities of the old stock, small town American. Business, for example, was loath to support immigration restriction because it desired a continuation of the flow of cheap foreign labor. By the second decade of the century, however, the growing militancy of the working class converted many businessmen, and the GOP moved to favor restriction. Many business leaders also opposed Prohibition as representing an unwarranted interference with a profitable business that might set a precedent for additional "socialistic" infringements upon property rights. When ultimately forced to choose, by the time of the Eighteenth Amendment, the business-oriented leadership of the Republican party often yielded to the demands of its most faithful constituents. In a crisis, the old stock, small town Republican lawmaker could generally be relied upon to uphold the prerogatives of the business community, while the latter could usually be expected to defer to the cultural and religious proclivities its leaders shared with traditional America.[16]

The major political condition fostering the Republican coalition of urban business interests and villagers in many states was the apportionment system, which generally overrepresented the rural and small town districts and underrepresented the urban ones. Much of this distortion was the result of failure to reapportion to accommodate the tremendous expansion in city population. In many cases, deliberate limitations placed upon urban representation transformed at least one house of the legislature into a rural bulwark. By far the worst conditions were in the "rotten boroughs of New England." Despite the dramatic growth of its cities, the lower house of the Connecticut General Assembly had not been reapportioned since 1818, at which time New Britain and Bridgeport did not even exist and New Haven and Hartford were scarcely more than overgrown villages. In 1818 nearly all towns, regardless of population, received the right to two representatives, except those that had customarily sent only one. This was amended in the 1870s so that only towns of over 5,000 people were entitled to two representatives and only those with at least 2,500 residents were entitled to one, but since the statutes permitted existing towns to retain their current representation the impact of the change was slight. By 1910 the situation was so inequitable that such towns as

Warren and Union, with respective populations of 412 and
322, had the same number of representatives as New Haven,
Hartford, and Bridgeport, whose populations were in excess
of 100,000 and heavily new stock. Contemporaries estimated
that a scant 12 percent of the state's population could elect a
majority of the lawmakers in the lower house. The senate had
been reapportioned in 1901 and 1903 to reflect population
distribution a little more faithfully, but the largest senatorial district contained seven times the population of the
smallest, and it still took only about one-third of the state's
voters to elect a senate majority.[17]

In neighboring Rhode Island, where only 29.5 percent of
the population was native-born of native parents, the apportionment system proved an equally effective weapon against
immigrant control. The new stock population was centered
in the highly populous Providence-Pawtucket area, in Woonsocket, and in a number of mill towns, but the distribution of
legislative seats effectively neutralized its political influence.
In the senate each of the state's thirty-nine towns was
allotted only one seat, so that West Greenwich, population
481, had the same representation as Providence, which had
224,326 people in 1910 and represented 40 percent of the
entire state's population. Since nearly all of the metropolis's
voters were immigrants or children of immigrants, the effects
are clear enough. The twenty smallest towns, with a combined total of 7.5 percent of the population and overwhelmingly Yankee, were in a position to control deliberations in
the upper house, prompting future Democratic congressman
George O'Shaunessy, an Irish immigrant from Providence, to
observe that the senate "is a strong power exercised by the
abandoned farms of Rhode Island." The lower house more
accurately reflected population distribution, but still created
considerable distortions by stipulating a minimum and
maximum number of representatives for each incorporated
area. Providence, for example, was limited to one-fourth the
total number of representatives, no matter what its population might become.[18]

Although Connecticut and Rhode Island were extreme

examples of legislative malapportionment, the situation in other industrial states differed mostly in degree. Boston and the other major cities of Massachusetts fared better than the urban centers of Connecticut and Rhode Island, but the New England tradition of representation by town still provided considerable protection for small town interests. In New Jersey, where the six northern counties of Hudson, Essex, Passaic, Union, Bergen, and Middlesex contained two-thirds of the state's population and three-fourths of its new stock inhabitants, urban elements were generally able to control the lower house of the General Assembly. Senate apportionment, however, allotted one seat to each of the state's twenty-one counties, placing the balance of power clearly in the hands of the old stock, rural populace. In New York, upstate interests had succeeded in limiting New York City to a fixed percentage of seats in the senate, making the upper house, in Al Smith's aphorism, "constitutionally Republican." In Illinois, too, downstate legislators generally succeeded in holding Chicago to a significantly lower number of representatives in both houses than its population might have dictated. Chicago Republicans also reaped advantage from the practice of cumulative voting for the lower house, which permitted voters to cast all their ballots for a single candidate and assured the GOP one representative even in many heavily Democratic districts. Ohio generally underrepresented its major areas, although the Republican party, except in Cleveland, was almost as dominant in the state's cities as it was in the rural areas. Reapportionment by a Democratic legislature after the 1910 census, however, added to the representation of the major urban centers after many years of Republican opposition.[19]

The importance of legislative apportionment was exacerbated by the inordinate power the state assembly exercised over the cities and their populations. Most cities were unable to alter their form of government, change their tax rate, regulate the price of utilities, or change the terms of service contracts without going through the state legislature. In many states, city officials were even appointed by the

General Assembly, and legislators occasionally punished uncooperative mayors by curtailing their right to choose their own subordinates. Between 1867 and 1870 the New York Legislature passed more laws for cities than did the English Parliament between 1835 and 1885; the city, said colorful Tammanyite George Washington Plunkitt, was "pie for the hayseeds." Although the Illinois constitution of 1870 augmented municipal power somewhat, the city of Chicago was still unable to grant concessions "for checking hats or selling popcorn on the new municipal pier without a special act of the state legislature. The city was the captive of the state and no meaningful municipal reform was possible without control of the General Assembly." [20]

In this antiurban atmosphere the Republican party constructed the statewide organizations that held sway in most of the Northeast between the Civil War and the Great Depression. Civil War General Charles R. Brayton devised the highly successful GOP party machinery in Rhode Island, based primarily "on the good old American stock out in the country." Although blind and holding no state office, he was still able to control the deliberations of the General Assembly by giving orders to the Republican leadership from his armchair in the office of the high sheriff of Providence, just off the legislative floor. Brayton dictated the choice of small town men as committee chairmen "because these were the 'old codgers' the General trusted. He didn't have much use for city slickers, who were likely to be Democrats anyway." As a director of several important corporations and an ally of Nelson W. Aldrich, Brayton was primarily concerned with fostering the state's industries, and he skillfully harmonized this end with a defense of small town Yankee political and cultural hegemony.

High on his list was the Republicans' insistence upon property qualifications for voting in common council elections, a tactic that disfranchised an estimated 60 percent of the electorate and guaranteed Republican control of city government even though the Democrats elected many mayors. Through "Brayton's Law," passed in 1901, the malapportioned, inevitably Republican legislature exercised veto power over the appointments of the popularly elected governor, with the right to appoint their own candidate instead. Brayton also undercut potential Democratic strength by running "safe" French-Canadians like six-term Governor Aram Pothier, a banker and industrial promoter.[21]

The same situation generally prevailed in neighboring Connecticut where the equally astute J. Henry Roraback led the Republican forces. Born in a small town and the president of the Connecticut Power and Light Company, Roraback was the personification of the alliance that ruled the state. As chairman and treasurer of the state central committee and a Republican national committeeman, he was virtual dictator of activities in the state capitol. From his suite in the Allyn House, he managed the legislature in measures defending the political, social, and economic status quo. Since legislative committees were joint ones, the Republican dominance of the lower house guaranteed them a majority membership even when the Democrats managed to squeeze out a narrow margin in the senate. As in Rhode Island, the Connecticut GOP had a small number of urban new stock legislators but they were a decided minority among a phalanx of Yankees.[22]

Elsewhere in New England the situation was much the same. In Maine and New Hampshire the Republicans welded the interests of the state's mineral and timber barons to those of its old stock population, both of which feared the potential of the Irish and French-Canadian laborers. Power was more evenly divided in Massachusetts, where the control of the Democratic party by the Irish alienated many in the newer immigrant communities, while the economic control exercised by Yankee Republicans in the mill towns attracted them. Still, the leadership of the GOP was provided by the best families of Massachusetts, and "in the rural towns and suburban cities (where the Yankees were still in the majority), almost uniformly, Republicans were the managers of municipal government." In the General Court, except for the small number of labor legislators, the Republican roll calls were largely devoid of names that would not have graced the commonwealth in colonial times.[23]

The Republican organization in the Empire State was fundamentally an anti–New York City coalition, perfected largely by U.S. Senator Thomas C. Platt. New York was by far the wealthiest state in the Union and Platt found early in his career that business leaders, "although they were constantly seeking government favor, were too loath to come under government control," and that "party funds were available to those who were regarded 'safe' by the big business interests." This connection between the GOP and the state's corporations was spectacularly revealed by Theodore Roosevelt in a quarrel with Platt's successor William Barnes in 1914, but the exposé failed to shake the party loyalty of most upstate New Yorkers because it was offset by the corruption of the Tammany Democrats. Except for a few large cities, upstate New York was heavily old stock and fearful of the alien masses that constituted almost 80 percent of the population of the metropolis at the mouth of the Hudson. "It is little wonder," Harold Gosnell observed in his book on the Platt machine, "that the inhabitants of the upstate regions, with their Protestant faith, their native parentage, and their local traditions running back a hundred years or more, looked with condescension upon the polyglot population of the great city." Hence the Platt group was careful to set the GOP on an anticity, anti–new stock course which guaranteed "the blind allegiance of the great mass of upstate farmers and shopkeepers to the Republican tradition." This orientation eventually led the GOP to a reactionary stance during the administration of Charles Whitman, governor from 1915 to 1919, when Republicans tried to undo many of the reforms enacted by the Democrats in the previous four years of the Progressive Era. Their fear, as one upstate senator expressed it, was of the "proletarians . . . crowding the seaboard cities. They elect legislators and are strong enough in number to enforce their demands for equality, according to their ideas, which are not American ideas." [24]

Elsewhere in the Northeast the divisions were less clear-cut, but the general orientation of the GOP was much the same. In New Jersey the party held its own in the struggle with the Irish Democrats for the votes of the foreign stock people in the six populous northern counties, thanks to the efforts of the machines of Colonel Sam Dickinson in Jersey City and Major Carl Lentz in Newark. Republican control of the other fifteen counties, however, gave the party almost unbroken control of the senate and a solid base in statewide contests. Their motto, well expressed by GOP Boss David Baird of Camden, was "never trust anyone who lives north of the Shrewsbury River." The GOP in Pennsylvania, developed by Simon Cameron, Matthew Quay, and Boies Penrose, was the most powerful party organization in the nation. Closely tied with the Pennsylvania Manufacturers Association, the party pursued an unswervingly conservative course for decades. "Callous, cynical, and indifferent to measures designed to lessen the burdens of the toiling masses [Penrose] served the vested interests with unceasing devotion." The efforts of the Vares, Flinn, and Magee secured the allegiance of the polyglot populations of Philadelphia and Pittsburgh, but the party's really solid source of strength "lay between these two metropolises in the rural districts." The Democratic party was captive, "nationally notorious for its alliance with the Republicans." [25]

The Ohio Republican organization was almost as all-inclusive as its Pennsylvania counterpart before the onset of the Progressive Era. The two most powerful Republicans in the state at the turn of the century were Joseph B. Foraker of Cincinnati, a wealthy attorney for Standard Oil, and Marcus A. Hanna, a powerful Cleveland industrialist. Although feuding over patronage and other benefits, Foraker and Hanna both labored to convince the state's business magnates that the GOP was "created in their own image." Through their lieutenants, such as George B. Cox in Cincinnati, they sought the new stock working class vote, but their greatest source of strength lay in the small town and countryside areas where, as Brand Whitlock reminisced, "one became, in Urbana and in Ohio, for many years, a Republican just as an Eskimo dons fur clothes." At its height, the party organization extended its sway "into every courthouse and city hall in Ohio." Foraker, in particular, was prone to appeal to the state's old stock Protestants by his stands on Prohibition and Sabbatarianism. As the Progressive spirit swept the cities up in a revolt against traditional business-Republican rule, the basic orientation of the GOP state machine became even more evident. It was heightened still further by a violent anti-Catholic reaction in the hinterlands at the presence of Irish Catholics on the statewide Democratic ticket, and by the Prohibition issue, for Ohio was the home of the Anti-Saloon League. As in New York under Whitman, the administration of Governor Frank Willis from 1915 to 1917 was essentially a rural Republican reaction sandwiched between two periods of urban Democratic progressive rule.[26]

Senator James McMillan, a Detroit traction magnate, and other industrialists ran the Michigan Republican party, but the GOP assiduously cultivated the outstate vote by its stand on Prohibition and generally won without carrying Detroit or Wayne County. In Illinois the Republicans were also successful in holding power during the Progressive Era, losing it only as a result of the Roosevelt-Taft split in 1912. They also did a better job of retaining the loyalty of some ethnic minorities in Chicago; by uniting their votes to those of the "country towns," Republicans were often able to control Cook County, if not the city itself. Outside the Chicago area, only a few larger cities downstate and the southernmost tier of counties had Democratic proclivities. As in Ohio, the offering of Democratic Catholic statewide candidates for office in 1912, 1914, and 1916 strengthened the Republican loyalty of old stock and many non-Catholic immigrant groups both in Chicago and downstate, as did the turmoil over Prohibition. Clearly, the Republican party in the major industrial states was based fundamentally upon a business–old stock–rural Protestant complex, even though it

THE EMERGENCE OF URBAN LIBERALISM

frequently could count upon large adjuncts among the foreign stock working class in the cities.[27]

Those Republicans who did emanate from urban new stock constituencies experienced growing discomfort within their party as many of the issues during the Progressive Era provoked labor-management, urban-rural, and native-immigrant dichotomies. The Massachusetts labor legislators found themselves viewed with increasing suspicion by the party of Henry Cabot Lodge and Winthrop Murray Crane, and often voted with the Irish Democrats on labor and cultural issues. The party leadership regarded them as Democrats in disguise and never permitted them to enter the ruling circle. Their counterparts in nearby Connecticut and Rhode Island had similar experiences, exacerbated by the fact that they themselves were often Italian, Jewish, or French-Canadian. New York City's Republican assemblymen often represented the silk stocking districts, but those who did not frequently deserted party leadership on such vital issues as the Sixteenth, Seventeenth, and Eighteenth Amendments. Hazen Pingree, a champion of the immigrant working class both as mayor of Detroit and governor of Michigan, found his efforts constantly undermined by the McMillan alliance's control of rural Republican legislators. He and his successors did bring the GOP to a slightly more prourban stance, but the basic antagonism remained. Toledo's pro–working class mayor, Samuel ("Golden Rule") Jones, was severely hamstrung by legislators of his own Republican party who restricted his appointive power. When he sought the GOP nomination for governor in 1899 he was read out of the party by Senator Foraker for his "municipal ownership nonsense and other populistic fads." Running as an independent, Jones carried Toledo and Cleveland and made inroads into the rest of the Republican urban vote, but lost because the "farmers had once again remained 'true blue' to the Republican party." [28]

By all odds, the bitterest intraparty struggle occurred in Pennsylvania between the Penrose organization and the

Pittsburgh and Philadelphia machines. Much of this conflict was a simple power struggle, but the need of Flinn and Edwin ("Duke") Vare to retain the loyalty of their polyglot constituents required supporting many measures that the Penrose people opposed. It is significant that while Penrose was a faithful lieutenant and successor to Nelson Aldrich as a leader in the U.S. Senate, both Flinn and Vare had reputations as progressives recognized both by such contemporaries as Gifford Pinchot and by such later scholars as Harold Zink. As a state senator Vare fought with the Penrose organization over many labor and welfare measures, the direct election of U.S. Senators, woman suffrage, election reform, and other political innovations, even though he stopped short of an open break. His lieutenant in the lower house, John R. K. Scott, assumed leadership of a progressive revolt in 1913 and worked for a constitutional convention, corrupt practices legislation, the direct election of U.S. Senators, a public utilities commission, and liberalization of the house rules. The following year Vare threatened to endorse Gifford Pinchot for governor and settled for Dr. Martin Brumbaugh, a moderate progressive who also clashed with Penrose. Vare's control of three-fourths of Philadelphia's assemblymen and one-half of its senators gave him considerable leverage and aided in the passage of child labor and workmen's compensation laws. Flinn had similar experiences as a state senator; his disagreements with Penrose led him to back Theodore Roosevelt in 1912, and helped carry the Washington (Progressive) party to victory. In 1913 he cooperated with the Scott forces on many issues but suspicion of each other's ambitions prevented Flinn and Vare from forging a permanent anti-Penrose coalition. Penrose's death in 1920 and Flinn's retirement allowed Vare to capture control of the state organization and shift it to a more urban orientation, but not thoroughly enough to save it from the Democratic onslaught of the 1930s.[29]

Given the Republican party's leadership and the frustrations of many of its urban politicians, it is not surprising that the new stock working class voters of many cities showed a

marked tendency toward Democratic lawmakers even before
World War I. The Republican split in 1912 facilitated this
trend at the most crucial juncture in the entire reform era.
Cleveland's polyglot population sent only Democrats to the
state senate between 1911 and 1921, and, after choosing two
Republicans for the lower house in 1911, returned a solid
thirteen-man Democratic contingent in the succeeding sessions. These lawmakers were generally a good cross section
of the city's ethnic composition, particularly in 1913 when
four of the five senators and eleven of the thirteen assemblymen were immigrants or second-generation Americans of
German, Austrian, Danish, Polish, Bohemian, or Irish derivation. In New York City, too, the predominantly new stock
voters returned primarily Democratic legislators after 1910.
In 1912 the party captured all thirty-five assembly seats and
the twelve senate positions in New York County. In Brooklyn they took eight of the nine senate posts and twenty-three
of the twenty-five assembly seats. More than half of these
legislators were of Irish derivation, but there were also
significant numbers of Jews and Germans and an occasional
Italian or Pole. Across the river, the New Jersey Democrats
also established a virtual monopoly on assembly seats in the
populous northern counties in both 1910 and 1912, with Irish
and German lawmakers again dominating. In 1913, thirty of
the fifty-one Democrats in the assembly were of recent Irish,
German, or eastern European extraction.[30]

In the 1909 election in Boston only twenty-nine Democrats
out of a possible fifty were elected to the state legislature. In
the next three years the total jumped to forty-four, forty-two,
and thirty-nine, leaving the Republicans in control of only a
few Back Bay districts. The overwhelming majority of these
Democrats were Irish-Americans, but there were a few
Italians and Jews and a handful of Democratic Yankees,
while the Boston GOP lawmakers were nearly all old stock
people. The major Connecticut cities, too, generally returned
Democratic representatives after 1910, although the apportionment system in the lower house restricted their potential
a great deal. New Haven regularly sent three Democrats to

the senate out of a possible four, while Hartford, all of whose senators were Republican in 1909, chose three Democrats out of four by 1917 and 1919. In addition, Waterbury, Bridgeport, and a few of the other larger cities returned more Democrats than Republicans for the decade 1909–1919. Nearly all the big city Democratic solons were Irish-Americans, except for a scattering of Yankees, German-Americans, and one Russian Jewish immigrant. The Republicans were solidly Yankee except for a lone Irish-American from Waterbury. Providence regularly yielded upwards of 80 percent of its seats in the lower house to Democrats, and Woonsocket and Pawtucket were generally close to that figure. In 1913 twenty-three of thirty-six Democrats in the assembly were of new stock origins: seventeen Irish and the rest of German, British, Scotch, Italian, and French-Canadian extraction. By contrast only eight of the sixty-five Republicans were anything but Yankees, a telling statistic in a state with a population of over 70 percent first- or second-generation Americans.[31] By 1917 the Democrats had captured thirteen senate seats and thirty in the house, mostly in the Providence-Pawtucket area and heavily dominated by Irish-Americans, with a few Italians and French-Canadians.

Chicago's polyglot population was somewhat less committed to Democratic lawmakers, partly as a result of cumulative voting, but the party generally captured at least a convincing majority of the city's seats. In 1910 it won thirty-two of the fifty-one assembly positions, and in 1912, thirty-five. In the senate it gained nine of seventeen positions in 1910, and raised its portion to eleven two years later. Irish-Americans held over half of these stations, but Germans, Poles, Italians, Danes, Bohemians, and Jews made up the remainder. By contrast, slightly less than one-half the city's Republican legislators in 1913 were of new stock backgrounds, much higher than in the GOP elsewhere but still low considering that the city was 76 percent first or second generation in 1910.[32] During the most crucial years of the Progressive Era, then, the majority of the urban new stock populace in New York, New Jersey, Massachusetts,

Connecticut, Rhode Island, Ohio, and Illinois were represented by Democratic legislators, most of whom were
themselves of Irish or New Immigrant extraction. It was to
these legislators above all that the urban new stock working
class looked to foster its interests, and it was their activities
that constituted the dynamics of urban liberalism.

The reformist impulse was slow to develop. Since their best
hope for survival and advancement seemed to lie in extralegal assistance rendered by the political boss and his
business allies, immigrants were initially reluctant to challenge the prevailing order. Moreover, those who courted new
stock support against the system rarely understood the urban
masses' needs or provided any worthwhile remedies for their
condition. Agrarian reformers such as William Jennings
Bryan proposed economic measures to aid the industrial
worker, but these were overshadowed by the ruralites' vocal
mistrust of city people and by their militant, revivalist
Protestantism that seemed to carry with it the threat of a new
wave of nativism. Bryan failed to win even such strongholds
of Irish Democracy as Boston and New York. No more
compatible were the patrician reformers who comprised the
good government associations and formed the backbone for
various mugwump, liberal Republican, and independent
movements. All too often their analyses of the urban malaise
involved firmly rooted, nativist, racist assumptions that held
the immigrant working class to be the major cause. Some
seemed to regard the urban immigrant as something less than
human. Superimposed upon this anti-immigrant prejudice
was often a feeling of class superiority, so flagrant that lower
class voters often concluded there was "too much Fifth
Avenue and not enough First Avenue." The combined effect
alienated rather than galvanized the foreign stock working
class vote since "one does not woo a girl by telling her how
ugly she is." It also gave the impression, at least, that the
reformers lacked that brand of human kindliness that was
the machine politician's stock-in-trade. Frederic C. Howe
and Brand Whitlock, who began life as patrician reformers,
came to despise many of their fellows as "without humanity,

without pity and without mercy," preferring the more personal methods of the ward politicians. "You can beat Tammany Hall permanently in only one way," Walter Lippmann cautioned reformers, "by making the government of a city as human, as kindly, as jolly as Tammany Hall." [33]

Their ethnic and class assumptions led many genteel activists to expend an inordinate amount of time and energy on moral crusades to uplift the new stock lower class. Prohibition, Sunday blue laws, censorship, and attacks on gambling and vice were often held to be viable solutions to the problems that plagued the city. To many of his own class, Whitlock observed sardonically, "there were no social problems that the Anti-Saloon League could not solve in a week." The old stock reformer frequently sought to impose his own standards of conduct upon the newer arrivals, and strongly advocated the breakup of institutions and customs the latter held dear.[34]

Beyond moral regeneration, the patrician based his program primarily upon what has been dubbed "structural reform," tinkering with the mechanics of the governmental system on the assumption that the introduction of more businesslike methods would be sufficient to remake urban life. The major thrust of this campaign was negative: promising to end graft, payroll padding, and favoritism. Many patrician politicians also tended to put their faith in such panaceas as civil service or the city manager form of government. If elected, they generally cut the payroll, limited expenditures, and succeeded mostly in "saving rubber bands" and "using both ends of the pencil." Most immigrant voters realized instinctively that honesty, efficiency, and economy in government would do nothing to alleviate their condition and could severely cripple the system's ability to dispense favors. Viewed in the broader perspective of historical development, many of these proposals were fundamentally undemocratic and contributed significantly to the alienation of city government from its constituents. At bottom many patrician reformers did not trust "the people" and sought to restrict their role in governing through the short ballot and other innovations, preferring instead professionals or those supposedly qualified by education, background, and wealth. Their structural changes permitted entry of "commercial and upper class elements into the centers of municipal power at the expense of the ethnic and lower classes." [35]

Most patricians also refused to acknowledge that the real beneficiaries of graft and corruption were not the politicians nor the lower classes, but rather the business leaders who generally came from the same social and ethnic background as the reformers. Deeply committed to unregulated capitalism, the patricians shrank from placing any kind of restrictions on industry. Richard S. Childs, the father of the city management system, staunchly denied that business was responsible for the ills of the city. "I am the son of a capitalist," he explained. With this belief in the essential goodness of the capitalist system and the beneficence of competition, the upper class reformer generally denied that government bore any responsibility for the welfare of the less fortunate. Patricians sought to destroy the political machine, but proposed no alternative to the very necessary functions that the boss system performed for the disadvantaged. The sociologist Robert Merton has concluded of their attack on the political machine that "to seek social change without due recognition of the manifest and latent functions performed by the social organism undergoing change is to engage in social ritual rather than social engineering." This failure to provide real solutions for the very vital problems of the urban masses was probably the biggest reason for the short-lived victories of the patricians. "In three elections out of four," Daniel Moynihan and Nathan Glazer observed, "the masses would choose to believe Charlie Murphy's version rather than that of the New York Times." [36]

From the 1890s on, however, it had become increasingly evident that those middle class reformers who made an attempt to understand and meet the needs of the immigrant working class might hope to count upon its support. Most prominent among these were Hazen Pingree, the four-time mayor of Detroit and two-term governor of Michigan; Samuel ("Golden Rule") Jones, the mayor of Toledo; Brand Whitlock, his successor; Tom L. Johnson, five-term mayor of Cleveland; California Governor Hiram Johnson; Mark Fagan, the mayor of Jersey City; and Carter Harrison, Jr., five-time mayor of Chicago. Nearly all these were successful businessmen or professionals from old stock, Protestant backgrounds who were first elected as candidates of good government movements. Jones was a Welsh immigrant and Fagan, an Irish Catholic and former Democrat, but both gained their earliest support from the old-line elements in their respective cities. Once in office, though, Jones, Fagan, and the rest were astute enough to recognize that the problems of urban industrial life were too complex to yield to the structural and moralistic palliatives of the patricians. Accordingly, they switched to programs that emphasized socioeconomic reform in the interest of the lower classes. They concentrated their efforts on attempts to win better service at lower prices from the cities' utility companies; their fight for municipal ownership of utilities, cheap gas, and three-cent trolley car fares earned the gratitude of the poor and the enmity of the well-to-do. Efforts to restrict the terms of franchises and redistribute the tax burden increased the hostility of the latter. The socioeconomic reformers also endeavored to extend better services to the urban masses in education, public housing, recreation, health, sanitation, and unemployment relief, and they advocated more humane hours, wages, and conditions of labor.[37]

At the same time, they generally soft-pedaled such issues as Sunday blue laws, enforced temperance, and curtailment of gambling and prostitution, preferring to let the masses enjoy their diversions as long as they were honestly run and properly regulated. Beyond this, these reformers were careful to defend the city's ethnic groups from discrimination and to ensure their loyalty by a judicious dispensing of patronage, granting each group a measure of recognition by slating its candidates for public office. In short, they sought to perform many of the functions previously provided only by the urban political machine without permitting the attendant graft and corruption; through taxation policy they moved to shift the financial burden for these services onto the public treasury to remove the need for informal government. In so doing they created in effect "reform machines" and became "reform bosses." At that point the socioeconomic reformers generally lost much of their original native middle class support but more than compensated for that loss by the accretions of ethnic working class voters.[38]

Pingree was first elected mayor of Detroit in 1889 as a good government candidate but later turned to a broad-guaged socioeconomic program that included a bitter fight against the traction companies for lower fares as well as the creation of his famous "potato patches" for unemployment relief. His policies and his skillful playing of the politics of recognition appealed primarily to Detroit's ethnic lower classes and their support carried him through to his various electoral victories. "The Age of Reform in Michigan was clearly not primarily dependent upon the native-born middle and upper classes. Behind a dynamic and compassionate leader newcomers had responded to the important issues of the age." [39] Jones, like Pingree a successful industrialist noted for his humane and forward-looking labor policies, was chosen as a respectable "front" by Toledo's business leaders. The idealistic Welshman stunned his backers by plumping for municipal ownership of utilities, an eight-hour day and minimum wage for public employees, playgrounds, kinder-gartens, and free public concerts, as well as for such political innovations as initiative and referendum, a nonpartisan ballot, and a new city charter. His activities succeeded in gaining the support of "the laboring men themselves and detaching many of the recent immigrant workers from the control of the local bosses." His successor Brand Whitlock pursued the same basic policies and won election five times with his main strength in the working class wards. Tom Johnson was a millionaire traction magnate who ironically had been one of Pingree's main antagonists in Detroit. After moving to Cleveland he won election in 1901 as a business

candidate, but his fight for a three-cent fare and municipal
ownership lost him the support of "men of property and
influence"; "the politicians, immigrants, workers, and persons of small means" flocked to his banner. His program
"appealed to the politically oppressed and to the underprivileged, and from the foreign wards came most of his support."
Johnson captured the city's Democratic machine from his
predecessor John Farley and welded it into a coalition of old
stock reformers and new stock politicians and voters that
made Cleveland "the city on a hill," nationally noted for its
progressive administration, and turned its delegation to the
General Assembly into the most progressive force in Ohio
politics.[40]

Hiram Johnson, who rose to prominence as the prosecutor
of Boss Abe Ruef and his Union Labor party in San
Francisco, initially was elected governor in 1910 as the
candidate of the Lincoln-Roosevelt League, receiving his
major backing in the old stock areas of southern California.
By his second term, though, Johnson shifted his emphasis
from governmental and regulatory reforms to labor and
welfare measures, and the base of his support veered to the
left. In the 1916 election, "the greater the number of
foreign-born and first generation immigrants in an assembly
district the higher the vote for Johnson." By 1920 Johnson's
main sources of support came from the San Francisco
machine, from Catholics, Irish, and other ethnic groups, and
from organized labor. In Jersey City Mark Fagan had
considerable ethnic support, especially Irish and Catholic,
from the outset, thanks to his own background; he enhanced
his popularity by naming three Irish Catholics to his cabinet.
He devoted his administration to altering the tax structure,
regulating the transit companies, and bettering "the physical
conditions of life" through schools, sewers, water treatment,
public baths, parks, free dispensaries, and free milk for
schoolchildren. His action alienated the business-dominated
GOP machine, but he lost in 1907 mostly because the
Democratic machine ran a second-generation German-
American on an equally progressive platform. Carter Harri-

son was descended from old southern stock and was the son of a highly popular mayor. Educated in Germany and married to an Irish Catholic, he enjoyed fantastic popularity among Chicago's two largest ethnic minorities, and he broadened his appeal with a platform of lower utility rates, an eight-hour day, union labor for city jobs, and better social services. Throughout his tenure he stood for "personal liberty" with regard to gambling, liquor, and prostitution, although he cracked down on the notorious Everleigh sisters and "Big Jim" Colosimo, who was a frequent political opponent. Harrison's support in the German, Irish, and other ethnic wards was his primary strength in his mayoral victories.[41]

The lesson of all this was not lost on the Democratic bosses whose continued success depended upon the allegiance of the ethnic working class. There can be little doubt that the growing popularity of reformers of the Pingree-Johnson-Jones school in the ethnic working class wards was a major factor in the switch made by many urban machines to a more progressive stance after the turn of the century. In New Jersey the advent of Fagan and the "New Idea" Republicans pushed the Democratic organization in the northern counties to endorse candidates and platforms that were, if anything, even more forward-looking. "All in all," the historian of the New Idea has observed, "progressive issues were becoming so popular that politicians of both parties ignored them only at their peril." The campaign of William Randolph Hearst for mayor of New York City on a platform of lower gas rates and municipal ownership of utilities made great inroads into the traditional Tammany vote. A year later the Hall endorsed Hearst for governor on a progressive platform and secured the backing of the publisher's Municipal Ownership League for many of its candidates, recouping many of its losses. Tammany Boss Charles F. Murphy was also impressed by the increase in popularity gained by Democratic lawmakers from their support of the labor and welfare measures proposed by such social workers as Frances Perkins and Belle Moskowitz. The capture of

Cleveland by "Golden Rule" Jones in his gubernatorial bid, plus the victory of Tom Johnson as mayor, made that city's professional politicians embrace reform as a means of survival, if nothing else. The winning of the Democratic gubernatorial nomination by a group of young mavericks headed by John B. Moran in 1906 also sent the Irish ward bosses of Boston scurrying for progressive candidates to back. Reform was the watchword of the era and no political organization could have survived for long if it did not adjust to that reality.[42]

The ranks of the urban political machine itself were also beginning to produce politicians of broader vision. In the nineteenth century the average machine politician saw politics almost exclusively as a means of personal advancement, one of the few ways to escape the drudgery of unskilled labor and achieve a measure of prosperity and security. Their credo was probably best expressed by George Washington Plunkitt of Tammany Hall who candidly remarked that his whole career could be summarized by the phrase, "I seen my opportunities and I took 'em." Many machine politicians never progressed beyond this "free enterprise" phase of politics, but for many others, especially the younger generation, it was but "an intermediate step between traditional conservatism and reform." For some, like Al Smith, this broadened vision resulted from experience gained by slow, steady progress through various levels of government. Smith, his friend Robert F. Wagner, and many others profited from contacts with social workers and intellectuals, who were able to identify for them the real cause of their constituents' plight and suggest remedial measures. The liberating effects of higher education had also heightened the social consciousness of men like Wagner, Edward F. Dunne in Chicago, and Joe Tumulty in Jersey City. Whatever the reasons, anyone who objectively examines the speeches, writings, and especially actions of Smith, Wagner, Dunne, Tumulty, David I. Walsh in Massachusetts, or their lesser known counterparts in Rhode Island, Connecticut, and Ohio cannot help but conclude that these were men whose social vision and political philosophy were as far removed from that of Plunkitt as the outlook of Pingree and the social reformers was from that of the mugwumps.[43]

By the second decade of the twentieth century this new breed of machine politician came to wield considerable influence in the organization's councils. In New York, Smith, Wagner, Jeremiah Mahoney, James Foley, Jimmy Walker, Ed Flynn, and a host of other young men prevailed upon Boss Murphy to give them a free hand in the legislature in return for the promise of electoral victories. Bob Davis in Jersey City also listened when Tumulty and a number of other young Irish-American lawmakers, mostly graduates of St. Peter's College, offered to let the boss have the patronage if they could choose the issues. Elsewhere it took the demise of an old-line boss and his replacement by a more flexible one to turn the tide. The replacement of "Big Jim" Smith in Newark by his nephew James R. Nugent altered the stance of Essex County Democracy. In Baltimore the substitution of the "open, generous, approachable, and democratic" John J. ("Sunny") Mahon for the "autocratic, withdrawn and conservative" Isaac Raisin produced a noticeable shift in the Democratic machine's orientation. Mahon freely supported a wide range of reforms and pledged to send a delegation to Annapolis so good "that not even a Mugwump can find fault with it." Realizing the changing situation, the former boss of the machine's safest ward stated that "a politician is not acting for his own interests or those of his party when he flies in the face of the people." [44]

In the case of Cleveland, as previously noted, it was the capture of the Democratic organization by an outside reformer that turned loose a host of young lawmakers, while in Chicago Dunne and his followers created their own organization that not only captured the state but helped move the city's acknowledged boss, Roger Sullivan, to a more progressive position. By the time of Sullivan's death in 1920, even the staunchly Republican *Chicago Tribune* granted that "it is not too much to say that the so-called 'reform laws' of the last ten or fifteen years bear more of

Sullivan's thumbprints than of the professional reformers."
Whatever form the transition assumed, most urban political
machines and their bosses adjusted sufficiently to the reformist clamor both from within and without their ranks to play a
major constructive role in the Progressive Era. Having
acquired an understanding of the uses of legislation to
ameliorate their constituents' condition, they acted as the
prime surrogates for the ethnic working class. Harold Zink
judged that six of eleven bosses active during the period
supported reform measures "frequently," two others occasionally, and only three "saw no farther than the ends of
their noses." As one prominent member of the New York
Citizens Union later reminisced about Tammany Hall, the
urban political machine was "in a flux so that . . . the
reformers were no longer in exclusive possession of reform.
That was a very subtle change which I have never seen
referred to very much." [45]

In the majority of the seven states studied the high point of
the reform tide came during Democratic administrations in
which the machine played a significant part. In Ohio the
Progressive Era on the state level coincides with the administrations of Judson Harmon from 1909 to 1913 and James M.
Cox from 1913 to 1915 and again from 1917 to 1920. In both
administrations Cleveland's heavily new stock delegation
was the most consistent source of support for reform
measures and many of its members assumed leadership roles.
Carl Greenlund, a second-generation Danish-American, was
chairman of two important committees, the sponsor of
several major reform laws, and the lieutenant governor and
presiding officer of the senate in the 1913–14 session.
Lawrence Brennan was the Democratic floor leader in the
lower house in 1913 and "his influence was felt upon all the
important legislation of the session." Scotch immigrant
Robert Crosser and German-American Carl Friebolin
"played a much more aggressive role in proposing and
guiding legislation than their years of experience seemed to
warrant," the latter serving as Tom Johnson's liaison to the
General Assembly. Various other ethnic Democrats in Cleve-

land served as committee chairmen and helped draft and sponsor significant pieces of legislation dealing with labor, welfare, business regulation, taxation, and political innovations.[46]

In New Jersey the urban Democrats, especially from Jersey City, began their key role in the state's reform era during the heyday of the New Idea Republicans. Tumulty and his cohorts formed the major source of support for proposals made by Fagan and his adviser George Record for railroad and utility regulation, as well as for electoral reforms. The victory of Woodrow Wilson in 1910 gave the Democrats control of the lower house and inaugurated the most productive legislative session in New Jersey history. With Tumulty as his chief legislative advisor, Charles Egan as the floor leader, and Edward Kenney as speaker of the house, Wilson was heavily reliant upon Jersey City's "Democratic liberalism." They and their colleagues were so faithful to Wilson's program in 1911 and 1912 that his biographer has deemed them "among his most loyal supporters." The Newark Democrats were much less friendly toward the Wilson program, especially after the governor blocked "Big Jim" Smith's try for reelection to the U.S. Senate, but they still supported measures of interest to their constituents. After Smith's death and during Wilson's presidency, Nugent and the Newark Democrats "gave Wilson his best latter-day support in New Jersey." In addition numerous other new stock Democrats such as Charles O'Connor Hennessy of Bergen, Allan Walsh of Trenton, John Zisgen of Bergen, Arthur Quinn of Perth Amboy, and John J. Griffin of Paterson were important cogs in Wilson's legislative machinery. All told, lawmakers of new stock origin and/or new stock constituencies constituted close to one-half the membership of the legislature during the years 1911–1914, and they gave Wilson and his successor, James F. Fielder, their most important backing, a situation that fully justifies the contention that "much of the leadership in this reform movement came from men with immigrant and Catholic backgrounds." [47]

A number of scholars have recognized the crucial position of the Irish Democrats and other minority group representatives in Massachusetts reform efforts. It is certainly implicit in the critical analyses of the Yankee reformers by such writers as Richard B. Sherman, Murray Levin, and Richard Abrams. Their findings show clearly that the leaders of the Progressive party never "understood fully the aspirations of the working man or the underprivileged," and that their insistence upon cultural uplift alienated the genteel reformers of that group from the ethnic groups, leaving the party "practically an A[merican] P[rotective] A[ssociation] side-show." In this circumstance the Irish Democrats and the labor Republicans from the polyglot mill towns emerge as progressives almost by default. Abrams has distinguished between "progressives," whom he defines as old stock intellectuals and professionals seeking to preserve traditional New England institutions and values, and "insurgents" who were seeking major political, socioeconomic, and cultural changes. The latter came "primarily from the large Irish-American segment of the population who purported to represent the newer Americans generally, and, to a lesser extent, from the growing class of labor unionists." Sherman states flatly that the Democrats were the major progressive force in Massachusetts. In a study of eleven progressive measures in 1911, Sherman found that these were supported by 81 percent of the Democrats and only 28 percent of the Republicans, leading to the conclusion that the administration of Democratic Governor Eugene Foss, elected with the strong backing of Boston politicians Martin Lomasney and John F. Fitzgerald, "coincided with the height of the progressive movement in Massachusetts." Lomasney himself served as Democratic floor leader in the lower house that session and later drew wide acclaim for his work in the constitutional convention in 1917. J. Joseph Huthmacher hails the administration of Foss's successor, David I. Walsh, the state's first Irish-American chief executive, as the high point of the reform years and insists that "in Massachusetts, non-Protestant newer Americans had supported many typically progressive measures even more zealously than the old stock inhabitants." [48]

In Illinois, where the reform movement never made the impact it did in many other states, Chicago politicians made the most important contributions. Republican Charles Deneen (governor from 1905 to 1913) and Frank Lowden (1917–1921) were both protégés of the city's "Blond Boss" William Lorimer, but they were generally regarded as moderate progressives. Edward F. Dunne (1913–1917), a Democrat, brought Illinois closest to the nation's reformist mainstream. The grandson of a prominent Fenian and a member of the Hearst-Harrison faction of the Chicago Democracy, Dunne first achieved prominence for his clashes with the Chicago traction companies as mayor from 1905 to 1907. In the 1912 primary he bested the candidate of rival boss Roger Sullivan for the Democratic gubernatorial nomination and went on to win election. His entire supporting cast on the victorious statewide ticket consisted of Irish-Americans, including his lieutenant governor and future congressman, Barratt O'Hara. Dunne was a vocal champion of the state's ethnic minorities, and his main support in the legislature came from a group of young Irish-Americans headed by Michael Igoe, a Georgetown University law graduate, and William McKinley, the speaker of the house in 1913. Despite factional rivalry with Sullivan, who made an unsuccessful try for the U.S. Senate in 1914, the governor forged a working coalition of Democrats, urban Republicans, Progressives, and Socialists and achieved a reasonably impressive record of reform legislation. [49]

Although the Progressive Era in New York is generally dated from the election of Charles Evans Hughes as governor in 1906, it was again the second decade of the century that was by far the most productive of legislative results. In those years the Empire State was governed primarily by the Tammany Hall–led Democrats, while the upstate Republicans played the role of obstructionists. From 1911 to 1915 governors John Dix, William Sulzer, and Martin Glynn and the Democratic legislature "compiled a record that has never

been surpassed in the history of the New York legislature."
New York "had not reached the millennium," the authors of
the state's best-known history have concluded, "but it had
adopted a body of forward-looking legislation that placed the
state in the front ranks of the progressive movement."
During the period, "the Democrats commanded a majority
in each chamber and Tammany commanded a majority of
the Democrats," and Boss Murphy was enough in control to
achieve Sulzer's impeachment. Al Smith and Robert F.
Wagner provided leadership in their respective houses, and,
according to Bronx boss and state senator Ed Flynn,
"nothing could have been done at Albany unless Charles F.
Murphy permitted or encouraged it." After a four-year
Republican interlude Smith himself was elected governor
and built a record that made New York the recognized
leader in the nation in social legislation. Wagner later applied
the lessons he learned in New York to national matters and
became the New Deal's most productive legislator, while
Flynn acted as Roosevelt's political right arm in the Empire
State. Clearly it was the urban new stock Democrats who
made the most significant and far-reaching contributions to
progressive reform in New York.[50]

In Connecticut and Rhode Island, where the regular
Republicans retained power throughout the Progressive
years, the urban new stock Democrats and a handful of
Republicans of similar origin stood out as the major force for
change. As the "party of the outs, the immigrants, the
Catholics and the poor," the Democrats in the Connecticut
legislature sought, generally in vain, to break the political
power exercised over the state by the rural Yankee minority,
to provide for the welfare of the workers and the disadvantaged, and to resist the enforced conformity imposed by
Sunday blue laws and Prohibition. The party had several
prominent Yankees, such as Governor Simeon Baldwin, but
the organizational and legislative hierarchies were largely
composed of Irish and newer Americans. The Democratic
leaders in Hartford and New Haven were Thomas J. Spellacy
and Davey Fitzgerald and their major rivals for power were

Herman Kopplemann, a Russian-born Jew, and Tony Zaz-
zara, an Italian. In 1911 Spellacy was the floor leader in the
senate assisted by Bryan Mahan, future congressman from
New London. In 1913 John McDonough of Naugatuck
served as majority leader in the upper house with Arch
McNiel of Bridgeport as his chief lieutenant. In 1917 Patrick
Sullivan of Derby assumed the role of parliamentary leader,
directing five other Irish-Americans plus Kopplemann and
German-American Frederick Neebe of Meriden. In Rhode
Island, the Democrats acted as "the spokesman for the
underdog and the disfranchised immigrants and offered a
nucleus for counter organization against the oligarchic
elements which ran the state." Except for such old stock
people as future U.S. Senators Peter Gerry and Theodore
Francis Green, who were descendants of figures prominent
in the American Revolution, the Rhode Island Democratic
party was once again dominated by Irish-Americans and
Italian-Americans pushing from below. By 1917, 68 percent
of Providence's ward committeemen were Irish and 4 percent
were Italian, leaving the Yankees only 28 percent, compared
with their 80 percent control of the GOP. The party's state
chairman was Frank Fitzsimmons and his chief rivals for the
post were all Irishmen, as were most of the party's mayors,
such as Joseph Gainer of Providence. Such Irish-Americans
as John Cooney, George O'Shaunessy, Thomas McKenna,
Patrick Dillon, and William Flynn provided most legislative
leadership, aided by Yankees Addison P. Munroe and Albert
West, Italians Luigi de Pasquali and Adamo Aiello, and a
few French-Canadians. In their struggles against the Brayton-
Aldrich combine, they were occasionally joined by a few
independent Republicans, primarily such urban ethnics as
Jacob Eaton, a Romanian-born Jew, Silverio Giannotti, Max
Levy, the German-born Carl Wendel, a few Irish and
French-Canadians, plus an occasional Socialist. Their successes were few, but occasionally they did force the Republi-
can majority to allow the passage of a weaker version of a
measure by sheer persistence. In both states the urban
Democrats constituted the most viable reform group during

the Progressive Era, and advocated many measures that came to fruition when the party gained power in later years.[51]

Whether achieving power or not, then, urban new stock Democrats, with their labor and Republican allies, played a major role in the reform efforts of Ohio, Illinois, New York, New Jersey, Massachusetts, Connecticut, and Rhode Island during the Progressive Era. The positions taken by these lawmakers generally reflected the aspirations of their constituents for a better life, aspirations not always shared by other reform groups. Despite natural variations from state to state, the general outlines of their activities formed enough of a pattern to justify labeling them the generators of a relatively new phenomenon in American life: urban liberalism. To examine that pattern in detail constitutes the major task of the next four chapters. In those seven states, as in the rest of the nation, there was no single progressive movement at work during the period, but rather many groups interacting and coalescing to produce meaningful legislative results. Rarely, if ever, were urban new stock lawmakers, or any other group, in a numerically strong enough position to produce reform legislation by their own unaided efforts. The passage of laws of statewide impact required the combined efforts of legislators from varied backgrounds; they often desired the same measure for different reasons, but each believed that enactment of the measure was somehow in the interest of the constituency he represented. The extent and duration of this cooperation varied immensely according to the type of reform proposed; for example, the makeup of the coalition that produced labor and welfare measures was substantially different from the one that brought about Prohibition. The contributions and motivations of farmers, small towns residents, the urban middle class of merchants, intellectuals, professionals, managers, and bureaucrats, and even of patricians and business leaders have been amply developed; the role played by the urban new stock masses has only begun to be appreciated. Focusing on their efforts in this study risks conveying the impression that urban new stock lawmakers were solely responsible for the legislative achievements of the Progressive Era in these seven states, but a detailed analysis of their positions is vital to establishing their crucial role in the period's reform process. The concluding chapter will undertake the task of placing these contributions in the perspective of the entire era and assessing urban liberalism as an important factor in the evolution of modern American society.[52]

CHAPTER 2

Bread and Butter Liberalism: Launching the Welfare State

The inauguration of the national welfare state during the New Deal Era was not a sudden departure from the nation's past history. The programs it embodied were essentially a broadening of those that had been developed in most of the major industrial states during the Progressive Era. Then, for the first time, serious efforts were launched to cope with such effects of industrial urban living as child and female labor, inadequate housing, low wages, excessive hours, dangerous working conditions, industrial accidents, and lack of retirement benefits. Although no state provided solutions for these problems in this period, the attempts at least established precedents for more comprehensive measures in future years.

This impressive record in the area of welfare legislation was in no small measure due to the activities of old stock, Protestant professionals and intellectuals, acting primarily out of a humanitarian concern for the plight of the underprivileged. Although the majority of their number probably continued to feel that the chief business of religion was individual moral regeneration and "paid scant attention to social reform," or professed the gospel of wealth that equated prosperity with God's favor and poverty with his displeasure, an influential minority were moved by the Social Gospel, with its "emphasis upon the saving of society rather than upon the salvation of individuals." By 1908 the Federal Council of the Churches of Christ in America and the National Methodist Conference proclaimed it "the duty of all Christian people to concern themselves directly with certain practical industrial problems" and endorsed a host of welfare proposals. Social workers, mostly from well-to-do families, went to live among the poor in settlement houses and became advocates of government action in social matters. Reform organizations such as the National Consumers League, the Women's Trade Union League, The American Association for Labor Legislation, the National Child Labor Committee, and the Social Reform Club of New York, with heavily native middle class memberships, lobbied for a variety of welfare laws. Professional economists, most of them trained in Bismarck's Germany with its welfare state, called for similar programs in the United States. The founders of the American Economic Association stated in their platform that they regarded "the state as an agency whose positive assistance is one of the indispensable conditions of human progress." The newly developed discipline of sociology, led by Lester Frank Ward, echoed the cry. Yankee Protestant politicians such as Hazen Pingree and Tom Johnson advocated welfare measures as a requirement for achieving political power in industrial, polyglot cities. Others from similar backgrounds endorsed such programs in the hope that legitimate aid programs would remove the need for the extralegal assistance furnished by the boss and the political machine and destroy their hold over the urban working class voter. The predominantly middle class, native, Protestant Progressive party devoted a section of its platform to "social and industrial justice," calling for dozens of far-reaching ameliorative measures. Middle class actions were instrumental in fostering the proper climate of opinion that led to acceptance of these new ideas and its lobbying efforts bore significant fruit. The actual enactment of legislation, however, depended upon the cooperation of "their natural allies," many of whom they found in legislators from similar backgrounds and from some segments of organized labor. Little could have been accomplished, though, without the strong support of the representatives of those whom these measures were designed to benefit. Although they originated few proposals themselves, urban new stock lawmakers provided much of the sponsorship, legislative skill, and the votes necessary to launch the welfare state.[1]

The receptiveness of the new stock working class to welfare legislation was conditioned by tradition and experience in both the Old World and the New. For most of them, life in the Old World had been one of stability and interdependence. The prevailing nexus of contractual obligations had restricted their opportunities for economic advancement, but it had also imposed corresponding obligations to them on the part of their overlords. The landlords, the church, the family, and the village all assumed some measure of obligation to care for those who were too ill or infirm to work. The individual who was a part of the whole process of economic life contributed as much as he was able in the years of his strength and vigor and was entitled to help when he was no longer fit. Whether he owned the land or not, the peasant was entitled to consume much of the fruit of his own labor, without the complications and distortions imposed by the wage system. While it is easy to exaggerate the security and stability of European peasant life, the experience certainly left most immigrants with definite expectations concerning society's obligations toward its members—the prevailing system in nineteenth-century America did not meet those expectations. Even in the cities of Europe the craft and merchant guilds had performed a variety of welfare functions for their members. The great majority of immigrants who thronged into America's cities during the Great Migration possessed neither capital nor marketable skills and hence had little reason to develop any fealty to the ideals of private enterprise capitalism.[2] Most, too, were non-Protestants who had had little exposure to the tenets of the Puritan Ethic that animated the lives of so many native Americans. The Catholic church had always urged that salvation was a social experience and, unlike the advocates of the gospel of wealth, had never claimed that prosperity was an indication of God's favor. "The blessedness of individuals," as St. Ambrose had phrased it, "must not be estimated at the value of their known wealth, but according to the voice of their conscience within them." The church's teaching that evils in the world could never be completely eliminated caused it to reject both laissez-faire and socialism and instead endorse ameliorative measures. The reiteration of those ideals by Pope Leo XIII in 1893 put the sanction of the church behind trade unionism and social legislation to improve the lot of the working class.[3] Ever since the days of the Old Testament prophets, the Jewish tradition had condemned any social order "based upon the exploitation of the weak, the helpless and the simple by the strong, the resourceful and the cunning," and had denied that human inequality was the inevitable result of "blind and purposeless" forces. The concepts of *hevras* and *tsedaka* ("charity conceived as justice") enjoined the Jews to seek remedies for social ills, and the reliance of many eastern Europeans upon social support in their native lands additionally conditioned them to accept the necessity for such programs. The acceptance by many eastern European Jews of various types of socialism further predisposed them against the prevailing social climate in the United States.[4]

Whatever predispositions toward the welfare state the immigrant possessed from his Old World experience were almost surely heightened by the conditions he encountered in industrial America. He soon discovered that his economic security depended not upon the cooperative efforts of family, village, and church, but rather upon his ability to hold a job and draw a wage. If for any reason—accident, illness, old age, or economic depression—he found himself unemployed, there was little or nothing to support him. "A philosophy that called for 'leaving things alone' to work themselves out seemed either unreal or hypocritical in the cities." The plight of the urban wage earner was too clearly the result of the workings of man-made institutions to be charged off to God or natural law; what was obviously required to redress the balance was the intervention of other man-made institutions.[5]

From the outset, therefore, the new stock city dweller accustomed himself to rely upon the ministrations of a variety of agencies. His churches devoted a growing amount of attention to meeting his physical needs by distributing food and clothing and by caring for the widows, orphans, and those incapacitated by alcohol or other disabilities. The Catholic church espoused a growing program of labor and welfare measures for its communicants and other working class people. By 1900 such ethnic groups as the German-American Catholics in the Midwest were looking to both the example of the old country and the teachings of their church to buttress their call for labor and welfare measures.[6]

Jewish immigrants also formed their associations, particularly the *lansmanshaften,* and stepped up their efforts to ameliorate life in the American ghetto. The Pittsburgh Platform of Reform Judaism adopted in 1885 called for efforts "to regulate the relation between rich and poor," and declared it "the great task of modern times to solve, on the basis of justice and righteousness, the problems presented by the contradictions and evils of the present organization of society." Many other Jews turned to trade unionism, socialism, and politics to effect these ends. Each nationality also established its own associations to provide a wide variety of services. The Polish National Alliance, the Sons of Italy, the Bunds, the Sokols, and the like lent money, provided burial expenses, issued inexpensive insurance policies, and acted as employment agencies. Added to these were the manifold activities of the machine politician discussed in the previous chapter. Taken together, the efforts of the clergy, the national societies, and the politicians provided at least a portion of the security that was so sadly lacking in American economic life and reinforced the immigrant's conviction that some such aid was a necessity. When proposals were forthcoming to allow government to intervene in the economy to insure decency and security, the foreign stock working class was predisposed by belief and experience to be among their most sympathetic supporters.

Machine politicians had additional reasons for favoring such legislation. Fulfilling the physical needs of the fantastic influx of immigrants into the cities in the two decades before World War I strained the machine's resources to the breaking point. At the same time patrician civic reformers stepped up their drives for honesty, efficiency, and economy in government, making it much more difficult for the organization to increase its revenues. Caught between those pressures, the boss and his lieutenants often found to their dismay that "with more applicants than places, each appointment made one friend and a half-dozen enemies." It is illustrative of the tremendous complexity of the Progressive Era's reform process that while the urban middle class backed the creation of the welfare state to divest the political machine of its main source of power, the politicians supported the same measures in an attempt to shift their welfare burden onto the public treasury and thereby preserve their positions. Many younger politicians within the organization had become familiar with the proposed programs of the American Association for Labor Legislation and its counterparts through higher education and personal contact with their members, and, reading the mood of their constituents, nursed "vague ambitions that they might make a name for themselves by helping those who elected them." [7]

Enactment of welfare-type proposals, in the judgment of one scholar, was the "first intimation of a shift of basic significance in American politics. It was something rather different from the Progressive movement: workingmen's support of welfare legislation through the urban machine." Al Smith later reminisced that Charles F. Murphy "took a keen interest in bills embodying social legislation," while future New Deal supporter Edward Flynn insisted that the Tammany leader "adjusted his thinking to a real belief that government might, through an expansion of its functions, serve the people in new and helpful ways." Even an otherwise anti-Tammany historian has acknowledged that the Hall under Murphy backed important welfare legislation opposed by the GOP, "provided it did not inconvenience their money-making." [8]

Much of the legislative output began with the work of the famous New York State Factory Investigation Commission, founded as a result of the disastrous Triangle Shirtwaist Factory fire; its recommendations were eventually translated into fifty-six separate welfare laws. The membership of the commission included labor leader Samuel Gompers, social worker Frances Perkins, and several prominent middle class reformers; but it was chaired by Robert Wagner with Al Smith as vice-chairman, and they and their Tammany colleagues assumed the major responsibility for shepherding the proposals through the legislature. Nearly all these measures were enacted in the years 1911 and 1913, when the governor's mansion was occupied by Democrats hand-picked by Tammany Hall and while the party had impressive majorities in both houses of the legislature. Nearly all of them were introduced by New York City Democrats or their allies, with the group as a whole forming the most consistent base of support for their passage. The 1913 legislature was so productive of worthwhile welfare legislation that the state Federation of Labor declared that no legislature in the period of the organization's existence in any state had ever surpassed it, and attributed the results primarily to the leadership of Smith and Wagner. None of these reform acts was ever struck down by the courts, a remarkable record given the generally hostile attitude of the judiciary toward such measures.[9]

A large part of the new welfare legislation dealt specifically with the protection of women and children working in factories. Women were prohibited from working between the hours of 10 P.M. and 6 A.M., while girls under twenty-one were barred from labor between 9 P.M. and 6 A.M. Other measures set daily and weekly maximum hours for both women and children. Women were also allowed to remain at home for a reasonable length of time after childbirth without risking the loss of their jobs. Minors were required to receive a physical examination before being employed, and their employment was absolutely prohibited in factories where dangerous equipment was in use. In 1913 the Democratic-dominated legislature appointed a fifteen-man commission to study the entire subject of child welfare and the Democrats again championed its recommendations in the face of opposition from the reactionary Whitman administration in 1915.[10]

Much of the other "Triangle" legislation dealt with the regulation of the inhuman conditions of labor the commission's investigations had uncovered. New York Democrats pushed for seats with backs on them for those who labored in garment factories. They endorsed the introduction of safety standards such as the enclosure of elevators and hoisting shafts. The danger of fire so graphically illustrated by the Triangle tragedy led to the enactment of laws requiring fire escapes, mandatory fire drills, a ban on smoking, and limitations on the number of occupants permitted in buildings. Special categories of business such as bakeries and canneries were the subject of health and safety laws. Canneries, most of which were located upstate and fiercely protected by their Republican legislators, proved particularly resistant to regulations regarding hours of labor, but the majority party brought them into line. Arguing for the end of Sunday work in canneries, Al Smith sardonically remarked that his Bible did not say, "Remember the Sabbath to keep it holy—except in canneries." [11]

To oversee these new regulations, the Democrats established a number of new state agencies. The State Industrial Board was authorized to enforce the health and safety codes. The Labor Department was reorganized to give it "ample power to enforce the law and initiate further reforms." Also placed under its jurisdiction were newly created public employment offices, designed to curb the nefarious activities of private employment agencies that often charged exorbitant fees for their services to those least able to afford them. A leading Republican legislator stigmatized the Employment Agency Act as "an illustration of open-hearted, generous-minded Democratic legislation" that "would soon bankrupt the state." A welfare commission was also structured to prevent the payment of protection to police officers by gamblers and houses of prostitution.[12]

New York City's new stock Democrats were the moving force behind a wide variety of other welfare measures. Two of their number introduced successful legislation providing for the regulation of working hours and paid vacations for railroad workers. Their efforts also produced a comprehensive regulation requiring one day's rest in seven for virtually all the state's workers. City Democrats also sponsored a bill stipulating a two-dollar-a-day minimum wage for laborers and mechanics on state canals. Democratic support was instrumental in the creation of pension funds for widows with children and/or retired public employees, despite GOP protests that these would make "a mollycoddle lot instead of increasing independence." They also provided the bulk of the votes that brought tenement dwellings under closer state supervision, and established a college scholarship fund for underprivileged students. In cooperation with the representatives of farming districts upstate, the city lawmakers endorsed a system providing for the formation of agricultural cooperatives on the one hand, and for the establishment of public markets for the sale of commodities on the other.[13]

Probably the most tenacious effort made by the Empire State's urban Democrats on behalf of the welfare of the workingman was in the development of a workmen's compensation system described by Samuel Gompers as the "best law of the kind ever passed in any state or any country." The reform Republican administration of Charles Evans Hughes had enacted a mild compensation measure based on voluntary compliance by employers. In 1911 the Democrats enacted a compulsory system, only to see the state supreme court invalidate it. In 1913 Charles Murphy's son-in-law James Foley introduced in the assembly a new compulsory workmen's compensation proposal and fellow Tammanyite Jimmy Walker followed suit in the senate. A group of independent Democrats from upstate, with organized labor support, sponsored a measure that provided for somewhat higher payments and excluded private insurance companies from participation. Governor Sulzer endorsed the latter bill, and when the Tammany Democrats mustered the votes to pass the Foley-Walker bill, he vetoed it. After Sulzer had been impeached at Murphy's insistence, the Democrats reintroduced the workmen's compensation bill at a special session with more generous rates than before, particularly in certain hazardous occupations, and restrictions on private insurers. The assembly passed the measure 110–0 with nearly all the body's ninety-eight Democrats concurring, while in the upper house all thirty-two Democrats voted in favor joined by only three Republicans. Wagner later claimed that the law was "the beginning of America's social security system." In 1917 the Democrats fought unsuccessfully against a Republican proposal to give private insurance companies more leeway in the compensation field.[14]

New York Democrats continued their support of welfare legislation in the 1915 constitutional convention. Smith and his cohorts not only sought to remove any constitutional restrictions on effective factory codes and wages and hours legislation for women and children, but also ferociously resisted the attempts of upstate Republicans to undo the accomplishments of the past four years. Charging that the Democrats' programs were creating proletarians and paupers, Republican state chairman William Barnes and GOP senate leader Harvey Hinman moved to abolish workmen's compensation and widow's pensions and to prohibit any further "class legislation." A coalition of Democrats and urban Republicans prevailed but only after several days of acrimonious debate. In 1917 the same combination in the legislature succeeded in sidetracking upstate Republican attempts to set aside labor and welfare legislation during the wartime emergency. So committed and well organized were New York's urban lawmakers that they continued to advance the frontiers of the welfare state even in the generally hostile atmosphere of the 1920s. With Smith providing the leadership from the governor's mansion, they pressed for rent controls, public housing, regulation of the milk industry, expanded public health facilities, and more generous state aid to education, as well as for the strengthening of the workmen's compensation and factory codes and the ratification of the federal child labor amendment.[15]

Across the river in New Jersey, urban new stock lawmakers compiled a similar record on behalf of government responsibility for the welfare of its citizens. The prime concern of Joe Tumulty and fellow Irish-Americans from Jersey City "lay even more in social than political democracy." [16] Although contemporaries credited Woodrow Wilson with the passage of social reform measures, he was much more interested in political reform and was, in the opinion of his most careful biographer, "in no sense the dynamic force behind them." As had their counterparts in New York, the Jersey City Democrats expended a great deal of time and energy on the issue of workmen's compensation. A bill introduced in the 1909 session of the legislature exempted industrial accidents from such common-law doctrines as the fellow servant theory, the concept that allowed employers to escape responsibility for industrial accidents if it could be established that a fellow worker's negligence contributed to the mishap. Its pernicious effect led one reform-minded editor to charge that New Jersey was "shamed by having the most ancient and unjust of any employers' liability laws in the country." The Hudson County Democrats not only backed the measure, but tried to strengthen it against the attempts of the conservative Republican majority on the judiciary committee to substitute its own bill. Mark Sullivan and his fellow Hudson assemblymen unsuccessfully introduced amendments to buttress yet another weaker bill substituted by the senate; they finally had to vote for the weaker bill as the only one that could pass both houses.[17]

With a Democratic majority in 1911, Cornelius Ford of Jersey City, president of the state Federation of Labor, introduced a more generous compensation bill and mobilized labor and Democratic support for its passage. Governor Wilson, however, was committed to a milder senate version drafted by state Senator Walter Edge providing for smaller rates of payment although it did give employers considerably less opportunity to avoid responsibility by prohibiting most of the common-law doctrines that had previously prevailed. Wilson was put out at Ford's insistence upon higher rates and finally asked the labor leader if he didn't "think it would be the better part of wisdom to accept the Edge bill and make sure of getting something?" In the end, the governor prevailed upon the state Federation of Labor president to accept the Edge Bill and the Jersey City assemblymen pushed hard for passage. When the law was finally enacted by the assembly, all twelve Hudson Democrats and ten of the eleven Essex Democrats cast their votes in favor.[18]

The Democratic representatives of Jersey City and Newark exhibited similar enthusiasm for a variety of measures designed to improve working conditions in New Jersey's factories. Ford in particular was the author of a myriad of such bills, including measures for proper lighting and ventilation in factories, a resolution petitioning Congress to outlaw the use of phosphorus matches in workshops, and a law requiring half-hour lunch breaks for workmen. With the exception of an occasional absence or abstention, the Jersey City and Newark Democrats voted for all these and similar bills such as the one requiring that industrial accidents be reported to the state Department of Labor. In addition, all but three of the twenty-five Essex and Hudson County Democrats voted for a bill that would regulate conditions of employment, while only four abstentions marred their support for a proposal to require fire escapes in factories.[19]

Although no law restricting the number of working hours in private industry was enacted, standards were established for public employment. Once again Ford proposed the limitation of hours for public employees, a measure backed by nearly all his fellow Democrats. The indefatigable president of the state Federation of Labor later proposed limiting convicts in the state's penal institutions to eight hours of labor per day, a bill that passed the lower house by a 51–1 count with all but one Hudson Democrat concurring.[20] Again usually avoiding measures that would directly affect

conditions in private industry, the urban Democrats sought
to establish precedents by dealing with wages paid to public
employees. Mark Phillips of Newark, the chief spokesman
for the Smith-Nugent machine, sponsored a minimum wage
for county employees in the most populous jurisdictions, and
he received nearly unanimous support from the representatives of those counties. The regulation of pay for firemen was
the subject of two successful bills introduced in 1911. Such
measures received similar support when introduced by
Republicans, as demonstrated by the fact that all the Jersey
City and Newark legislators, with the exception of two
absentees, favored a bill stipulating the wages of workers on
public projects.[21]

Efforts to improve pay scales did not end there. New
Jersey's urban Democrats also backed a variety of efforts to
make the worker's often meager wage stretch as far as
possible and to keep him out of the clutches of the often
unscrupulous people who operated the credit business. To
lessen the necessity of borrowing, state laws were enacted
that would require the semimonthly payment of wages in real
money to railroad workers. The attempt to extend the
principle of semimonthly payment to cover all state employees died in the Republican-controlled senate. In the event
that borrowing did prove necessary, Cornelius Ford drafted
legislation to regulate the activities of the wage loan companies that lent money using the laborer's potential pay as
collateral, and his fellow Hudson County Democrats unanimously backed its passage.[22]

Efforts to deal with unemployment were less noteworthy in
New Jersey during these years, but they again stemmed
largely from the activities of the urban machine politicians
since the problem was almost always at its worst among the
ethnic minorities. Although New Jersey did not enact a
system of unemployment insurance during the Wilson era,
Hudson and Essex County leaders secured approval for
regulation of those private agencies that sought to procure
jobs.[23]

Urban new stock liberals in New Jersey also devoted a

great deal of their time to guaranteeing adequate income for
the aged. Bills that would have provided pensions for public
employees with thirty years of service passed the assembly
with the overwhelming endorsement of Hudson and Essex
County Democrats only to be cut down in the Republican-
controlled senate. Failing in this broader purpose, Democrats lent their backing to pension plans for selected groups
of public employees such as policemen and wharfingers, but
one of Wilson's numerous 1912 vetoes blocked the latter
attempt. Even more significantly, New Jersey's urban Democrats gave substantial support to efforts to create a commission for the study of a statewide system of old age insurance.
The resolution passed the assembly in 1910 with only three
negative votes, and again in 1911 by 41–0, but the senate did
not endorse it on either occasion.[24]

As further evidence of their concern for the unfortunate
victims of industrialization, Hudson and Essex County
Democrats were among the most effective proponents of
legislation dealing with the problems of child and female
labor. A resolution was introduced in 1912 to create a
commission for the study of women's wages, with the goal of
establishing a minimum wage law. A few days later, Cornelius Ford continued his efforts on behalf of New Jersey toilers
by sponsoring legislation to prohibit the use of women as
coremakers or molders in factories and foundaries, a proposal probably motivated both by humanitarian concerns
and by a desire to limit the work force. Both measures failed
in the Republican-controlled house, but a law providing for a
ten-hour day for women, also drafted by Ford, did pass.
Hudson County Democrats supported all these as well as an
earlier proposal by an Essex County Republican ordering the
construction of seats for female employees in mercantile and
manufacturing establishments.[25] The protection of minors
working in factories was an ongoing proposition throughout
most of the Progressive Era in New Jersey, and the urban
representatives were usually in the vanguard of the reformers. The state law enacted in 1903 that established a
minimum employment age proved ineffective, and nearly

every session brought attempts to tighten it. Finally a bill was passed that raised the age limit to sixteen. 1910 also saw the enactment of another law that proscribed night work for children, although the Republicans added a number of undesirable exemptions.[26]

Cleveland's heavily new stock delegation of Democratic legislators played a leading role in the enactment of a wide variety of welfare measures in Ohio. Their major allies in these endeavors generally came from the representatives of Ohio's other major cities and from working class representatives of the coal-mining districts in the southeastern part of the state. Most prominent among these was William Green, the son of English immigrant parents, a miner since boyhood, and the future president of the American Federation of Labor. On many welfare issues, particularly those involving the protection of women and children, the working class lawmakers generally had the backing of the middle class leadership of their party—men such as Tom Johnson, and Governors Harmon and Cox—but occasional proposals to benefit special groups of able-bodied male workers brought the two factions into conflict. In all cases the Cleveland delegation proved to be in the vanguard of those working for constructive social legislation.

The so-called Mother's Pension Law, considered one of the major achievements of the period in this area, was drafted by state senator William Greenlund in the 1913 session. It represented a comprehensive attempt to reorganize the state's welfare program for indigent mothers with dependent children. Besides providing for pensions, the law—known as the "Magna Carta of the children of Ohio"— also regulated the conditions of child labor and stipulated compulsory education until the age of fifteen for boys and sixteen for girls. The entire Cleveland delegation in both houses of the General Assembly backed it unanimously. When the Republican administration in 1915 tried to weaken the intent of the measure by allowing county sheriffs to investigate welfare recipients, the Cuyahoga lawmakers abstained from voting.[27]

Welfare reform in Ohio included a compulsory workmen's compensation law, which received strong backing from Cleveland's delegates. The original bill was introduced in 1911 and provided for the creation of a state insurance fund financed primarily out of employer contributions. It stipulated an automatic payment to the worker without the necessity of proving negligence and also created a state Liability Board of Awards. The measure passed both houses over the token opposition of some rural Republicans and with the unanimous support of Cleveland lawmakers. In 1913 the Cuyahoga delegation backed an amendment making workmen's compensation compulsory, although it allowed some employers to provide for self-insurance. When the Republican superintendent of insurance ruled that the private liability companies could provide coverage, the state Federation of Labor sponsored a successful measure, via an initiative petition, to prohibit this activity; the Cuyahoga lawmakers voted almost unanimously for it in the 1917 session. Governor Cox was so pleased with the state's workmen's compensation system that in his second inaugural he insisted that he knew of a man who was injured in Pennsylvania and crawled over the Ohio state line in order to be eligible for benefits.[28]

The regulation of working hours, especially for women, found similar favor with the Lake City lawmakers. The original bill, introduced in 1911, provided for a nine-hour day and a fifty-four-hour week. Opposition to the measure in the house inspired a Cleveland Democrat to amend the proposal to a ten-hour day and a sixty-hour week, over the objections of all his colleagues, but on the final vote the entire Cleveland group concurred. In 1913, German-American union official Harry Vollmer sought to lower the limit to eight hours and to include women working in hotels and mercantile establishments as well as factories. Under threat of a veto by Governor Cox, Vollmer and his associates finally agreed to a nine-hour day and certain other limitations, but not before they had demonstrated their desire for the strongest possible law. As further evidence of their concern

for shorter working hours for women, the Cuyahoga delegation approved an extension of the law's provision in 1917.
Although the issue of maximum hours for male workers did
not engender much interest in the legislature, the Cuyahoga
delegation did back a law, drafted in 1913 and eventually
passed, stipulating an eight-hour day for public employees as
an example for private industry.[29]

Cleveland lawmakers were in the forefront of those who
sought to establish a strong industrial code for Ohio and to
provide for a statewide commission to oversee it. They
unanimously supported a 1911 measure requiring employers
to report to the chief inspector of workshops and factories
any serious accident that resulted in more than two days'
absence. In the following session they backed a proposal to
punish any violation of the statutes regarding abuses in
sweatshops with a fine ranging from 25 to 100 dollars; they
also voted for a bill requiring any business employing more
than five people to report the number, wages, hours, and
conditions of labor of any females or workers under eighteen
years of age. To oversee these laws Cleveland's Democrats
backed the creation of a state industrial commission that
would assume the powers of all the existing labor boards and
bureaus, administer workmen's compensation and all laws
relating to health and safety of employees, oversee free
employment bureaus, provide arbitration, and enforce legislation dealing with the hours of women and children.
Although some labor leaders reportedly feared that the
board would exercise too much control, the bill eventually
received the complete support of the Cleveland delegation as
well as that of all the other labor-oriented legislators. During
the same session the Cuyahoga lawmakers upheld an amendment to the industrial commission bill stipulating that the
newly established commission would accede to all the powers
of the state Board of Awards.[30] The wages of Ohio's
industrial workers also concerned the state's new stock
legislators. In the 1911 constitutional convention, Cleveland's Thomas S. Farrell, an Irish-American labor leader,
introduced a minimum wage proposal, noting that the state's

unions had originally opposed such a measure, trusting to collective bargaining, but that the continuing weakness of the union movement caused most leaders to experience a change of heart. The idea was adopted, but Governor Cox prevailed upon the lawmakers to refer the matter to the Industrial Commission for study. Despite earlier opposition, by 1915 William Green was debating Samuel Gompers on the floor of the AFL convention in favor of a minimum wage. Organized labor in New York and elsewhere was being pushed by Socialists and was moving toward a pragmatic position of asking government for things that could not be gained by collective bargaining. Although Ohio did not enact a minimum wage law in this period, labor-oriented lawmakers did endeavor to protect the worker's earnings in other ways. In 1913 the Cleveland delegation backed a law that required the semimonthly payment of wages, successfully frustrating attempts of conservatives to riddle it with exceptions. All but two of their number, who did not vote, also supported a 1915 bill strengthening the provisions of a law to license and regulate wage loan corporations.[31]

Among other disadvantaged groups singled out for special consideration by the General Assembly were the state's public school teachers, and Cleveland's urban new stock lawmakers sympathized with the reform efforts in this area. In 1911 a bill providing for retirement pensions for teachers passed the senate by a 23–3 count, with most Democrats voting in favor. In the lower house all but two of the Cleveland lawmakers present lent their support to passage. In the 1914 special session, eleven of the thirteen Cuyahoga representatives in the lower house and two of the five senators voted for the establishment of a forty-dollar-a-month minimum wage for teachers, with the state making up the difference if the local school district was unable to do so. Cleveland's new stock politicians were likewise agreeable to the efforts of William Green and other labor leaders to better the condition of the state's sizable number of coal miners. In 1914 Green successfully proposed that the workers be paid on a "run of the mine" basis rather than by the amount of coal weighed after screening. Unanimous support from the Cleveland delegation in both houses considerably aided passage of the measure. The Cleveland machine also backed other mining regulations proposed by Green, including the requirement that all men be cleared out of the mine before blasting, the right of any next of kin to sue mine owners in the event of wrongful death, and the mandatory enclosing of all mine shafts.[32]

If anything, Cleveland's legislators were even more interested in the welfare of Ohio's railroad workers than in that of the state's miners. Except for four who did not vote, they all backed the bill to provide for eight hours of rest after fifteen hours of work and another measure to require the use of air brakes on 85 percent of all railroad cars. On two separate occasions during the period, they gave substantial support to full train crew bills sponsored by lawmakers with railroad union approval, as well as to one requiring seats for railroad employees. Everyone but four absentees voted in favor of a bill to appoint a state inspector of brakes and couplings.[33] Cleveland's Democrats also supported the creation of free employment offices, the prevention of occupational diseases in plants producing noxious fumes, and the prohibition of convict labor.[34]

As did their Cleveland counterparts, the Chicago Democratic delegation consistently supported labor and social welfare measures, particularly when they were responding to the leadership of Governor Dunne. The latter's own views on social legislation were well formulated and extremely advanced for the period. Dunne was fond of repeating his belief that the "primary object of government is to promote the happiness and well-being of the people." He was particularly insistent that anyone who was weak or helpless should receive first, "kindness and sympathy," and second, "skillful and scientific treatment." Rejecting any laissez-faire position, Dunne gloried in the welfare legislation of his own and other "progressive" states, and hailed its enactment as part of "a great social awakening." Social democracy, with the labor movement as its bulwark, held for Dunne the only viable formula for the future. "Democracy could only be preserved," he argued, if "all men have an equal chance to participate in the opportunities, the work, and the profits of our national development." Seeing wage earners as the producing class, "the backbone of the nation and the real ruling class," Dunne urged them "to carry the light of reason and humanity into dark places." Recognizing the problems inherent in the wide variation of welfare legislation, he called for joint efforts by the major industrial states to standardize their provisions, a call that went largely unheeded even though echoed by such contemporaries as Governor Cox of Ohio. For the enactment of his own welfare program, the governor relied primarily upon his own Chicago Democrats in cooperation with downstate Democrats, urban Republicans, a few Progressives, and a handful of Chicago Socialist representatives.[35]

The creation of retirement pensions for several categories of public employees was high on the list of priorities. Pensions for firemen resulted from a proposal passed with the nearly unanimous backing of city lawmakers. Chicago House of Correction employees similarly benefited from a measure introduced unsuccessfully in 1909, but later passed. Urban lawmakers also solidly favored retirement plans for civil service employees and a resolution to investigate the possibilities of a statewide system of pensions. The Dunne administration provided for state contributions to teacher's pension funds, which the governor claimed doubled the size of the benefits.[36]

Although Illinois also failed to enact a statewide minimum wage law during the Progressive Era, urban lawmakers evidenced a great deal of concern about the issue. Chicago Democrats sponsored a resolution to consider the feasibility of a minimum wage law for women. The administration also created a vice commission, chaired by Lieutenant Governor Barratt O'Hara, that spent most of its time documenting the theory that low wages paid by department stores and sweatshops drove girls to a life of prostitution. Its major recommendation was a minimum wage for female workers.

Chicago Democrats also voted for the resolution of a Progressive representative to determine the need for a general minimum wage standard. Having failed in all these attempts, they contented themselves with more modest efforts. Following the recommendation of the Illinois Federation of Labor, Dunne and his legislative cohorts succeeded in having a law passed that would require the semimonthly payment of wages in order to save workers from the necessity of borrowing from loan sharks, who often charged 10 to 15 percent interest. For those who still had to borrow, the administration proposed the establishment of wage loan corporations chartered by the state and limited to a 3 percent interest charge. Although some Chicago lawmakers objected that the rate was too high, most voted for its passage.[37]

On the closely related issue of maximum hours of employment, Chicago lawmakers again took the lead. They introduced bills to control the hours of interurban railway employees. They also supported an hours limitation statute for firemen, and backed Dunne's unsuccessful campaign for an eight-hour day for state employees. The fight to establish a limitation on the hours of female workers was bitter and frustrating because of the opposition of the Illinois Manufacturers Association, but administration supporters and a few Progressives pushed hard for the reform. Most Chicago lawmakers opposed an earlier Republican measure providing for a seventy-hour week and a twelve-hour day. In 1913 they succeeded in passing a fifty-four-hour week bill after a great deal of compromising, but Dunne vetoed it on the grounds that it permitted too many exemptions and set no daily limit. In ensuing sessions, urban lawmakers generally backed more comprehensive measures introduced by Progressives.[38]

The abuses connected with child labor also proved a vital concern for most urban legislators in Illinois, although some were reluctant to prohibit the employment of minors altogether. The low wages paid to heads of households often made child labor a necessary, if regrettable, evil. If the father were dead or unable to work, children would often be the sole support of the family. Not all Chicago lawmakers agreed with that reasoning, and so voted for outright prohibition of child labor; but both groups generally supported the unsuccessful 1915 bill that provided for the strict regulation of the practice, even though a Peoria department store owner claimed that it would "develop a first-class bunch of loafers," and another opponent felt it would lead to "bringing up a nation of sissies." Many new stock representatives voted for exemptions for newsboys and other occupations and clashed with reformers and organized labor over the question of children being allowed to perform on stage, since the theater had become a career ladder out of the working class for many recent immigrants. Most urban lawmakers were unimpressed by the testimony of a famous actress that "a child is more apt to be completely and irrevocably ruined by the artificiality of the stage than to be elevated and ennobled," or that of social worker Jane Addams that the prohibition of child actors "removes these children from temptation and safeguards their social life." To minimize the need for child labor, Chicago lawmakers also backed a state aid measure for mothers with dependent children.[39]

Dunne himself served notice of his sincerity in providing humane standards in the state's factories by his appointment of Oscar Nelson, president of the Chicago Federation of Labor, as chief factory inspector. He followed this with a law requiring sanitary washrooms in factories, and with amendments to the state's Health, Safety, and Comfort Act providing for a power shutoff switch, enclosed elevators, seats for female employees, better lighting facilities, and doors that opened outward. His followers in the legislature enacted a safety code for chauffeurs, as well as a law requiring that factories producing noxious fumes be situated aboveground. The administration also provided for a commission to investigate working conditions in factories and make recommendations for further legislation.[40]

Chicago Democrats were the most consistent proponents of measures designed to provide better working conditions for two major categories of laborers: miners and railroad employees. The urgency for the former was underscored by the terrible Cherry Mine disaster of 1909, which took 259 lives. That year a number of safety measures as well as a resolution to create a commission to investigate mining conditions were introduced. Chicago's representatives generally supported these, despite the fact that most of the state's mine workers were located downstate. Included in the list of successful mining measures were establishment of a mining investigation commission, a shot-firer's act, a stronger health and safety law, the establishment of rescue stations, and the mandatory placement of fire-fighting equipment in the mines. In 1915 a miners examining board was established, limitations were placed on the number of consecutive hours of labor, the certification of miners was required, and mines were required to have two places of egress. Chicago's Democrats strongly endorsed all of these. Their efforts on behalf of railroad workers extended to such measures as equipping all trains with adequate headlights and requiring the frequent inspection of safety devices. Urban Democrats in the house also expended a great deal of effort on behalf of a bill to limit the number of cars on freight trains, a favorite cause of the railroad brotherhoods.[41]

· Chicago lawmakers and Governor Dunne led the fight for unemployment legislation. In 1915 the administration pushed through a proposal for a commission to investigate the question of unemployment compensation, but Dunne's defeat the following year meant the end for any of its recommendations. His proposal for free employment offices was supported by the Windy City delegation in both chambers of the legislature. The administration received similar backing for the regulation of private employment agencies and for merging the employment office with the Bureau of Labor Statistics. Chicago Democrats also were instrumental in the creation of a commission to investigate the causes of unemployment in the state; their votes in the senate were primarily responsible for saving the commission's appropriation. Finally, Dunne himself struck a very modern note by recommending public works projects for the unemployed, particularly in building the state's deep-water-way system. He was sophisticated enough to see the latter proposal not only as a political or humanitarian one, but also as one that would "furnish opportunities for future employment in the commerce that will inevitably develop." [42]

Illinois's urban lawmakers proved as concerned about payments to the victims of industrial accidents as did their counterparts in other states, but they divided between outright workmen's compensation and the employer's liability approach. The former, endorsed by the Illinois Federation of Labor, gave the injured party an automatic payment with no need to affix responsibility for accidents. The latter, favored by the railroad brotherhoods and the Chicago Federation of Labor, held out the possibility of more lucrative awards, but only if negligence on the part of the employer could be proven. All but four Chicago Democrats voted for an employer's liability bill in 1909, and it is likely that the dissenters were holding out for workmen's compensation. In 1911 an employer's liability law was passed with solid city backing, but Republican Governor Charles Deneen vetoed it. Chicago lawmakers also favored a resolution introduced in 1909 to study the merits of both approaches, and voted for the first workmen's compensation law in 1911. Four years later they backed Dunne's recommendations for strengthening the system by taking the power to make awards out of the hands of the courts and turning it over to an industrial board with the power to issue subpoenas, administer oaths, appoint physicians, and fix the amount of compensation. The Illinois and Chicago Federations of Labor supported all these changes, and Dunne himself judged that no other form of legislation was "more humane, more just, and more earnestly demanded by the public." [43]

Welfare legislation was also the overriding interest for those Irish and newer Americans who comprised the bulk of Boston's representation in the General Court. The Bay State had pioneered in this area in the nineteenth century when it enacted the first child labor law, state factory inspection codes, the limitation of working hours for women and children, and compulsory rest periods. This legislation was

greatly augmented and improved during the progressive
years.

Massachusetts law permitted private citizens and groups to
petition the legislature for action, and a great portion of the
declarations in favor of reform measures emanated from
Irish and newer Americans and from labor organizations.
The Democratic platforms during the height of the Progressive Era always featured a large number of welfare proposals,
and governors Walsh and Foss urged these upon the
legislature in every session. "The roll calls of the Senate and
the House," as Walsh himself observed of welfare issues,
"will show a majority of the Republicans always on record in
the negative, and victory always due to the practically solid
Democratic vote reenforced by an independent Republican
minority chiefly from the labor districts." On occasional
questions such as wages and hours legislation, organized
labor influenced the Boston lawmakers to oppose seemingly
progressive proposals, but in the context of their overall
record their actions were consistent.[44]

The establishment of decent wages concerned Boston's
Democratic lawmakers, but their advocacy was tempered by
the Massachusetts Federation of Labor's fear that a statutory
minimum wage might undermine its efforts to achieve even
higher pay scales. In 1912 the state's labor organization lent
its backing to the creation of a minimum wage commission
for women and children. By the time of the constitutional
convention in 1917, though, union leaders voiced their
opposition to the idea of a statewide standard and most
Boston Democrats took the cue and voted in the negative. A
Boston Democratic labor leader set the scene by reading a
letter from Samuel Gompers urging defeat of the proposal.
Most urban lawmakers favored a minimum wage for classes
of employees who were too weak and disorganized to engage
in productive collective bargaining, a stance often endorsed
by labor. Minimum wages for women and children employed
in factories generally received backing from both groups, as
did efforts to set a standard for state employees. A minimum
wage for state employees passed the lower house with solid

Democratic support in 1913, but the senate did not act upon it. The following year the Democrats unsuccessfully opposed a Republican attempt to postpone the measure until the following session. Along the same line, Boston's Democratic delegation in both 1916 and 1917 backed a proposal favored by the Massachusetts Federation of Labor that sought to protect workers from being fined for tardiness, an action amounting to a reduction in wages.[45]

The same principle of providing protection for workers in weak bargaining positions and maximum latitude for those who were well organized animated Democratic attitudes toward the regulation of hours of labor. In both the 1916 session of the General Court and in the constitutional convention, the Hub City's representatives voted to oppose granting the legislature power to establish a maximum number of hours for all workers. On both occasions, their action followed statements by the labor federation that it opposed the measure for male workers employed by private enterprise but favored it for women and children and state employees. True to that position, Boston's Democrats pushed for a fifty-four-hour week for females and minors in 1910 and 1911, voting against GOP attempts to raise the maximum. In 1916 they backed an unsuccessful attempt to lower the maximum to forty-eight and the following year sought to settle for fifty. In 1913, Boston Democrats in both houses backed a measure establishing an eight-hour day for public employees. After defeating Republican attempts to submit the question to a referendum in the lower house they were unable to prevent the senate from attaching an amendment providing for a state supreme court opinion on the measure's constitutionality. In both 1909 and 1910 the Democrats and their labor legislator allies voted to strengthen the eight-hour-day law for construction workers by outlawing the practice of allowing workers to "consent" to work overtime, but they failed to muster the necessary numbers to override gubernatorial vetoes. In 1914 the same coalition fought for a two-week paid vacation for public employees and for declaring Saturday a half-holiday. After frustrating Republican attempts to postpone the bill to the next session, they were forced to accept a senate substitute providing merely for investigation of the matter. In 1917 the Boston lawmakers continued their support of a humane work week by voting for one day's rest in seven for hotel and restaurant employees and for a reduction in the hours of paper mill employees.[46]

As did their counterparts elsewhere, Boston lawmakers pressed for compensatory payment for victims of industrial mishaps. In 1911 they and the labor legislators were out-maneuvered by the Republican regulars in their attempt to strengthen the existing law. Although able to fend off attempts to permit private insurance companies to partici-pate in the program, they eventually had to agree to postponement until the next session. In 1913 the house, at the urging of a host of Irish-American petitioners, voted to extend the time period covered, include hospital costs, and allow patients to select their own physicians, but the senate refused to concur. The following year Governor Walsh, supported by numerous petitions from Irish-Americans and organized labor, reintroduced the same provisions along with an increase in maximum benefits; this time the bill passed both houses. In 1915 another Boston Democrat moved successfully to cover workers who were only temporarily incapacitated; two years later city lawmakers failed in an attempt to include workers hired in the state for employment outside of it.[47]

Boston's Democratic lawmakers also supported a myriad of other proposals designed to improve living and working conditions in the state. They and the labor legislators prevailed in an effort to establish a commission to investigate conditions under which women and children labored. When the state's manufacturers sought to amend the child labor law to allow fourteen-year-old children to work if they had a certificate, a solid bloc of Democratic votes helped hold the line. In response to a petition by Boston Mayor John F. Fitzgerald, Democrats staunchly backed a proposal that would allow city governments to regulate the construction of multiple-resident dwellings. They sought to no avail to include such specific provisions as a requirement for sealed garbage cans in tenements, and also failed to prevent the Republicans from adding a referendum clause. Their concern for decent housing led to their efforts to allow cities the right of eminent domain to build public housing in overcrowded slums. The measures passed the senate in 1915 with only seven Republicans opposing, but failed twice in the house, whereupon the Democrats, with Governor Walsh's backing, successfully introduced a constitutional amendment to that end.[48]

Boston Democrats led the fight for adequate safety signals and fire escapes in factories, but were outvoted when they refused to accept a watered-down version. They also declared overwhelmingly in favor of allowing cities to purchase and sell such necessities of life as food and clothing, and they worked for a free home for people suffering from consumption. The movement to establish a statewide system of old age pensions was sponsored by a number of Irish Democrats in conjunction with labor legislators, but the regular Republicans generally succeeded in sidetracking all such attempts. The city's working class representatives sponsored a number of measures designed to make education available to their constituents and to protect the position of teachers. Two lieutenants of Martin Lomasney persisted in efforts to prohibit inquiries into the religious or political affiliation of public school teachers. After two unfruitful attempts the measure finally passed both houses in 1915. Lomasney himself sponsored bills for the creation of evening schools whose graduates could qualify for bar exams. In 1911 Mayor Fitzgerald petitioned the General Court to create tenure for public school teachers and raise their salaries. The measure passed both houses but Governor Foss, by now feuding with the Boston Irish who had been largely responsible for his election, vetoed the bill. Lomasney, the minority leader of the lower house, and his fellow Bostonians led the successful fight to override the veto, but in the senate Lomasney's brother Joe and the other city Democrats failed in a similar attempt on 25–14 vote.[49]

For the most part the positive record on welfare legislation compiled by Boston's new stock lawmakers was matched by similar contributions from their counterparts in the constitutional convention of 1917. As previously noted, the opposition of organized labor and their own fears that any fixed standards would hinder collective bargaining generally led Boston Democrats to oppose allowing the General Court to set minimum wages and maximum hours. Boston's Irish delegates enthusiastically favored a statewide public trading section. When the introduction of a large number of specific amendments complicated the measure, Martin Lomasney proposed a substitute resolution that simply granted the General Court the power to permit the state and its cities and towns to sell the necessities of life in "times of war, emergency or distress." Although many proponents of the original idea felt that Lomasney's version was too general, the Mahatma insisted that it was "so plain that no one can misunderstand it and so broad that the legislature can act in time of emergency." In the end, the convention adopted the Lomasney substitute and voters approved it by the biggest margin accorded any of the new provisions. The official historian of the body dubbed its introduction one of the most surprising and important incidents of the entire convention. Lomasney and the other Boston working class delegates also pressed for a homestead proposal, which would have allowed the city to construct housing and sell it at cost. After much debate the measure was rejected 90–94, but it had the support of almost all the body's Irish or new American delegates. They also fought unsuccessfully to create a system of social insurance. Lomasney maneuvered to protect those former public employees who already held pensions by requiring their continuation under the existing system, but otherwise he and his fellow Bostonians favored the idea while the Massachusetts Federation of Labor delegates split on the issue. The Boston delegates also backed proposals for a one day's rest in seven provision but it perished in committee.[50]

Rhode Island's urban Democrats were by far the most consistent and conspicuous supporters of welfare legislation in that state's legislature, aided primarily by other representatives of working class districts. Rhode Island had the nation's heaviest proportion of foreign stock peoples, was among the leaders in infant mortality and number of industrial workers, and was lowest in home ownerships. Two-thirds of the state's work force were immigrants or second-generation Americans and most of them were found in "the occupational groups which are the least remunerative and the least skilled." The Democrats' ultimate rise to power in Rhode Island depended heavily upon their espousal of "social and economic ideas beneficial to these groups." The domination of the legislature by the Brayton forces seriously inhibited the enactment of effective ameliorative legislation, but the constant pressure applied by the Democrats and urban Republicans sometimes forced the majority party into sponsoring or accepting weaker versions. This pressure was especially evident on the issue of child and female labor. At almost every legislative session Democrats or urban Republicans introduced bills designed to reduce the hours and improve the conditions of labor for women and children. Organized labor, religious leaders, civic groups, women's clubs, and social workers supported their moves, while opposition generally came from representatives of the textile mills, department stores, jewelry manufacturers, telephone and telegraph companies, and other employers, and even from state officials such as the superintendent of the Board of Health who argued that Rhode Island's rank of second in mortality rates was not due to child and female labor but to his efficiency in reporting statistics.[51]

In 1909 a bill limiting the work week to fifty-four hours for women and children was introduced by the Democrats and eventually enacted into law after the Republicans amended it to fifty-six. In 1910 the more urban house unanimously passed a Republican-sponsored bill to prohibit night work for women and children in department stores, although the

Republican-controlled senate amended this to exempt Saturday nights and the Christmas rush season. The following year urban lawmakers successfully opposed Republican attempts to remove the educational test required for minors to obtain work certificates and tried in vain to bring telephone companies under the night work ban. In 1912, aided by the legislature's lone Socialist, the Democrats sought to lower the work week to fifty-four hours, investigate the wages of women and children, and provide for payment of damages to minors injured on the job. They continued this course in 1913 by backing a fifty-four-hour bill, which was eventually adopted, and by seeking to provide women with maternity leave at full pay. In 1915 they endorsed a bill to prohibit hiring minors unless they could speak English and sponsored bills to increase the coverage of existing laws. Concern for children also motivated the Democrats' endorsement of industrial and vocational education, a stance favored by the state's labor unions.[52]

The Democrats expressed a great deal of interest in the wages, hours, and working conditions of other groups of workers as well. They regularly introduced legislation for an eight-hour day for state and municipal employees and people on public works projects, not only to benefit the workers in question, but also to provide an example for other employers. The Republicans usually stymied the attempts. Unsuccessful Democratic measures would have regulated hours for telephone, telegraph, and railroad employees, set minimum pay scales for public employees, especially for schoolteachers, and petitioned Congress to establish uniform hours and conditions of labor for all industries in interstate commerce. Since the industrial commission reported in 1912 that income was below the cost of living in most Rhode Island industrial centers, a constitutional amendment for a statewide minimum wage scale was proposed, but it did not carry. In the same session an attempt to prevent the attachment of wages in payment of debt also failed, as well as a bid to establish a two-dollar-a-day scale for workers on public projects.[53]

The high incidence of disease and accidents among Rhode

Island's workers led to several Democratic proposals to
regulate conditions of labor. A 1909 study, revealing that
30.3 percent of all male laborers in the preceding decade had
contracted lung diseases from "industrial dust," gave impetus
to measures that would have established an industrial
accident commission, but they were all killed in committee.
So too was a proposal that factory inspectors be dismissed if
they were not performing their function properly. Democrats
also endorsed bills to require first aid stations in factories, to
provide for full train crews, to prevent the firing of employees
who made mistakes in weaving, and to outlaw the use of the
suction shuttle, a weaver's device that had to be started by
the worker's breath and that was so dangerous it was
popularly referred to as the "kiss of death." [54]

Since few of these measures were enacted and industrial
accidents occurred with alarming frequency, the Democrats
expended a great deal of energy on the enactment of an
adequate workmen's compensation system. Threatened by
unsuccessful Democratic attempts in 1910 and 1911, the
Republicans introduced a bill of their own in 1912. The chief
differences between the measures were that the Democratic
one provided for higher rates and for administration by a
board instead of by the courts. The senate Judiciary Committee further amended the proposal by exempting small
business, cutting the length of time covered by the system,
and setting up a series of conditions under which workers
would be ineligible. The Democrats sought to remove these
objectionable features, but in the end all but one of their
number supported its passage. For the remainder of the
Progressive Era they sought to strengthen the system by
providing for more complete reporting of accidents, com-
pelling employers to join, and allowing workers to decide
for themselves if they wanted to apply for compensation.
Despite proposals in 1913 and 1915 for a constitutional
amendment to change the entire system, no significant
alteration occurred until 1921 when the decision was finally
taken out of the hands of the courts and turned over to a
commission.[55]

A wide variety of ameliorative measures, including public housing and tenement inspection, retirement pensions for public employees, public bathhouses and auditoriums, playgrounds, comfort stations for commuters, and reduced trolley car fares for workmen and schoolchildren, received attention and support from Rhode Island's urban Democrats. To take care of the needy and the unemployed during the pre–World War I depression they proposed the creation of a public market and public works projects in Providence. Their concern for their constituents who ran afoul of the law led them to seek the barring of physical coercion to obtain evidence, the so-called third degree, as well as the prohibition of the use of confessions as evidence. In the midst of all this, they found time to petition Congress on several occasions to lower the tariff on necessities and to propose appropriating money to aid flood victims in Ohio and Indiana.[56]

The alliance of the Roraback Republicans with Connecticut's business interests generally proved even more detrimental to the chances of welfare legislation there than did the similar situation in Rhode Island, particularly since the party's urban representatives seemed less willing to challenge the leadership on such issues. Under the circumstances the state's urban Democrats stood out in even clearer relief as the champions of social legislation. For the most part the GOP regulars used their control of the legislative process to strangle or emasculate such measures, but the Democrats were not without their victories. One of the chief ones was the adoption of workmen's compensation. After a coalition of Democrats and urban Republicans narrowly missed pushing such a bill through the senate in 1909, both parties introduced workmen's compensation bills in 1911, the Republican bill being endorsed by the state's businessmen. Republican-proposed amendments exempted agricultural establishments and allowed the employer to claim an "assumed risk" on the part of the worker as a defense against any legal action. Democrats argued vociferously against the changes, but eventually had to acquiesce and voted for the bill on final passage, while six Republicans found even the watered-down version too much to accept. In the lower house urban Democrats led the fight but were overwhelmed by the Republican majority 46–144. The senate then voted to refer the matter to the next session of the legislature.[57] In 1913 a compromise measure, finally hammered out by the judiciary and labor committees, passed the senate unanimously and even managed to gain acceptance in the house. The bill's success could clearly be attributed to the unusually large number of Democrats in the General Assembly, a result of the Republican split in the 1912 election, and to the popularity of the idea of workmen's compensation that forced even the Roraback Republicans to make some concessions. In ensuing sessions urban Democrats made unsuccessful attempts to strengthen the law, while the senate's Democrats led the fight to abolish the upper limit of damages possible for accidental death. The party was pledged to removing the upper limit entirely, but Bryan Mahan of New London, theorizing that half a loaf was better than none, amended the bill to double the limit from $5,000 to $10,000. Mahan was accused of violating a sacred pledge and the chamber's Democrats split down the middle on the final vote.[58]

Urban Democratic lawmakers also worked to better the conditions of child and women's labor if not eliminate it altogether. They led the senate fight for a 1911 bill that would have prohibited the employment of minors in hazardous occupations, but the Republicans riddled it with exemptions. In 1913 a bill forbidding women and children under eighteen to work in certain occupations passed with a Republican amendment giving factory owners sixty days to remedy working conditions. During that same session senate Democratic floor leader John McDonough introduced a package of nine bills drafted by a commission of experts that covered various aspects of child and female labor: hours of employment, accident reports, minimum wages, conditions of labor, and factory inspection. Most of these were either tabled or rejected by the Republican-dominated Labor Committee, which successfully substituted its own more limited bill. In the end, the house version of the bill was so diluted that the senate rejected it, as it did two other house-passed child labor measures that same session. In 1915 the senate rejected two Democratic bills abolishing night work for women and children, and establishing maximum hours; similar bills were rejected in 1917.[59] The urban Democrats were also solidly in favor of state aid to dependent children and unsuccessfully fought for imposition of an estate tax to cover the cost of keeping dependent children in state institutions and to aid mothers with dependent children.[60]

Urban Democrats were also the driving force behind the many efforts to appropriate state money for dependent children and to allow the state to establish humane standards in hours, wages, and conditions of labor. These were either rejected by committee or superseded by weaker substitute measures, and in any case they failed to get anywhere in the lower house.[61] Urban Democrats also failed in their efforts to prohibit the attachment of pensions in payment for debt and to prohibit garnishment of wages in payment of back rent.[62] In 1911 Thomas Spellacy of Hartford advocated the establishment of a comprehensive office of labor commissioner to replace the system of factory inspectors; he also proposed the creation of a committee to investigate working conditions in factories and make recommendations. Neither of these measures passed. Nevertheless, urban Democrats continued to press, generally without success, for the elimination of such specific abuses as factory wastes, occupational diseases, lack of washroom facilities, and unhealthy conditions for telephone and telegraph operators, as well as for an industrial commission.[63]

Railroad employees were singled out for special consideration, probably because they were the most highly unionized workers in the state. Democratic support was especially evident for a bill providing for a full train crew. The representative of the railroad unions argued the necessity of the measure for safety's sake, while spokesmen for the railroad industry denounced it as featherbedding. The debate was long and bitter, and most of the arguments in favor were voiced by urban Democrats. In the end, the Republicans forced the passage of an amendment allowing the state Public Utilities Commission to decide the number of crewmen needed, and all but two senate Democrats held out for a stronger bill. The senate rejected an attempt to revise the law in 1913.[64]

Connecticut Democrats acted on behalf of the disadvantaged in other areas as well. They sought state funds for the education of the blind, and they led the movement to create pension funds for policemen, schoolteachers, custodians, and other public employees. They waged a more ambitious, although unsuccessful, fight to establish an old age pension system in 1917. Several Democrats introduced measures to investigate the high cost of living and proposed to no avail the establishment of public markets.[65]

Thus, in several major industrial states, urban new stock Democrats served as a major force working for the enactment of welfare measures during the Progressive Era. The emphasis placed upon specific approaches varied somewhat from state to state, but in the main they sought similar solutions for similar problems. High on the list everywhere was some form of compensation for those incapacitated by industrial mishaps. Close behind were the passage and enforcement of strict safety and health codes for factories and other places of employment. To a greater or lesser degree, urban new stock lawmakers also endeavored to establish decent wage scales and reasonable limitations on the number of working hours. Since many of them shared the attitude of organized labor that male workers could probably gain better standards in these two areas by collective bargaining than by statute, they were reluctant to establish across-the-board requirements. Nearly all of their number, however, favored statutory limits for women, children, and public employees, who were unorganized and in need of special protection. In every state the working class representatives were in the vanguard of those seeking to extend the protection of the state to women and child workers in the fullest degree possible in the face of the powerful opposition of the industries that employed such labor.

Taught by the experience of those closest to them that unemployment was probably the most serious threat to the prosperity and security of the nation's wage earners, urban legislators sought to commit the state to action. Generally the proposed remedies aimed at the creation of free employment agencies or the regulation of private ones. A few farsighted leaders even argued for public works projects or the distribution of food and other necessities to those without work. These same lawmakers generally favored the establishment of pension funds for a wide variety of workers, as well as for their widows and children. Although no state adopted any comprehensive system of retirement benefits in the era, various categories of workers benefited and much of the credit was due to the efforts of urban new stock representatives. Beyond these commonly favored measures, city lawmakers in a few states proposed action in the area of housing, even to the extent of having the government finance low-cost dwellings. Some also pushed for public markets and other forms of direct aid to the disadvantaged.

In sum, the urban new stock lawmakers in these seven states consistently took positions on the major welfare issues of the day that were at least as advanced as any other identifiable group in the political or social spectrum. In no instance was the enactment of this enlightened social legislation due entirely to the impetus provided by the representatives of the urban working class operating through the Democratic party. The success of any such measure depended upon Democrats' effective collaboration with numerous other elements both within and without the legislature. Those Republicans who represented working class districts were often courageous enough to challenge the probusiness leadership of their own party and to support these measures in the interests of their constituents. Organized labor made major contributions both by lobbying and by having many of its own officials serve in state legislatures. A wide variety of intellectuals, social workers, and humanitarian agencies also contributed constructively by drafting legislation and creating a climate of public opinion more favorable to ameliorative legislation. Their efforts doubtless accounted for a large measure of the support that non–working class representatives gave to welfare measures. In some states these forces were aided by a few Socialist lawmakers, acting in the revisionist tradition of the European Social Democrats. None of these, however, could have effected the enactment of the solid body of welfare legislation produced during the Progressive Era without the leadership, parliamentary skill, and votes of the urban new stock Democrats. The pressure for reform and the disarray of the Republican organizations that previously dominated the state political scene placed them in a strategic position at a crucial period, and they generally proved equal to the challenge. Whether in control of the legislative machinery or acting as a prod to those forces that were in control, urban new stock Democratic lawmakers played a major role in committing their states to a course of governmental responsibility for the well-being of its citizens from which they would never turn back.

CHAPTER 3

The Politics of Amelioration: Unions, Business Regulation, and Taxation

In addition to fostering a wide variety of welfare measures, urban new stock legislators were also notable for their support of other attempts to alter the socioeconomic status quo. Prominent on their list of priorities was strengthening trade unions in their dealings with management during the difficult days of organized labor's infancy. Significant, too, were their endeavors to provide for state regulation of business, particularly of those corporations that provided the necessities of life for their constituents. Urban new stock lawmakers also generally proved highly sympathetic to attempts to develop a more equitable system of taxation on the state and federal level, based as much as possible on the ability to pay. Their allies and opponents on these questions were much the same as those generated by the welfare issues discussed in the previous chapter, although some middle class reformers who favored humanitarian legislation were put off by labor's militancy or by restrictions on business methods and profits. In some cases the city lawmakers played only a supporting role, but in many instances they defined the issues and provided the legislative leadership. At any rate, the efforts of the urban Democrats in the areas of union recognition, business regulation, and taxation were

usually consistent with the broad outlines of twentieth-
century American liberalism, and constituted one of the most
effective methods possessed by their constituents of amelio-
rating their socioeconomic condition. Many of their specific
proposals, although unacceptable at that time, anticipated
the legislation of the New Deal era.

The affinity of urban new stock representatives for the
labor union movement was largely a product of their own
working class backgrounds. The biographies of the vast
majority of city lawmakers clearly identified their origins,
and many listed themselves as union members or officers. In
New Jersey, the Democratic ranks included Cornelius Ford
of Jersey City, president of the state Federation of Labor,
Allan Walsh of Trenton and the machinists union, Arthur
Quinn of Perth Amboy, president of the Brotherhood of
Carpenters, and Frank Shalvoy of Newark and the hatters
union. The Cleveland delegation at the state capital during
the period had James Reynolds, president of the machinists
union, James Kennedy, secretary-treasurer of the plumbers
union, George Doster of the carpenters and joiners, and Tom
Reynolds of the city federation. Connecticut's Democrats
included labor leaders Garry Paddock of Bridgeport, Jeri-
miah Donovan of Norwalk, and Martin Gorman and Peter
Lawlor of Danbury who were codefendants in the famous
hatters case. New York Democracy also far exceeded the
Republicans and Progressives in the number of union
members on its ticket, and even in Massachusetts the
predominance of union officials on the GOP ticket in the mill
towns was often matched by the number slated by the
Democrats in Boston and other large cities. Many of the
urban legislators who were lawyers were frequently retained
to represent labor unions in disputes, as the careers of Robert
Wagner, Senator Billy Hughes of New Jersey, and Boss
Thomas Spellacy of Hartford illustrate.[1]

The leadership and membership of the nation's unions
were largely drawn from the same immigrant stocks as the
lawmakers. An Illinois Bureau of Labor study in 1886
revealed that only 21 percent of the state's trade union

membership were of native stock, while 33 percent were of German derivation, 19 percent Irish, 12 percent Scandinavian, 10 percent British, and 5 percent Polish, Bohemian, and Italian. The Old Immigration, particularly Irish, British, and German-Americans, provided most of the leadership of the National Labor Union, the Knights of Labor, and the American Federation of Labor. In Rhode Island, Irishmen occupied most of the leading positions in the state's unions, while Connecticut's labor movement was headed by such new stock officials as E. C. Terry of the Trainmen's Association, Sol Sothheimer of the Hartford Central Labor Union, and Thomas Sweeney of the plumbers union. Although accurate figures are difficult to obtain, many qualified observers have concluded that the majority of the rank and file members of the American Federation of Labor were Roman Catholics, mostly of Irish and German derivation. Between 1900 and 1918 one-half of the vice-presidents of the federation were Irish-Americans, and their fellow countrymen headed no less than sixty-two of the organization's major craft union affiliates.[2]

Workers from southern and eastern Europe and French Canada were less likely to be union affiliated since they were concentrated in the unorganized mass production industries and had to be prepared to work harder for less reward in order to be employed at all. In certain industries, however, such as mining, textiles, and clothing, unionization of new immigrant groups was proving to be successful; they played a large role in the bitter strikes in Paterson, New Jersey, and Lawrence, Massachusetts, as well as in the Pennsylvania coal mines. The growing willingness of organized labor to endorse at least some measures designed to aid unorganized workers probably helped bridge the gap and made it easier for the urban politician to keep the support of both groups. The AFL's position on immigration restriction, the continued opposition of some leaders to wages and hours legislation, and its general distaste for a system of social insurance were still potentially divisive issues, but they did not rule out effective cooperation on a wide variety of other socioeconomic matters.[3]

The growing involvement of organized labor, and particularly the AFL, in political action after the turn of the century was prompted by a number of considerations. One was that the increasing antiunion militancy of various employer groups, especially the National Association of Manufacturers, threatened to destroy what few gains the movement had made under Samuel Gompers's strategy of "pure and simple trade unionism." In addition to applying such direct methods as coercion, spies, and strikebreakers, manufacturers made increasing use of the nation's complaisant court system to rob unions of their meager arsenal of effective weapons. Obliging judges responded to employer's requests with injunctions, protection for strikebreakers, and severe restrictions on striking, picketing, and boycotting; they even made individual union members financially liable for judgments as the result of a job action. At the same time, the Federation's conservative orientation was being severely challenged by more radical bidders for working class support, mainly the Socialist party and the Industrial Workers of the World. Gompers's elitist philosophy and his refusal to challenge the existing social order led to numerous defections from the ranks and augmented the backing of those calling for a class-conscious reform movement and a vast quantity of social legislation. Perhaps even more significantly, the harsh realities were forcing the AFL leadership to face its inability to pit its economic power against that of management without the government acting as a makeweight. As long as organized labor remained a political cipher, government intervention would continue to be at the pleasure of management.[4]

Labor's response to this worsening crisis was twofold. Many of its leaders sought to modify their opposition to certain types of social legislation of primary benefit to workers not affiliated with the AFL, as their changing attitudes toward wages, hours, and workmen's compensation in New York, Massachusetts, Ohio, and Illinois strongly indicate. Such action might not only blunt the appeal of more radical labor groups, but also broaden the base of support they needed for measures of more pressing concern. Gompers himself was most reluctant to take such a course, but the growing debates over such issues in the Federation's convention and the more advanced positions taken by some state officials demonstrate that others in the AFL were more willing. More crucial to Gompers and organized labor generally was the support of politicians for legislation that would remove the legal disabilities against organization, bargaining, striking, and boycotting. Both on the state and federal level after 1906 the AFL and other union organizations worked increasingly for such measures and their actions brought them steadily into a political alliance with the Democratic party, even though they professed nonpartisanship.[5]

Although this coalition did not proceed nearly as far as it was to do in the 1930s, and despite the fact that a few prominent union leaders such as Daniel Keefe of the longshoremen and John Mitchell of the United Mine Workers were prominent in Republican or Progressive ranks, the national leadership and most state and local organizations clearly expressed their preference for Democrats with increasing regularity. In 1906 the AFL presented a list of grievances to President Theodore Roosevelt and many members of Congress. Of those who replied, forty-seven of the fifty Democrats and only twenty-three of the seventy-three Republicans expressed views that Gompers regarded as satisfactory. In the Congressional elections that year the AFL president took some credit for GOP losses, although the results were hardly conclusive. In 1908 Republican nomination of the "injunction standard bearer," William Howard Taft, and the platform committee's rejection of labor-proposed planks coupled with the Democrats' acceptance of three-fourths of them led to the AFL's endorsement of William Jennings Bryan. Although the leadership failed to deliver the vote in 1908, its position helped accustom the rank and file to political action. The enactment of twenty-seven prolabor measures by the Democratic House of Representatives in 1911, the rejection by the Republican Senate of eighteen of them, and the GOP's refusal to accept six of labor's nine planks in 1909 led to the endorsement of Woodrow Wilson in 1912. Although the Progressive platform was more prolabor than the Democrats', Gompers's mistrust of Roosevelt and his business associates George Perkins and Frank Munsey precluded support. Wilson's efforts on labor's behalf were sufficient to merit another endorsement in 1916.[6]

On the state level, the situation was much the same. The political realities generally dictated that labor establish a working relationship with the dominant urban political machines since the latter had the votes and the organization to achieve labor's goals. Given the small town orientation of the Republicans, the Democrats generally proved more receptive; experience soon proved that labor's endorsement paid off in votes more often than not. In New York, the state Federation published a yearly honor roll and blacklist and, except for 1913 when Tammany's impeachment of Governor Sulzer aroused labor's ire, city Democrats generally appeared on the former rather than the latter. In fact two years earlier only two of the forty-two legislators on the NYFL's blacklist were Democrats and in 1915 Samuel Gompers himself ran as a Democratic delegate to the constitutional convention.[7]

In Massachusetts James Michael Curley assured his Tammany Club that it was his "duty to be right on labor measures," and his biographer has observed that "any hint from organized labor was enough to cause an order requiring action." The close working relationship between the Boston Irish in the legislature and the state's unions has already been noted in the previous chapter, as has their frequent coalition with the labor representatives of the mill towns. The similarity of the Democratic legislative program to that of organized labor in all seven of the states was generally striking and the newspapers frequently reported meetings between the two groups to work out bills and strategy. Governor Dunne of Illinois ran with labor's endorsement both in 1912 and 1916

and did such a conscientious job of fulfilling the state
Federation's program that the organization's 1916 convention accorded his record a virtual eulogy. Dunne was so
certain of labor's support that he felt safe in publicly urging
unions to concern themselves with "the rights of those
masses who toil as you do but are not affiliated with your
movement," and to use their "ability to improve the condition of the whole people." Although local political conditions
prompted some prominent union leaders affiliated with the
Progressive party and others as well to cooperate with
Republicans, the vast majority of unions placed increasing
reliance upon the Democratic party during the second
decade of the twentieth century. The party representatives in
the legislature usually responded with strong backing for
labor's rights.[8]

The Tammany Democrats in New York showed increasing
concern for labor's welfare with the ascendancy of Smith and
Wagner after 1910. Even before that time the Hall had
received its share of labor backing, since labor was often
forced to accept the lesser of two evils. The temporary
setback caused by the Sulzer incident in 1913 damaged the
relationship somewhat, despite the party's enactment of
nearly all of labor's programs, but the advent of the
reactionary Whitman administration cast the Democrats and
the unions as dual defenders of the state's working class.
Labor leader Peter J. Brady styled Boss Murphy "one of
labor's best friends" who "never failed to help us when we
needed his powerful aid to push labor legislation." Although
they worked together to establish the 1915 constitutional
convention, upstate Republicans controlled the convention,
causing both groups ultimately to cooperate against the
proposed document. By 1915 prominent labor leaders were
making public testimonials to both Smith and Wagner,
offering the organization's support should either decide to
run for governor. Wagner responded in nearly every legislative session by introducing bills aimed at strengthening
labor's position. One exempted unions from prosecution

under the state's antitrust law, specifically providing that wages and hours agreements concluded through collective bargaining were not conspiracies. Another limited the use of injunctions in labor disputes, while a third sought to protect labor's right to organize, picket, and strike. These failed to get by the Republican-controlled legislature but Wagner went on to further efforts on behalf of organized labor both as a judge and a U.S. Senator, while his Democratic colleagues continued to work for the same cause on the state level.[9]

Massachusetts urban Democrats also exerted themselves on behalf of the state's unions, again working in close alliance with the Republican labor legislators. In 1910 a bill to allow unions to discipline their members, by fining those who crossed picket lines or failed to honor a boycott, passed the senate on the strength of the Democrat–labor Republican coalition. The lower house rejected the proposal on a 97–109 vote, after the same coalition had sought to amend the proposal to allow unions to fine members who resigned. In the same session city Democrats and labor legislators failed to carry a bill to limit the use of injunctions and to provide jury trials for violators of court orders. Democrats were more successful with a modified version of the same bill in 1911, after floor leader Martin Lomasney and his followers frustrated Republican attempts to substitute a weaker version. The entire Boston senatorial delegation, including Lomasney's brother, voted for a measure that permitted strikers to picket, and nearly all those in the lower house followed suit. When Governor Foss vetoed the act on the grounds that it violated the rights of nonparticipants, the Boston Irish sought unsuccessfully to pass it over his veto. Five years later they also endorsed an unsuccessful effort to regulate the practice of hiring strikebreakers. They continued their support of organized labor in the 1917 constitutional convention by favoring a resolution declaring that labor was not a commodity and limiting injunctions during a strike unless serious property damage resulted. Although the provision failed of adoption, labor and the Democrats salvaged some small victory by defeating a compulsory arbitration provision.[10]

Urban Democratic lawmakers in Connecticut also led the struggle for union recognition. They exerted their biggest single effort on behalf of legalizing boycotting and picketing. Senate Democratic floor leader Spellacy introduced a proposal to do so in 1911. The main lobbyists in favor included most of the state's union leaders as well as social worker Robert Hunter, author of *Poverty*, and Socialist Jasper McLevy of Bridgeport. Those who testified against included the president of the state Manufacturers Association and D. C. Loewe, plaintiff in the landmark hatters case that threatened to destroy the union movement by holding individual members liable for damage done during a strike. The bill failed, as did Arch McNiel's attempt to revive it two years later, but the Democrats continued to press for other advantages for the state's unions. Spellacy tried unsuccessfully to impeach an antilabor judge in 1911 on petition of several unions, and also failed to outlaw the practice of blacklisting. In 1917 Frederick Neebe and floor leader Patrick O'Sullivan led the vain fight for proposals to require employers to acknowledge that they were being struck when advertising for employees, to prohibit the use of private police during labor disputes, to require that two witnesses were necessary to prove intimidation or boycotting during a strike, and to outlaw the use of contract prison labor.[11]

Their equivalents in Rhode Island were just as active, though no more successful, in attempts to aid union development. As late as 1926, a study on labor conditions in the state concluded that "it is traditional that wage settlements and working conditions in most plants are on an individualistic basis." Even so, unions were very active during the period and the state's employers, generally backed by the press and public opinion, launched a ferocious counterattack featuring blacklists, spies, strikebreakers, injunctions, and "yellow dog" contracts. Under the circumstances the Democrats emerged as the most prominent prounion force in the government, seeking to deprive the state's employers of their main weapons and to strengthen labor's bargaining position. Assembly Democrats unsuccessfully introduced a bill to outlaw blacklisting in 1912. The proposal to create a board of conciliation, because the Rhode Island unions considered themselves much weaker than did the Massachusetts ones, failed in 1912 and again in 1915. "Yellow dog" contracts, specifying that the employee would not join a union, were attacked in 1913, but the Republicans killed that bill in committee, along with one that would have required companies to advertise that they were being struck when seeking new workers. Efforts by various Rhode Island Democrats to outlaw the use of contract convict labor and to require that convict-made goods be labeled as such proved equally fruitless. A few urban Republicans again joined the Democrats on all these proposals to seek discharge from committee, but the majority party was always able to hold the line.[12]

Several similar bills were introduced by working class representatives in New Jersey, and backed by their fellows. Paterson Republican James Blauvelt, a labor lawyer, and the state Federation of Labor president, Cornelius Ford of Jersey City, combined in 1909 to seek limitations on the power of the chancery courts to punish violations of labor injunctions. The measure had the backing of Gompers and the AFL but failed in the lower house by a 22–36 vote with Hudson and Passaic County representatives of both parties forming the major source of support. Ford later continued to press for laws that would prohibit advertising for strikebreakers, appoint union representatives to the state labor board, require full train crews, and outlaw the use of contract prison labor. Urban Democrats in the lower house gave overwhelming support to all these, but almost none was able to get through the roadblock of the malapportioned senate.[13] Urban Democrats in Illinois were similarly concerned about the well-being of the state's unions. In 1909 they generally backed an abortive effort to require proof of an actual conspiracy before an injunction or restraining order could be issued. The efforts of the Illinois Manufacturers Association and the Associated Employers of Illinois helped prevent the enactment of an anti-injunction law until 1925. Urban Democrats were also the moving force behind legislation permitting unions to label their products and bargain collectively. In response to the state's powerful railroad brotherhoods, city Democrats also pressed for a full train crew bill.[14]

In their efforts to strengthen the state's unions, Ohio's urban Democrats formed a coalition with labor and sometimes with such middle class leaders of their party as Johnson and Cox. The latter were not always willing to create what they considered special privileges for able-bodied workers. The unions for their part were not always consistent either, insisting upon their right to bargain for the best terms on most occasions, but seeking government assistance on others. Tom Johnson worked hard for the passage of an anti-injunction law and urged it upon the national Democratic platform committee in 1908, but his followers in the legislature were unable to make any headway with the idea before 1911. That year, in the constitutional convention, a Cincinnati labor leader proposed to restrict severely the use of injunctions and to guarantee jury trials for workers who violated the ones that were issued. Labor and urban representatives gave vigorous support to the bill and passed it by a large majority, but rural and business opposition defeated it on the referendum vote. Labor and urban delegates also fought unsuccessfully for other measures in the convention, including a specific guarantee of the right to organize and strike, and prohibition of the blacklist and the hiring of strikebreakers. They continued to support these aims in the 1913 session of the legislature, but Governor Cox's opposition led to the defeat of the effort, prompting the state Federation of Labor to deny him its support in 1914 despite his record on other labor and welfare issues. Ohio's urban delegates to the constitutional convention also worked to table a proposal for compulsory arbitration, since organized labor, as in Massachusetts, felt that it could get better results if the bargaining process were left to run its course. In addition all but three of Cleveland's new stock lawmakers voted for a measure to prohibit the use of contract prison labor, while only two of their members failed to support a bill to punish companies making fraudulent use of the union label on their products.[15]

In the main, urban new stock politicians were probably the most consistent supporters of the trade union movement in their respective states during the Progressive Era. Their positions were generally identical with those of organized labor itself, a predictable situation since many state legislators were themselves active in the labor movement. They strove to guarantee labor's right to organize, bargain collectively, strike, picket, and engage in boycotts. They also sought to deprive management of some of its most effective ammunition against unions, such as the blacklist, "yellow dog" contracts, labor spies, private police, and strikebreakers. On such questions as arbitration and conciliation, most urban new stock lawmakers responded to local circumstances (as they did on wages and hours legislation), supporting the idea where unions were weak and stood to gain, opposing it where they were stronger and hoped to fare better by direct confrontation. Despite occasional disagreements over some issues, the general trend in the second decade of the Progressive Era was one of growing interdependence between the urban political machine and organized labor.

The realization by the urban lawmakers that the state might play a more active role on behalf of their constituents carried over into the area of business regulation. This issue was so central to the reform impulse of the age that it often served to obscure the significance of other major concerns. Scholars have identified many different sources and motives for such activity, and have differed strongly over the sincerity of its advocates and the efficacy of the results. The earliest analysts saw the movement for regulation as an agrarian one, a series of efforts by disgruntled farmers to halt the machinations of the railroads, insurance companies, grain elevators, and banks that increased their cost of doing business. Others have emphasized the role played by merchants and small businessmen seeking to minimize the advantages bestowed

by bigness and restore themselves to a more competitive
position. Such recent scholars as Gabriel Kolko have seen
the movement for federal regulation as part of the design of
the nation's major corporations to extend their sway over the
economy. Nearly all those who have investigated the phenomenon have also pointed out the disagreement between
those who wanted to "bust the trusts" and enforce competition, and those who desired only to outlaw certain unfair
practices through government supervision, a debate that
formed at least the rhetorical difference between Roosevelt's
New Nationalism and Wilson's New Freedom in 1912. A
similar split was often noticeable on the question of regulation of utilities versus outright municipal ownership and
operation. Most recently, some scholars have perceived the
efforts of reformers to use governmental power to ensure
better products and services at reasonable prices as the early
flowering of consumer consciousness. The interaction of the
representatives of the urban new stock working class with all
of these other social groups produced a flurry of regulatory
legislation in the seven states.[16]

The motives of the urban Democrat were primarily those
of his constituents, reflecting their need for adequate and safe
heating, lighting, transportation, food, and clothing at prices
the wage earner, office worker, civil servant, and shopkeeper
could afford to pay. Laissez-faire had never established a
very firm footing in most of the countries of continental
Europe or Ireland, and those who had proceeded from that
environment were used to the regulation of economic
enterprise by the state, the church, and merchant and craft
guilds. They usually favored regulation over trust-busting,
sought municipal ownership of utilities when mere regulation
seemed ineffective, and in all cases worked for greater
business responsibility to workers and consumers. Most of
the states under investigation took significant steps in this
direction during the Progressive Era. Kolko, who dismisses
the federal regulatory legislation of the period as either
ineffectual or a blind for big business control of the
economy, acknowledges that many states were more success-

ful, and views the fear of effective state regulation as one of the prime motivations causing big business to turn to the federal government.[17]

The one regulatory measure that received the strong backing of urban Democrats in all seven states was the creation of some type of commission to oversee the rates and services of public utilities. In New York the first such effective agency was formed during the administration of Republican reformer Charles Evans Hughes, but even at that point its passage was aided in large measure by the decision of the Democratic caucus to back the bill. As they did on so many other occasions, many GOP regulars refused to follow the governor's lead. The Democrats' contribution was so significant that the staunchly anti-Tammany *New York World* editorialized that the Hall's lawmakers "have heard from the people. Their decision merits the highest praise." During the landmark 1913 session the Democratic majority in the legislature endorsed measures designed to strengthen and expand the commission's powers. Democratic leadership also embraced the concept of municipally owned and operated gas and water facilities for New York City, after William Randolph Hearst had first popularized the idea. Expanding this concept to the state level in 1913, the party's representatives, led by Lieutenant Governor Martin Glynn, supported legislation for the ownership and operation of hydroelectric plants in upstate New York over the objections of upstate Republicans representing the privately owned electric power companies. Al Smith, as governor, sought to expand the idea, stating that "we are poor citizens if we allow the things worth most to get into the hands of the few." In 1918, Democrats pressed for a more comprehensive municipal ownership bill in cooperation with the Tammany mayor of New York City, John ("Red Mike") Hylan. In January Wagner and assembly floor leader Charles Donahue introduced legislation that included a repeal of the requirement that the city could only build utilities on a pay-as-you-go basis. The measure allowed municipalities to issue bonds in anticipation of revenue to finance such efforts. Senate

Republican leader Elon Brown of Watertown stigmatized the
proposal as anarchistic, Bolshevistic, and "German," an
obvious attempt to smear Wagner with the anti-German
hysteria of the World War I era. He was answered sharply by
James Foley, Murphy's son-in-law, but the Republican
succeeded in substituting a commission to study the question.[18]

In New Jersey efforts to bring the state's common carriers
and utilities under regulatory control were primarily the
work of a coalition of urban Democrats and New Idea
Republicans. When Newark Democrat Edwin Wright first
proposed a regulatory plan in 1907, the Hudson and Essex
County delegations unanimously supported him. The bill
passed the assembly on a 36–22 vote, but the heavily
Republican senate defeated it. Newark Boss James R.
Nugent reportedly opposed a measure granting the commission somewhat less authority, but it still received the votes of
nearly all the Hudson and Essex Democrats; it failed to pass
in the lower house by a 28–31 margin. In both 1908 and 1909
the Jersey City Democrats, in conjunction with reform
Republicans, again backed the stronger of the two proposals,
only to have the senate again stymie their efforts. In 1910
Democrats held out for the enactment of an almost exact
copy of the New Idea bill, even though the Republican
regulars eventually undercut their support by passing a much
more innocuous version. The following year the Wilson
administration finally succeeded in enacting the stronger
measure, with Hudson and Essex Democrats constituting
twenty-one of the forty votes cast in its favor in the assembly.
The resultant law "was one of the most thoroughgoing public
utilities statutes in the country at the time," and "incorporated all the provisions for which progressives had been
struggling for the past decade." [19]

Democrats were equally committed to the creation of a
public utilities commission in Cleveland, but the generally
rural orientation of Ohio state government motivated them
to hold out stubbornly for municipal regulation or ownership
of utilities in the state's largest cities. In 1911 several

Cuyahoga legislators voiced their opposition to placing regulatory power completely in the hands of the state agency. They also argued that utility rates should be based on physical valuation of property, and not on reported capitalization, since the latter was easily subject to manipulation. Snubbed on both these points, the Cleveland delegation split on the final vote, six assemblymen voting no and seven yes. All three city senators voted obstinately in the negative. In 1913, though, legislation to increase the latitude of municipalities in dealing with public utilities provoked a Democratic-Republican division. At a 1914 special session all the city's lawmakers in both houses supported amendments to this bill that would clarify the powers and duties of the commission. When the Republican administration in 1915 sought to weaken the home rule provisions of the law by permitting city councils only to request the state Public Utilities Commission to review rates and property valuations, most Cuyahoga lawmakers refused to concur. In the senate three Clevelanders voted no and the other two abstained. In 1917 all but three city Democrats voted for the successful proposal of another Cleveland legislator to bring the state's railroads under the supervision of the Public Utilities Commission.[20]

The same concern for municipal regulation colored the attitude of Chicago lawmakers toward the Illinois Public Utilities Commission. This was a precondition to which all three Chicago Democratic leaders, Harrison, Sullivan, and Dunne, had firmly committed themselves. The governor had made his reputation, both as judge and mayor, on the issue, and in his inaugural address he came out flatly for municipal ownership of utilities and traction companies where feasible and for state regulation elsewhere. When legislation was introduced providing for actual municipal ownership of certain utilities in Chicago, all but the followers of Roger Sullivan supported it. As a major stockholder in one of the city's largest gas companies, Sullivan reportedly instructed his lieutenants to refuse assent. In 1913 the leader of the Harrison forces in the senate, with Dunne's concurrence, introduced legislation granting the city the right to regulate the rates charged by Chicago's telephone, gas, and electric companies, but the attempt failed. Efforts to incorporate the provision into Dunne's public utility measure in the same session also miscarried, despite urging from all three Democratic leaders that the principle be adopted. Because he was committed to the establishment of some form of commission, Dunne reluctantly signed the Public Utilities Bill despite advice from many Chicago Democrats to veto it. Several times in ensuing sessions Chicago Democrats introduced local regulation amendments, but failed in votes sharply divided between Cook County and downstate. By the end of his administration Dunne, despite his dissatisfaction with the defeat of the home rule section, was lauding the commission's record of saving the consumers two million dollars a year and of having only 5 of its 3,925 rate decisions reversed by the courts.[21]

Boston's Democrats also supported efforts on behalf of state regulation of utilities and transportation facilities. Massachusetts had a railroad commission, but in 1911 Governor Foss proposed to replace the body with a public service commission empowered to regulate other utilities as well. "The Republican majority," according to a contemporary expert, "denied the necessity for the change," while the Democrats backed the governor's efforts. The Republican-controlled Ways and Means Committee first refused to discharge the bill, despite several Democratic petitions. When they did, the majority members attached a railroad-sponsored amendment permitting common carriers to issue long-term debentures at rates equal to twice the amount of their existing capital stock. Foss charged that this was the "price enacted by the railroads for their permission to enact the other provisions of this bill," but nearly all the General Court's Democrats were anxious enough to see the commission established that they accepted the amendment. When Foss vetoed the bill, the lower house overrode him on a 170–58 count, with most Boston Democrats following the lead of Martin Lomasney in voting to uphold the act. In so doing they concurred with Joseph B. Eastman, secretary of the Public Franchise League, who wrote in the *Quarterly Journal of Economics* that it was still a worthwhile bill, particularly for regulation of gas and electric companies. In 1915 the Democrats endorsed Governor Walsh's recommendation to have the Public Service Commission investigate the activities of the New England Telephone and Telegraph Company.[22]

Democratic agitation in Rhode Island in 1911 forced the majority party to propose the creation of a public utilities commission the following year. The GOP measure provided for a commission appointed by the governor, with the consent of the malapportioned senate, empowered to fix the rates subject to judicial review. The house Judiciary Committee, with several Republican members and only two Democrats, further amended the measure to allow railroads to issue free passes and to prohibit commission control of stock issues. The Democrats objected to all these provisions and also insisted upon the appointment of one member of organized labor to the commission as well as the right of the agency to fix wages and conditions of labor for utility workers. In the end the minority party was forced to accept the Republican version, although it continued its efforts to strengthen the commission in 1913.[23]

Similar arguments over details complicated urban Democratic support for utilities regulation in Connecticut, but the party again emerged as the champion of the strongest possible agency. As in Rhode Island, the Democrats ultimately pressured the Republicans into espousing the establishment of an appointed commission with control over all the state's utilities. Democrats sought two elected agencies, one for transportation and the other for utilities, on the grounds that the former was statewide and the latter primarily local. Most of the state's unions reportedly favored this approach also, but the move failed in both houses and most of the proponents acquiesced in the Republican version. In ensuing sessions urban Democrats continued unsuccessful efforts for elected commissioners and home rule.[24]

Besides their endorsement of utilities commissions, urban new stock legislators were also conspicuous in their support of a wide variety of other regulatory measures. New York Democrats were again especially active in 1911 and 1913. In the latter session Tammanyite Jimmy Walker introduced legislation to bring fire insurance companies under state regulation. Democratic votes were also largely responsible for giving the insurance department powers over the promotion of new insurance companies, the sale of their securities, their capital stock, and the rates they could charge under the employer liability system. Businesses with a particular relevance to the everyday lives of the working class, such as loan companies, cold storage food plants, and tenement housing corporations, were brought under the watchful eye of the state between 1911 and 1913. Aaron J. Levy, a representative of John F. Ahearn's Fourth Assembly District, introduced legislation incorporating the New York Stock Exchange, which stipulated that brokers must reveal to their customers the details of their transactions and made it illegal to buy or sell securities without the customer's permission. City Democrats also favored the creation of a commission to investigate and propose alterations in the state's banking laws. A stringent antitrust law was proposed by a New York City Democrat and favored by his fellows, while the organization also gave backing to a truth-in-advertising bill and a small loans regulation bill. During World War I Wagner and house Democratic leader Charles Donahue of New York City took the lead in proposing price regulation of commodities and even public purchase and distribution, measures also favored by Herbert Hoover, the federal food director.[25]

Urban Democrats consistently backed regulatory measures in New Jersey. Most noteworthy was their support for Wilson's famed "Seven Sisters" laws designed to curb the growing concentration of control in the state's industries by forbidding stock watering and other enumerated practices, making corporate directors personally responsible for such infractions, and prohibiting the creation of future holding companies. These seven regulatory bills were voted upon separately during the 1913 session of the legislature, and not a single Democratic vote was cast against any of them. In addition city lawmakers consistently proposed and backed numerous other less ambitious measures. Thomas Donnelly of Jersey City was the author of an unsuccessful bill to create a bureau of rapid transit in 1912, as well as one to regulate the price of electricity per kilowatt-hour, which failed despite the overwhelming support of Hudson and Essex Democrats. Thomas Martin of Jersey City proposed several bills to regulate street railways and power companies that same year, while his fellow Hudsonites unanimously backed a fifty-year limitation on streetcar franchises and two pure food and drug acts. Nearly all the assembly's new stock legislators also voted for a bill drawn up by a Newark Democrat in 1912 to fix telephone charges in first-class cities, and were similarly enthusiastic about attempts to control smokestack emissions and water pollution.[26]

Cleveland Democrats followed a similarly forward-looking course on issues affecting public control of business. The Cuyahoga lawmakers were consistent in their support of home rule with regard to efforts to curb the influence of private traction companies in the state's municipalities. One of the hardest-fought battles of the Progressive Era in Ohio resulted when attempts were made to repeal the so-called Rogers Law of 1896, which permitted cities to grant fifty-year franchises to street-railway companies. Although the bill introduced specifically negated the franchise in Cincinnati and legislators from that city provided the leadership, the Cleveland lawmakers lent considerable support. They were unanimous in their backing of the strongest possible measure, which passed the lower house by a 69–42 margin. When the opposition of the traction companies forced the introduction of a compromise bill later in the same session, two Cleveland senators and two representatives did not vote, while the remainder accepted the substitute.[27]

The regulatory principle was also involved in the adoption of a "blue sky" law that regulated the sale of bonds, stocks, and other securities, and of real estate not located in Ohio. It passed the house by a 107-0 vote, supported by the entire Cincinnati and Cleveland delegations. Two Republican senators voted against passage, but the measure received the votes of all the Democrats present in the upper chamber. Four years later, Cleveland lawmakers in both houses backed the creation of the office of commissioner of securities who, in addition to having absolute authority in issuing and regulating licenses of concerns selling securities within the state, was to regulate and license the loaning of money without security, upon personal property, and of purchasing or making loans upon salaries.[28]

In addition to these better-known ventures into the area of business regulation, Cleveland's new stock lawmakers were instrumental in several similar attempts. The regulation of the insurance business was the peculiar province of Herman Fellinger, himself an official of the German National Alliance Insurance Company. Among other things, Fellinger sponsored bills to supervise insurance companies (except for life insurance), to regulate fire insurance companies and their agents doing business in the state, and to create a state superintendent of insurance. In the main all these bills were supported by his fellow Cleveland Democrats. Fellinger also introduced a truth-in-advertising measure in 1913, which had their unanimous backing. Regulation of various aspects of banking likewise had the complete concurrence of the Cuyahoga delegation in the senate and of all but two in the house. A bill for the creation of a state inspector of building and loan associations also received the nearly universal support of Cleveland's Democrats. Proposals for establishing a bureau of markets and a state superintendent of public works enjoyed similar fealty.[29]

Chicago's Democrats also sought to assert the police power of the state over a number of vital industries. Dunne illustrated their position by lashing out at Illinois insurance companies in his inaugural address. Charging that rates were "fixed arbitrarily by a combination of the great fire insurance companies of the state," the chief executive urged the legislature to "invoke and require government regulation."

His followers in the General Assembly responded by endorsing attempts to control all forms of insurance activity. Dunne also was a strong advocate of supervising railroad rates, especially on local and interurban lines. One of his most frequent claims was that his administration had prevented rate discrimination against schoolchildren. The Chicago Democrats also sanctioned uniform standards for weights and measures and pure food and drug acts. They began the movement for the development of a comprehensive hotel code in 1909, brought to fruition in 1913, for the suppression of fumes and odors aboveground, and for mandatory inspection of oil companies. It was Chicago Democrats who introduced a successful joint resolution asking Congress to prevent and suppress monopolies by appropriate legislation.[30]

The Boston Irish were similarly involved with regulatory measures. In 1911 they backed a measure designed to forbid price discrimination in the sale of commodities that failed the senate by a paper-thin 16–17 count. They also gave full support to efforts to prohibit price discrimination by oil producers and distributors. In 1913 an attempt to extend the principle to such necessities as milk, eggs, and butter and to direct the attorney general to initiate suits failed of passage. The position of the Boston Irish in the long-drawn-out struggle over the merger of the New Haven and Boston and Maine Railroads was not always consistent, but neither was that of the state's other groups. In 1910 they divided on the issue of the New Haven's purchase of the Berkshire Street Railway Company, but generally refused to allow savings banks to purchase bonds of the Boston Railroad Holding Company. In 1914 they voted to force the holding company controlled by Republican Governor Eben Draper to dispose of its Boston and Maine stock. The attempt of the New Haven to charge its new subsidiary a switching fee later caused a rift between the followers of floor leader Lomasney and those of Governor Walsh. In the constitutional convention the boss of Ward Eight led the fight to allow the state to transfer utility franchises if companies failed to provide adequate service. Such agreements, the Mahatma argued, "should forever remain subject to revocation and amendment." He and his fellow Bostonians also endorsed the resolution that all the state's resources belong to all the people.[31]

Urban Democrats in adjacent Rhode Island, aided by some Republican counterparts, pressed the state's businesses on all sides. In 1909 they attacked the gas, ice, and electric companies for levying "a shameless tax on the poor" with no marked success other than blocking the merger of the Blackstone Valley gas and electric companies. At the same time they backed efforts to regulate pawnbrokers and loan sharks, and to oversee the sale of coal by weight and kind "to protect the poor who buy coal in small lots." In 1910 they joined a coalition of city officials, grangers, and ministers to seek the banning of billboard advertising, and endorsed efforts to regulate the weight and price of bread. The following year they sought a truth-in-advertising bill, and in 1912 Providence Democrats worked for measures to provide for state inspection of loan companies. They also backed an unfruitful attempt to investigate the price of coal and failed on a largely partisan vote to prohibit free railroad passes to legislators. In 1913 the urban Democrats secured house concurrence for the investigation of the New England Trust Company, and failed by one vote to get a state antitrust law discharged from the Republican-controlled judiciary committee. Democrats led the effort to develop an effective pure food and drug law and moved to investigate the ice trust and to prohibit the sale of spoiled eggs. Most of these attempts failed of ultimate adoption because the Brayton-Aldrich-Wilson forces controlled the legislative process, but their introduction clearly marked Rhode Island's urban new stock Democrats as the state's staunchest champions of business regulation.[32]

The same general patterns prevailed concerning regulatory issues in Connecticut. All but the Hartford representatives consistently backed measures aimed at regulating insurance companies. Numerous urban new stock lawmakers prepared bills to control interest rates and trusts and prohibit illegal practices, while Herman Kopplemann distinguished himself as a champion of stock and securities regulation. Other urban Democrats worked steadily for meat and cold storage inspection, a plumbing board, the limitation of extra charges for extension phones, a fuel commission, a truth-in-advertising bill, and heated vestibules in streetcars. Democrats sought to ensure against water and air pollution, and several emerged as defenders of low streetcar fares, especially for workers and schoolchildren.[33]

With such actions, the representatives of the urban new stock working class generally proved themselves to be staunch protagonists of positive state action, especially with regard to those enterprises that provided the necessities of life for their constituents. Their major concern was on the practical day-to-day level of prices charged and the quality of service and products rendered, an outlook that led them to seek controls over a wide variety of corporations ranging from local ice and coal dispensers to subsidiaries of such monoliths as the American Telephone and Telegraph Company. Many of their efforts in this regard failed to materialize into statutes, mostly because many other segments of society were not yet willing to grant such a wide latitude of action to the state. Except for the Socialists and a few intellectuals it would be difficult to single out any other single group in the period whose record demonstrated such an advanced position on the question of the authority of the state over the economy.

These same urban lawmakers were not quite so active in the field of taxation, but their actions again demonstrated readiness to seek redress of economic inequality. Although the issue of taxation did not arouse the popular imagination to nearly the degree that trust-busting did, it was certainly at least as significant in the long run. For the most part, the groups that dominated the political and economic life of the industrial states had succeeded in escaping at least part of the burden of taxation to which their financial status should have committed them, primarily because their wealth was

mostly in such intangible property as stocks and bonds, while
the tax system was designed to reach such tangible assets as
buildings. Estimates indicate that some cities and states
failed to reach as much as three-fourths of potential taxable
wealth by the general property tax as it was originally
constituted. This inevitably meant that the slack had to be
taken up to an inordinate degree by the urban working class,
either in the form of higher taxes or decreased social services.
The urban middle class, as the owners of homes and
businesses, paid the lion's share of city taxes, while farmers
found it difficult to avoid the property levy since it was
difficult to conceal barns, machinery, and livestock from the
assessor. All three groups eventually reached a consensus
that the intangible wealth of the upper income groups had to
be taxed a fair share, although they often disagreed over the
best method of accomplishing this. On the national scene, the
old stock representatives of the seven states had been among
the leaders in the effort to prevent the enactment of an
income or inheritance tax based upon the ability to pay and
to keep the taxes on the lower and middle classes through
import duties and excise exactions. In the words of the
French historian Mathiez, taxes everywhere "are a charging
product of earnest efforts to have others pay them" and the
well-off "are inclined to burden themselves as lightly as
possible," while "those who have little to say are expected to
pay." For a long time the middle and working classes had
acquiesced in this state of affairs, but the consciousness
signified by the proposal of the federal income tax amendment altered the situation to at least some degree. Many
people who became aware of the inequalities present in the
nation's tax system worked to alter the situation in their
respective states and to effect the ratification of the income
tax amendment. No group in the major industrial states was
more active in this area than the representatives of the urban
new stock working class.[34]

In Illinois, their efforts took the form of changing the
method of assessment and removing the constitutional
barriers to taxing the wealth of its leading citizens. The

Illinois revenue system was based primarily upon a personal property tax that was assessed by an elected board of equalization, thus making taxes a political football. The 1870 constitution specifically forbade the levying of any graduated tax or discrimination in rates between different categories of property, twin restrictions that all but ruled out any possibility of a graduated income tax falling heaviest on those other than wage earners or salaried employees. Governor Dunne took the lead in seeking to correct both these conditions, with the backing of most Chicago Democrats. Floor leader Michael Igoe introduced the governor's proposal to replace the equalization board with a nonpolitical, appointive tax commission, and the measure passed the assembly 79 to 44 in 1913. Nearly all the Chicago Democrats voted in favor of the change, with the exception of several lawmakers who usually were regarded as followers of Roger Sullivan. The measure was killed in the senate by the Republican-controlled Election Committee and the governor's efforts to revive it in the next session of the legislature were to no avail. The administration was more successful in its plan to amend the constitution to provide for graduation of rates and the right to levy divergent rates on different categories of property. Although the proposal failed in 1913, it was adopted by both houses of the General Assembly in 1915, with most Chicago Democrats voting in favor. The proposal failed in a referendum vote, but the fact that it carried polyglot Cook County comfortably and lost downstate serves to illustrate the popularity of tax reform among city dwellers.[35]

Cleveland's representatives were equally involved in efforts to alter Ohio's tax structure. They unanimously supported the enactment of a graduated inheritance tax in 1919, and were in the vanguard of those who fended off conservative attempts to shift the burden of the tax onto small inheritors. Cleveland Democrats resisted legislative restrictions on the city's ability to raise the necessary revenue and to prevent discrimination against city dwellers in the state's tax structure. In 1911 Cleveland lawmakers in the lower house led the fight against a provision in the Smith One Per Cent Tax Law which placed an aggregate limit of ten mills on taxable property (five mills for municipal corporations). Eventually, all but three Clevelanders who did not vote acquiesced in the final passage of the bill. Although state senator William Greenlund introduced a measure in 1913 to increase the amount of levy possible, endorsed by the mayors of the state's largest cities, the bill was kept in committee and the limitations remained on the books.[36]

Cleveland's representatives continued to press for tax reform, and particularly for the type of adjustments best suited to an urban industrial society. A proposal to introduce the home rule principle in taxation passed the senate in 1913, but did not come to a vote in the house. Another bill in the same session, which would have made municipal bonds tax exempt and would thus have encouraged investment in city projects, passed the legislature but failed in a referendum vote, largely because of rural opposition. Six years later, the Cleveland lawmakers supported a joint resolution providing for the classification of property for the purpose of taxation, and took the lead in successfully resisting an amendment that would have placed limitations on the amount of the levy.[37]

The biggest taxation issue of the era was the establishment of a state tax commission in 1913, and the Cleveland Democrats were again on the positive side. Previously the evaluation of property had been in the hands of local assessors, resulting in a wide variation throughout the state. The Cox administration backed a measure creating a state tax commission to insure uniform levies. The Republicans and some rural Democrats fought the proposal vigorously, but in the end it prevailed, 24–8 in the senate and 73–42 in the house. In both chambers the Cleveland contingent provided a solid phalanx of support, along with most other urban lawmakers. The Republican administration of Governor Frank Willis failed in an attempt to repeal the law in 1915, but the state supreme court found it to be unconstitutional in 1917, thus returning authority to the local assessors and weakening the efforts of reformers to raise the revenue needed to operate a modern state. The Cuyahoga lawmakers continued to support the cause of better methods of taxation and were unanimous in their support of the creation of a joint tax commission to study the state's problems in 1917.[38]

Their counterparts in Rhode Island concentrated on frustrating Republican attempts to protect the state's vested interests. When popular agitation forced the Republican party to propose a corporation tax in 1910, the Democrats and some urban Republicans objected to the measure's mild provisions and its stipulation that the GOP lieutenant governor serve as chairman of the proposed tax commission. Despite the efforts of the Brayton forces to secure passage, the urban coalition succeeded in deferring the measure until the next session. When the same combination prevailed upon Governor Pothier to allow a joint bipartisan committee to write a stronger bill in 1911, corporate lobbyists and the Brayton machine killed the attempt. The following year, the GOP proposed the same measure that Democratic leader Albert West styled a "rich man bill" and found objectionable on several grounds. The Democrats were especially adamant against provisions that exempted the New Haven Railroad, stocks and bonds, and the stockholders of public service corporations from taxation, placed the burden on real estate, set the maximum rate at 3 percent, and allowed the tax commission to be appointed with the consent of the mal-apportioned senate. Despite their objections the measure passed the lower house 79–17 on a partisan vote, and the senate concurred with only one Democrat opposing. Democratic spokesmen also resisted a GOP proposal in 1911 to allow real estate appraisers to reassess property values for the previous six years, terming it "vicious." In the end they concurred in a modification to two years proposed by a Providence Republican. They also joined the opposition to funding the so-called good roads bill by the property tax because the cost of highway improvements would be borne by the "poor man and he isn't the one who is going to ride over these roads." Their efforts to substitute a levy on intangible property failed, however, as did the proposal for an inheritance tax.[39]

Connecticut's urban legislators bent most of their efforts toward the repeal of the state's personal tax, and initiated attempts to tax various business enterprises. The personal tax levied a flat rate on each person regardless of income or worth and fell heaviest on the working class, since the employer simply passed the cost along to the consumer. The Central Labor Unions and the Socialists joined the Democrats in repeal efforts, while spokesmen for the state's industries staunchly defended the tax, one small town legislator claiming that it was the "only way to get money from aliens who work here and send money home." Democratic control of the senate in 1913 led to its passage there but the house refused to agree. The Democrats introduced the same proposal in every succeeding session during the Progressive Era but were always frustrated. In addition they sponsored a corporation tax that the state's industrialists claimed would drive out business, and proposed levies on such specific enterprises as banks, trust funds, insurance companies, and trolley car operators.[40]

The biggest taxation issue in Massachusetts was the enactment of a state income tax. The urban Democrats consistently supported the principle of the tax, although the details of the measures and Republican maneuvering caused Martin Lomasney and his closest followers to take some serious exceptions. The main argument revolved around the difference in rates for income from stocks and bonds versus income from wages or salaries, a differential most Democrats accepted as the price for Republican agreement but that Lomasney was unwilling to swallow. In 1911 the Democrats supported the bill through its second reading, even though they were unable to add penalties for failure to file. Republican speaker Joseph Walker of Brookline succeeded in amending the bill over Democratic opposition to provide for uniform tax rates and numerous exemptions. The Republicans also maneuvered successfully to turn the proposed statute into a constitutional amendment. The nascent amendment failed to receive the required two-thirds vote as several Democrats held out for a statutory tax. The same divisions continued to apply for the next several sessions of the General Court, but the enactment of the federal income tax amendment and mounting popular pressure finally led to a rapprochement between the two parties in 1915. Most Democrats agreed to accept the idea of taxing income from securities at a lower rate than wages or salaries, but Lomasney and his four closest followers held out to the end. The amendment had barely been enacted when the constitutional convention again opened the question for debate. Once again Lomasney and his supporters attacked the principle of taxing securities at different rates, but another Boston Irishman introduced the proposed article and most of his fellows, as well as labor spokesmen, worked for the retention of the tax. New York City Democrats gave near-unanimous support to that state's first corporation tax in 1917. Two years later, under the leadership of Governor Al Smith, they joined several independent Republicans from upstate in forcing through a state income tax. After a bitter struggle, Smith agreed to drop his expanded welfare program in exchange for Republican compliance. The GOP was forced to agree because of the state's dire fiscal situation. At Smith's prodding and "usually moving against the grain of middle class prejudice," New York became the first major industrial state that "discarded the general property tax and substituted a general income tax on both individuals and corporations." [41]

By far the most important contribution made to the cause of equitable taxation by the urban Democrats in all seven states was their role in the ratification of the federal income tax amendment. This was the measure regarded by many prominent historians as the most far-reaching passed in the Progressive Era; "perhaps the most profound reform passed in the course of recent American history," in the opinion of George Mowry, the dean of the period's chroniclers. Its ratification by several of the major eastern industrial states provided the necessary margin of victory, since the standpat Republicans in Congress had designed the amendment in the hope that these states would refuse their assent and thus frustrate the Democratic-Insurgent coalition pushing for immediate enactment of a statutory income tax in 1909. The crucial factor was again the temporary setback suffered by the small town–business Republican coalitions and the consequent ascendancy of the predominantly urban Democrats. In Ohio and Illinois ratification took place just before the transition was accomplished but the Chicago and Cleveland delegations nevertheless were important in the victory. In New York, New Jersey, and Massachusetts ratification was a clear-cut triumph for the urban Democrats, aided by other working and middle class representatives. In Connecticut and Rhode Island, they were the only organized groups pressing for adoption and eventually went down to defeat before the Roraback and Brayton Republicans.[42]

Ratification occurred in 1910 in Illinois, where support was bipartisan, reflecting the unwillingness of any political faction to risk the consequences of opposing a seemingly popular measure. Governor Charles Deneen, a Chicago Republican of moderately progressive leanings, recommended ratification although he added that it "is a disputed question whether or not such a tax should be imposed by the nation in ordinary times." The *Chicago Tribune*, soon to endorse Theodore Roosevelt for president, also favored ratification, challenging the other industrial states to follow suit. The ratification resolution passed in the senate 41–0, with twelve of the thirteen Democrats and twenty-nine of the Republicans voting in favor. Nine of the ten who abstained were also Republicans, including Frank Funk of the Bloomington Seed Company who was shortly to be the gubernatorial candidate of the Progressive party. In the assembly, the tally was 83–8 with sixty-two members either absent or not voting. Of the eight negative votes, two were cast by downstate Democrats and six by Republicans, including the speaker, while the GOP floor leader abstained. A few prominent Chicago Democrats were not recorded, such as

Anton Cermak and Sullivanite leader John J. McLaughlin, but the rest of the city's representatives voted to ratify. Governor Dunne later praised the enactment of the first income tax for the revenue it would bring and because it would make the rich bear their proportionate share of the burden of government.[43]

Ratification was more clearly a Democratic victory in Ohio, although the intervention of President Taft undercut any possible Republican opposition. The Democrats pledged ratification in their 1910 platform and victorious Governor Judson Harmon urged it upon the General Assembly. The party also sought to put the Republicans on the defensive by introducing a resolution to have Taft, an Ohio native, address the legislature. The Republicans smothered the proposal in committee, but the president was able to communicate with the legislature through letters to leaders of both parties. With bipartisan support, the ratification resolution easily passed both houses, with a total of only four Republicans in opposition.[44]

In New York the eventual success of the income tax amendment was indisputably due to urban Democratic efforts, since it came after the Republican administration of Charles Evans Hughes had defeated ratification and had been supplanted by a Democratic governor and legislature in 1911. Hughes himself claimed to favor the idea of a federal income tax but urged the legislature to deny ratification on the grounds that the amendment's wording opened the door for federal taxation of state and municipal boards. Although his contention was highly debatable and strongly denied by several members of Congress and some prominent economists, it provided a handy rationale seized upon by the state's considerable number of wealthy citizens. As the Democrat-oriented, pro–income tax *New York World* observed, it "furnished the opponents of the income tax amendment the one thing they have been seeking . . . a plausible argument from a highly respected source." These opponents included such formidable people as John D. Rockefeller, his chief attorney John Milburn, Austen Fox of the bankers associa-

tion, banker Stuyvesant Fish, corporation lawyer Joseph
Choate, former Republican Congressman Charles South-
wick, former Supreme Court Justice David Brewer, George
Baker of the First National Bank, Charles Peabody of the
Mutual Life Insurance Company, Herbert Saterlee, son-in-
law of J. P. Morgan, and Francis Lynde Stetson, Morgan's
attorney and former law partner of Grover Cleveland. Since
nearly all these powerful individuals were inclined to work
through the state's Republican party, the Platt-Barnes group
of lawmakers lined up solidly against ratification. They were
joined by several followers of Governor Hughes despite their
rift with the regulars on other issues. There were some
Republicans, mostly from New York City districts, who were
willing to cross both Barnes and Hughes.[45]

From the outset the Democrats formed the most sizable
bloc of supporters for ratification, led by Smith and Wagner.
The latter praised the measure as "a tax on plenty instead of
necessity. It will lighten the burdens of the poor." With the
Democratic caucus committed to vote for the measure,
Wagner twitted the GOP by introducing a resolution to have
U.S. Senator Elihu Root, a prominent Republican supporter
of ratification, address the legislature. The Republicans
tabled the motion on a 21–18 vote, and Root was forced to
address the body in the form of a letter read by progressive
Republican senator Frederick Davenport. Davenport also
introduced the ratification resolution as did Republican
Assemblyman Andrew Murray of the Bronx. When the
resolution passed the senate thirteen of the fourteen Democrats voted for it, but only thirteen of the thirty-two
Republicans. In the assembly the measure failed of the
necessary two-thirds vote, even though it received a majority
in a vote of 74–66. Forty-eight of the fifty Democrats present
voted for the bill, while the Republicans split with twenty-six
in favor and sixty-four against. Fourteen of the twenty-six
Republicans were from New York City as were a majority of
the Democrats. Murray's attempt to revive his resolution
failed in an almost identical division.[46]

The Democratic landslide of 1910 gave the party control

of the governor's mansion and both houses of the legislature, making Smith and Wagner majority leaders in their respective houses. This time they introduced the income tax measure and Governor John Dix and the party caucus pledged themselves to ratification. A number of important businessmen sought to destroy party harmony on the issue by appealing to a few prominent anti-Tammany Democrats led by Edmund R. Terry of Brooklyn in the assembly and Franklin D. Roosevelt in the senate. The business group offered to provide Republican support for a non-Tammany Democrat for the U.S. Senate against Murphy's candidate, William F. ("Blue-Eyed Billy") Sheehan, in exchange for blocking such radical economic proposals as the income tax. Murphy got wind of the proposed deal, and used it to discredit the erstwhile rebels and secure the selection of Tammanyite Judge James O'Gorman. In the end Terry was the only Democrat in the lower house to vote against ratification. The other eighty-two Democrats joined with nine Republicans, six from New York City districts, to put the measure over the top. In the senate, the Democrats beat back a Republican attempt to hold the resolution in the Judiciary Committee on a partisan 30–21 vote. The final count was 35–16 with only one Democrat (from Buffalo) opposing. Even the Democrat who had voted no in 1910, Howard R. Bayne of Richmond, switched because his previous stand had "met with the extreme disapproval of my constituents, and I deem it my duty to reflect their views." The Democrats alone had provided enough votes to carry in both houses and Tammany Hall commanded the loyalty of the vast majority of those.[47]

The pattern was much the same in New Jersey: defeat by a Republican senate in 1911 despite the efforts of urban Democrats, and ultimate triumph after the Democratic landslide of 1912. The victory of Woodrow Wilson in 1910 gave his party the lower house, but left the upper one in the hands of the Republicans. Wilson wholeheartedly urged ratification upon the legislature, declaring it to be necessary because of a "decision of the Supreme Court based upon erroneous economic reasoning," and insisting that "liberal opinion throughout the country clearly expects and demands ratification of the amendment." He stressed the Republican origins of the proposal to the senate and warned them not to put selfish interests ahead of those of the nation. The urban Democrats handled the measure in the lower house, which passed it by a vote of 42–0 with nine of Newark's eleven Democrats and ten of Jersey City's twelve comprising half the affirmative votes. The senate rejected the resolution on an 8–12 vote which saw only one Republican join the Democrats in support. The 1912 election gave the latter party a 50–10 margin in the assembly and a 13–8 one in the senate, and that paved the way for ratification. Charles O'Connor Hennessy again introduced the resolution, arguing that "only the rich will pay." The vote was a strictly partisan 49–8 count, with all the Republicans hailing from south Jersey. In the senate Democrat Peter McGinnis of Paterson sponsored the resolution and spoke out against Republican attempts to substitute a state income tax. He denounced the ploy as a ruse and argued that it would simply result in an exodus of the state's wealthy. Only one Democrat, Wilson's soon-to-be successor James F. Fielder of Jersey City, joined the Republicans on the 12–9 vote.[48]

The struggle for ratification in Massachusetts took four years and three defeats but in the end the Democrat–labor legislator coalition prevailed. In 1910 the GOP floor leader stigmatized the amendment as a plot to despoil the East for the benefit of the western states and the Republican-controlled Committee on Federal Relations recommended defeat. The senate concurred on a 23–11 vote, with eight Boston Democrats and three labor legislators favoring ratification. The lower house followed suit, rejecting a ratification resolution by a 126–101 margin. All but one of Boston's twenty-nine Democrats and nine of Cambridge's ten voted yes, as did nearly all the other members of the party. Only six of the Hub City's twenty-one Republicans favored ratification, a percentage that the GOP reflected generally.

Democratic gains in 1910 resulted in ratification by the

house on a 130–69 vote. The victory was clearly the result of
Democrat–labor legislator cooperation, with fifty-two of
Boston's fifty-six Democrats voting affirmatively. A motion
to reconsider failed to carry. The same combination in the
senate fell short by one vote, with the chamber's thirteen
Democrats, nearly all Irish-Americans, joining the body's
four labor legislators from New Bedford, Lynn, Haverhill,
and Taunton. The following year almost an exact replica of
the 1911 developments occurred. The Democrats and labor
legislators again prevailed in the lower house, but failed in
the senate by a 14–17 vote. Finally in 1913, after the
Democrats had carried the state and the amendment had
been assured of the necessary number of adoptions, both
houses agreed to ratification. Although there was no recorded vote, the previous history of the issue coupled with
the election results left no doubt that ratification was
primarily the result of Democratic and labor legislator
efforts.[49]

Their counterparts in Rhode Island and Connecticut
worked as diligently for the income tax amendment, but were
never able to overcome the opposition of the Republican
organization. Rhode Island was especially significant because it was Nelson Aldrich's home base, and the Republican leader of the U.S. Senate had been one of those who
devised the amendment scheme in the first place. If he had
been seriously seeking ratification, the Brayton organization
from which he rose to national prominence would have
carried out his request, but, as the *Providence Bulletin*
observed in 1910, Aldrich had proposed the amendment only
as a means of "staving off the immediate enactment of an
income tax law." Accordingly, it was the urban Democrats
and not the Brayton-Aldrich Republicans who undertook
responsibility for the measure. The Republicans buried
ratification resolutions in house and senate committees. In
1911 and 1912 the resolutions met the same fate. In 1913 the
house approved the amendment on a voice vote, but the
malapportioned senate again did the bidding of the state's
small town–business coalition.[50]

Connecticut's urban Democrats had to fight not only the Roraback organization but their own old stock governor, Simeon Baldwin. Echoing Hughes in New York, Baldwin urged the legislature to wait to see how the courts ruled on the question of taxing state securities. Elaborating upon that theme, the Republican floor leader in the senate, Stiles Judson, reminded the legislators that Connecticut had just issued ten million dollars' worth of securities and that "you, as business-men ought readily to see the impairment of the state's resources by the taxation of these bonds on the part of Congress." Warming to his task, Judson added that the state would pay an unjustly large share of the tax to finance "the billion-dollar projects of the west." Another opponent opined that it would be a different story if Connecticut got the benefit from the tax, while a Republican insisted that the burden would fall heaviest upon the workingmen. This last was a particularly dubious proposition since, as a Republican schoolteacher-legislator observed, the tax was unlikely to be levied on incomes of less than $5,000 per year. In the face of the opposition of most Republicans and their own governor, the urban Democrats mounted a futile effort to secure ratification; it failed 6–19. The six affirmative votes were cast by Democrats from New Haven, Waterbury, Bridgeport, Norwalk, Danbury, and Hartford, floor leader Thomas Spellacy accounting for the last one. In the confusion engendered by Governor Baldwin's position, three of the other four Democrats abstained, leaving only one to join the opposition. The house eventually adopted the unfavorable recommendation of the Committee on Federal Relations by an 89–74 vote. Nearly all the body's urban Democrats joined against the report. The attempt to resuscitate the resolution in 1912 never even left the committee, but the state's urban Democrats had already proven themselves the only significant group working for ratification in the state.[51]

Whatever the ultimate fate of the federal income tax amendment in their respective states, the urban new stock Democratic legislators consistently distinguished themselves as ardent supporters of ratification. This desire to construct a taxation system based more equitably on the ability to pay was also frequently manifested on statewide questions, leading them to endorse changes in the method of assessment, more flexibility for urban communities in setting tax rates, and efforts to shift at least some of the burden from workers, consumers, home owners, and small businessmen to corporations and holders of intangible property. This same basic orientation led them to compose and back an assortment of legislation intended to lessen at least to some degree the influence that big business exercised over the daily lives of their constituents. These ranged from measures regulating the operation of banks, insurance companies, and stockbrokers to the checking of industrial waste. Primarily, they were attempts to exercise the police power of the state over the prices and quality of those goods and services most vital to the urban dweller: fuel, lighting, transportation, water, ice, and so on. The capstone of these attempts was usually their concurrence with the establishment of a public utilities or public services commission, although some of their number often held out for the right of the city to regulate its own utilities. The inclination of the urban lawmakers to seek redress of the socioeconomic imbalance made imperative the closest possible cooperation with organized labor and the strongest possible stand in favor of its right to match its strength against that of the corporations. When the contest proved unequal, the urban lawmaker supported labor's demands for more direct government assistance. In the three areas of taxation, regulation, and the recognition of labor unions, they occupied a position squarely in the mainstream of twentieth-century United States socioeconomic reform.

CHAPTER 4

Revamping
the Political System

Political innovation at all levels of government was a hallmark of Progressive Era reform. The variety and currency of proposed changes in the mechanics of governing was virtually unmatched in any other period in U.S. history. Some of these proved to be of only transient significance, vintage pieces identifiable only to scholars as relics of the era. Others, such as the direct election of U.S. Senators, woman suffrage, or new constitutions, were of more solid and lasting value. Some proposals were successful in altering the distribution of political power and the conditions under which it was exercised, while others had virtually no practical impact at all. Although nearly all political change was advocated as a means of returning government to "the people," many measures really had the opposite effect, sometimes because the proposal failed to deliver as advertised but often because its designers had a very narrow conception of just who "the people" were. Like all else in this volatile and complex period, political reform was characterized by a myriad of groups pressing for a plethora of reforms for even more variegated motives.

For all the diversity present in progressive political innovation, two reasonably distinct strains did emerge. The one, fostered by the upper and middle classes, aimed at removing the machinery of government as far as possible from the great mass of voters because they held the latter responsible for the failure of government to cope with the problems of modern America. The other, favored by groups acting either from self-interest or from an intellectual commitment to democracy, sought to open up the political process still further, broadening the franchise and allowing popular participation at levels of decision making where it had never before been permitted. The sponsorship of these two strains fluctuated from issue to issue and the nature of the division was often obfuscated by two salient tendencies. One was that nearly all would-be alterers of the status quo invariably presented themselves as representatives of "the people" against "the interests," even if their proposals ended in shrinkage of the degree of popular participation. "Although reformers used the ideology of popular government," Samuel Hays has said in an observation that has broad application, "they in no sense meant that all segments of society should be involved equally in municipal decision making." [1] With everyone representing "the people" and almost no one willing to admit to being one of "the interests," it was very difficult to gauge the actual effect that a proposed change might engender.

This fact flowed from an even more fundamental tendency, the habit of innovators to push for political change in order to realize some larger goal, such as political power or the mechanism of producing socioeconomic reform. Insurgents often espoused a measure like the direct primary to wrest the nominating power from the old guard, and when successful, promptly dropped the method. "Political reform," Hays concludes, "was an instrument of political warfare. Reformers demanded electoral change not because they believed in certain political principles but because they hoped that new techniques in politics would enable them to overcome their opposition." [2]

Even so, the two dominant trends are possible to sort out. The patrician strain preoccupied itself with structure and purification and "resulted in concentrating control in the hands of 'experts' who would exercise their professional discretion free from the pressures of electoral politics." The short ballot would severely cut the number of elective offices. The removal of party labels would minimize political conflict. Civil service regulations would circumscribe patronage, that inevitable source of corruption. Professional city managers and commissioners, who would be immune from popular pressure, would govern the cities. Citywide elections would eliminate the machinations of the ward heelers. Corrupt practices legislation would be strengthened and commissions established to ensure efficiency and economy of operation. The result would be to centralize "the process of decision-making rather than distribute it through more popular participation in government." [3]

The popular strain sought to effect nearly opposite results. Rather than removing large numbers of officeholders from the need to stand for election, this trend proposed to increase the number through such devices as recall and the election of judges and other previously appointed officials. Officials such as U.S. Senators who were then chosen by indirect means would be subjected to direct election. The introduction of primary elections would open the nominating process, previously the province of the professional politicians, to popular participation. The adoption of woman suffrage and the abolition of property and other qualifications would enfranchise wholly new groups. Using the secret ballot, keeping the polls open longer, and taking steps to prevent intimidation by employers would ensure the voting rights of the lower classes. The enactment of initiative and referendum would broaden even the legislative process. Such devices as home rule and reapportionment of the state legislatures would end rural domination of the cities. In many cases, the magnitude of the task required the adoption of an entirely new ruling instrument to replace constitutions written in preindustrial, preurban days. In short, the popular strain sought to follow the dictum that the answer to the problems of democracy was simply more democracy.

The identity of the sponsors of these two diverse strains is still very much in doubt among scholars of the period. The status revolution school generally acknowledges the presence of the two strains but attributes them to ideological differences between two factions of genteel reformers, some of whom trusted the great mass of voters while others did not. Other scholars have seen the patrician strain as largely the program of status revolution–type reformers, while concluding that the popular strain emanated from the same small town, midwestern roots that produced Bob La Follette, William Jennings Bryan, and George W. Norris. The most recent studies of municipal reform in the Progressive Era have made an apparently irrefutable case for associating the patrician strain of political reform with the activities of the upper class business and professional leaders who were the core of the reformist movement, according to the status revolution theory. These findings also clearly identify the urban political machine and its constituents as the major opponents of the patrician strain of municipal reform, placing these scholars in substantial agreement with the status revolution school. Their agreement ends here, however, for the status revolution theory seems to view the patrician reformers as sincere protectors of the public interest, while the municipal reform scholars generally hold them to be pursuing narrow, self-interested aims. More importantly, the status revolution school has also argued that the machine and its followers were generally equally indifferent or hostile to the popular strain of political reform, while the students of municipal reform open up the possibility, at least, that they were much more sympathetic to democratic innovation. As noted, Melvin Holli identifies Hazen Pingree and his ethnic working class constituents as the most potent force striving for democratic government in Detroit and Michigan. It is the central thesis of this chapter that the representatives of the urban political machine in the seven states under consideration were likewise the strongest force for popular government and, with certain exceptions, the major opponents of patrician reform for reasons that were often both understandable and sound.[4]

The argument that the urban political machine opposed patrician reforms is sound enough as far as it goes. The patrician reformers struck at the heart of the organization's method of operation. Civil service would destroy the patronage system upon which the machine depended for workers and voters. The short, nonpartisan ballots would prevent party leaders from balancing the interests of the city's ethnic and economic groups. Citywide elections would sever the vital cords between the ward boss and his constituents, rendering the whole system obsolete. The movement for honesty, efficiency, and economy in government would curtail the funds upon which politicians depended both for personal aggrandizement and for aiding their constituents. Worst of all, the advent of supposedly disinterested professional administrators might mean the end of politicians, since the art of getting elected would no longer have any significance in the governing process.[5]

Granting all this, some important qualifications still have to be made concerning the urban politician's attitude toward the patrician strain. Despite their general opposition to such reforms, urban lawmakers did lend occasional support to certain ones, especially where the state was so controlled by small town–business interests that the city politicians reaped little benefit from the spoils of governing. Where the Republicans controlled virtually all the patronage, civil service was about the only way for deserving Democrats to acquire state jobs. A few astute politicians recognized in some patrician measures the potential to increase rather than decrease their influence. In Jersey City Frank Hague used the newly created commission form of government as a springboard for making himself one of the most absolute bosses in the nation. In Boston James Michael Curley joined the patricians in their efforts to have the city council elected at large in order to break the power of his rival ward bosses and build a citywide machine of his own. Once the enactment of a particular patrician reform became assured, the urban politician generally accepted the fact, and either sought to adjust his tactics or to amend its operation to be less damaging to his interests.[6]

Many urban new stock legislators backed certain good government reforms, especially in those states where their adversaries controlled the machinery. The Boston Irish divided on the new reform charter for the city, particularly over the question of electing aldermen at large rather than by wards. Mayor Fitzgerald and Governor Walsh reportedly favored the idea, while Lomasney and Curley voiced strong opposition. The motive of the first two was most likely a desire to break the power of the ward bosses and strengthen their own control over the city and state party organizations respectively. In the lower house the Boston Irish, supported by Lomasney, failed to amend the charter to allow election by ward, with the city lawmakers dividing on the question. A final effort to submit the issue to a referendum also failed. In the senate only one Boston Democrat voted against the measure. Despite his initial distaste, Curley later turned the charter to his advantage as mayor by building a citywide machine much freer from the restraining influence of the ward bosses than before, thus demonstrating both his own virtuosity and the inability of structural reform to destroy the boss system. Lomasney remained a power in his own and adjoining wards, but his citywide influence was weakened considerably.[7]

Urban Democrats in New Jersey proved equally able to adapt to such innovations as the commission form of city government and jury reform. The former was sponsored by Allan Walsh of Trenton in 1911, with Wilson's belated backing. Newark Boss James Nugent connived with old-guard Republican leaders to render the proposal innocuous by requiring that it first had to be submitted to a referendum and receive 40 percent of the votes cast in the 1910 election. The amendment passed the assembly by a vote of 36–16 with about three-fourths of the Hudson and Essex County delegations in favor. Wilson threatened to veto the measure unless the requirement was lowered to a more modest 26 percent and a compromise was finally struck at 30 percent. All but four of the Jersey City and Newark representatives then concurred. The commission form of government failed to end boss rule in New Jersey as elsewhere, but instead provided the opportunity for Frank Hague to establish a much more stringent organization than his predecessor enjoyed. Commissioners elected at large without a local constituency proved unable to resist the power drive of the most powerful of their number.[8]

Jury reform also aroused the ire of Nugent and his supporters but not that of all the urban Democrats in New Jersey. A proposal to remove the selection of jurors from the machine-controlled sheriffs was introduced; several Democrats voted against a Nugent-drafted amendment to submit the measure to a referendum. Despite the opposition of two Essex lawmakers, about one-half the Hudson ones, and several other north Jersey Democrats, the amendment carried and the dissenters then voted for the bill as modified. Once again Wilson balked, and alternate proposals were drafted providing for joint selection of jurors by sheriffs and a commission appointed by the state supreme court, and containing no referendum clause. Several urban lawmakers went down the line for the alternate measures before bowing 23–31. Nearly all their number then concurred with the referendum provision, except for the Bergen County representatives.[9]

In New York, Ohio, and Illinois, urban representatives lent significant support to governmental reorganization programs. In the constitutional convention of 1915, Al Smith had led the unsuccessful fight to reorganize the state's 169 separate agencies, many of which were not even responsible to the executive branch. When he became governor, Smith appointed a commission to recommend reorganization and succeeded in funding it from private sources when the legislature refused to concur. The body's findings called for centralizing authority under the governor, but the Republicans prevented implementation of the proposals for several years. In 1925 the legislature agreed to submit the questions to a referendum, which returned a 60 percent affirmative vote. The Republicans sought to forestall enactment by creating their own commission but Smith outmaneuvered them by suggesting Charles Evans Hughes as chairman. Hughes's findings concurred with those of Smith's original commission and led finally to the reorganization of the state's agencies into sixteen bodies. Smith also insisted that the judiciary and local governments be rearranged, but the legislature successfully resisted his pressures. Similarly, the Tammany Democrat was a leader in reorganizing the state budget and eliminating the "pay-as-you-go" principle that upstate Republicans had used to stymie urban programs. Under Smith's direction, the Empire State acquired a reputation as the most efficiently and economically run administration in the nation.[10]

Cleveland's representatives also supported a variety of efficiency measures. In 1911 they voted unanimously for Governor Harmon's plan to bring the state's penal institutions, charity hospitals, schools, and homes under one centralized board; the measure passed in both houses over strong Republican opposition 20–14 and 70–38. The establishment of a streamlined board of clemency in 1917 marked a similar victory, over heavy Republican opposition, for the idea of this improved method of handling requests from prisoners. The 1917 bill creating a state board of rapid transit was backed by all of Cleveland's senators and three-fourths of its voting representatives. Another proposed the establishment of a legislative reference department and received the complete backing of the Cleveland and Cincinnati delegations. All but three Cuyahoga representatives voted for the introduction of a state budget system in 1913, and nearly all of them endorsed the various efforts to reorganize the state court system. Even on the highly explosive liquor question, the Cuyahoga Democrats endorsed a centralized approach, backing the proposal of William Greenlund for the establishment of a state liquor-licensing board. About the only measure designed for more centralized administration that encountered the active opposition of the Cleveland lawmakers was the Republican-sponsored bill to establish a state agricultural board. Motivated either by urban prejudice or a desire to retaliate against rural intransigence on matters of interest to the cities, all five Cleveland senators and six of her representatives refused to concur, with four not voting, out of a total of thirteen.[11]

Governor Dunne of Illinois took the lead in the creation of the Efficiency and Economy Commission and the Democrats in the legislature generally backed him. The Chicago governor later lauded its accomplishments, although they proved to be of a short-run nature. Dunne also received the support of a majority of urban Democrats for measures to improve the operation of the General Assembly and to bring state agencies under closer executive control, but generally failed in his attempts. Urban Democrats in Connecticut and Rhode Island also endorsed at least the rhetoric of efficiency and economy on numerous occasions when the dominant Republican organization sought proliferation of agencies in order to increase the amount of available patronage.[12]

The urban political machine's concern for its own patronage positions generally made its representatives hostile to the civil service system, but their opposition was not absolute. Such old-line politicos as G. W. Plunkitt viewed the merit system as "the greatest curse of the day," and many scholars have agreed that civil service was a major blow to machine politics. The Republican organizations had also demonstrated the possibilities of "freezing" their appointees into jobs against that rare occasion when the Democrats captured the state. Accordingly, urban Democrats showed themselves highly skeptical of such proposals, except when their chances of benefiting from the patronage system on the state level were negligible. A few, perhaps, also saw that they could protect their own functionaries from Republican wrath by similar means, since, as Eric McKitrick has noted, "a considerable sector of Tammany's former patronage preserves in New York City is blanketed by a very effective system of Civil Service." The capture of several state governments after so many years of exile gave them a rare opportunity to entrench their own people. At any rate, urban Democrats generally insisted upon two qualifications to any civil service law: they urged that large numbers of people be exempted from its provisions, and that all civil service employees be entitled to due process and show of cause in dismissal proceedings. The latter was naturally designed primarily to protect Democratic civil servants; in Illinois Dunne's Secretary of State Harry Woods created a furor by seeking wholesale dismissal of civil service employees on the grounds that the previous Republican administration had packed the state bureaucracy. Even the official party history acknowledged that Woods was an "unabashed advocate of the spoils system." [13]

As a result, the attitude of the urban Democrats toward civil service was somewhat mixed. In New Jersey the Smith and Davis organizations joined with the Republican bosses in 1907 to defeat a civil service law 15–40 in the assembly; only Joe Tumulty and three young Jersey City representatives defied the north Jersey leaders. The following year, though, Republican opposition was overcome by the personal intervention of Governor John Franklin Fort and the work of Essex Republican William P. Martin, while Mark Sullivan of Jersey City made the measure more palatable to his Democratic colleagues by adding a series of amendments providing for numerous exemptions and an elected civil service commission. When the senate deleted these provisions, only Tumulty and one other Hudson Democrat were willing to accept the bill. In Illinois the Democratic caucus gave qualified endorsement to the merit system in 1911, but sought to amend the Republican bill to provide for exemptions, an elected commission, preference for veterans, political participation, maintenance of current officeholders without examination, a ninety-day probation period, and a public trial for employees removed for cause. When the new system seemed to work to the advantage of the GOP, many urban Democrats withdrew even qualified endorsement. As Woods began his abortive purge of Republican officeholders, measures were introduced to repeal civil service in both the state

and Cook County. The measure was finally killed in committee by a 9–7 count, but nearly all the urban Democrats on the
body voted for passage.[14]

The same general pattern characterized the attitude of the
Boston Democrats toward civil service. The efforts of machine politicians such as Martin Lomasney to provide for
exemptions to the system brought them into conflict with
Governor Foss in 1913. The urban lawmakers favored
special consideration for veterans, lowering the age limit to
seventeen, forbidding the use of police records against
applicants, and striking such questions as religious affiliation.
These were generally either rejected by the senate or vetoed
by Foss. Three years later most Boston Democrats opposed
attempts to extend the functions of the Civil Service Commission, tried to exempt employees in Boston and Worcester,
and sought to submit the question to a referendum, all
unsuccessfully. Lomasney prided himself on being "probably
the father of Civil Service in the city"; he supported it partly
because he had almost been dismissed from his first political
job as a lamplighter, and partly because it proved a handy
device for avoiding bloody patronage fights among ward
leaders. At the same time he insisted that he had never
appointed an unqualified man to any position and remained
skeptical of the merit system's potential for mischief in
unfriendly hands. The Mahatma reportedly remarked to
Curley that civil service, along with woman suffrage, killed
the political machine. The Purple Shamrock himself once
went to jail for taking the civil service examination for a
constituent to whom he had promised a job. Connecticut's
urban lawmakers showed somewhat more sympathy to the
merit system as a possible device to break the Roraback
machine's stranglehold on patronage jobs. Democratic floor
leader John McDonough proposed the creation of a state
civil service commission in 1913, even though freely admitting he believed in the spoils system and felt it "essential to
the party's welfare." In the height of reform euphoria of that
year the measure passed, but the GOP severely undercut its
effect in 1915 by appending a long list of exemptions that

passed over solid Democratic opposition. As a result, minority leader Patrick O'Sullivan moved to abolish the entire
system in 1917, but his effort failed. Two years later the
Democrats voted en masse against a Republican bill to allow
state employees to be exempted from taking the examination
on their own application.[15]

In Ohio the middle class leadership of the Democratic
party carried most Cleveland lawmakers along with it in
enacting a civil service system, a development that was
probably less distasteful because it held out the promise of
protecting Democratic bureaucrats once the Republicans
regained their normal control of state government. The bill
that created a statewide system was introduced in 1913 and
passed the senate with four of the five Cuyahoga members in
agreement. In the lower house, representatives of organized
labor, including several Cleveland Democrats, refused to
concur unless election board clerks, bailiffs, and all laborers
were exempted. With these changes William Green reluctantly voted for the bill but four Cleveland assemblymen
with labor backgrounds still abstained. The thirty-two votes
against the system were mostly cast by rural Republicans
who sought to protect the party's profitable patronage
system. New York's urban Democrats generally opposed
civil service, but did make certain adjustments once it
became a reality. In 1913 they worked for a sizable increase
in salary for state commissioners, an effort the Times called
"Tammanyizing" the commission. During that same session
Jimmy Walker introduced a bill requiring an open hearing
and proof of incompetency, misconduct, or insubordination
before a civil servant could be removed. Where possible
Democrats also sought to protect their appointees with the
security of the civil service umbrella.[16]

Most urban Democrats were only slightly more enthusiastic about corrupt practices legislation, although their position
varied again according to whose corrupt practices were being
proscribed. The entire Cleveland delegation in both houses
voted in favor of the Lobbyist Registration Act of 1913, and
were all but unanimously behind a bill making it a crime to

bribe a legislator. When charges of soliciting bribes were levied against several senators in the 1911 session, the Cuyahoga representatives supported vigorous prosecution of the accused, and John Krause and William Green even refused to serve on a committee that was generally regarded as being packed so as to produce a "whitewash." On the other hand, when one of their own people was suspected of accepting a bribe in 1919, his colleagues were less interested in prosecution. On the joint resolution calling for an investigation of the charges, four of the thirteen Cleveland representatives and two of the four senators abstained.[17]

By the same token, Cleveland lawmakers demonstrated a general interest in preventing abuses in the electoral process. The legislators were in substantial agreement with the Corrupt Practices Act of 1911 which sought to control campaign expenditures and prohibit coercion of voters. Because the city's three senators desired a somewhat stronger law, they abstained on the final vote. In the same session, the three senators and six of the ten representatives voted in favor of a stronger voter registration law. In the 1913 meeting of the General Assembly, the Cuyahoga delegation gave nearly solid backing to several bills designed to guarantee an honest count of the ballots by requiring that they be kept for a specified length of time in sealed envelopes and that the returns be handed over promptly to the county board of election or to the secretary of state. Two years later, all but one senator and three representatives voted for a bill that stipulated a fine for circulating false rumors about candidates. In 1917 all but two members of the lower house favored a joint resolution to create an electoral commission. Only on the issues of filing election expenditures and investigating the election of 1916 did they show any reservation, and even then it was expressed by the abstention of three senators rather than by open opposition.[18]

New Jersey Democrats were very receptive to Woodrow Wilson's corrupt practice legislation in 1911, partly in response to popular pressure but also because illegal practices in Newark and Jersey City were "on an amateur scale" compared with those in such Republican bailiwicks as Atlantic County. Democrat John Bracken of Newark did attempt to offer a version of the bill milder than Wilson's, but all save two urban lawmakers voted instead for the administration proposal. In Illinois Edward Dunne called for limiting campaign expenditures, requiring publication of expenses, and making breach of campaign promises a felony. Many Chicago Democrats did not share his enthusiasm, though, and none of the recommendations were ever acted upon favorably. Robert Wagner introduced a proposal in the New York Legislature requiring a report on campaign expenditures and putting a limitation of $10,000 on individual contributions, but the opposition of the Republican leadership and some Democrats prevented its adoption. Urban working class opposition was generally evident on proposals to abolish free railroad passes for legislators. In view of the meager salary paid to lawmakers, they viewed the free pass as a necessary subsidy without which no laboring man could afford to sit. Consequently they insisted upon coupling abolition with an increase in salary or a travel allowance. The failure of the measure was thus largely due to urban Democratic votes, but their opposition put the finger squarely on one of the most significant questions in American politics: how to avoid making officeholding the exclusive province of the moneyed leisure classes.[19]

Urban new stock lawmakers in Connecticut and Rhode Island proved to be more conscientious and consistent champions of electoral and financial purity, since their Republican opponents enjoyed a virtual monopoly over the possible sources of corruption, although when one of their number was accused of taking a bribe in 1913, the Democratic majority in the senate found him innocent and commended him for his cooperation. In 1911 Hartford's Thomas Spellacy introduced a bill requiring the registration of lobbyists that passed the senate with solid Democratic support. Although it failed in the house, urban Democrats were the leading spokesmen in its behalf, and they tried unsuccessfully to revive it in 1917. During the same session floor leader O'Sullivan failed in an attempt to limit campaign contributions of over $1,000, a measure clearly aimed at the business-Republican alliance. As did their working class counterparts elsewhere, Connecticut Democrats also pressed for higher salaries and transportation allowances for legislators. Rhode Island's urban Democrats fought a number of valiant but fruitless battles to trim the fat from the Brayton combine. One major effort was to cut excess jobs and spending from the GOP budget in each session. Another was to prohibit dual officeholding in town and state government, and to prevent government officials from doing business with the city or state. The barring of lobbyists from the floor of the legislature was another favorite cause, as was preventing public service companies and other corporations from making campaign contributions. When future U.S. Senator Theodore Francis Green introduced a bill to regulate paid lobbyists, one of the latter responded: "Oh, paid lobbyists. Hell, that doesn't include me. I haven't been paid yet." The prohibition of free railroad passes was also frequently proposed by urban lawmakers, despite the reluctance of their counterparts in other states.[20]

From the perspective of over half a century it is clear that the machine's attitude toward the patrician strain is anything but grounds for branding it as reactionary, despite what contemporary reformers concluded. There can be little doubt that the success of the patrician strain of reform was a major contributing factor to the current malaise of city and state government. "Behind the debate over the method of representation," as Samuel Hays has observed, "lay a debate over who should be represented." The patrician reformers "made little or no sense as a democratic phenomenon." They sought to make the lower and middle classes politically ineffectual in order that the city and the state could be run in the interests of those who owned it. This alienation of government from the mass of citizens, in turn, led to the neglect of pressing socioeconomic problems until they had become crises or worse. The worker and the shopkeeper were deprived of their line of communication to city hall, and the politicians were stripped of much of the wherewithal to distribute welfare with as little red tape as possible. Although the machine politician undoubtedly stood his ground primarily out of an instinct for self-preservation, his action often served the general interest.[21]

The charge that the urban political machine opposed popular reform has been levied on two levels. The leadership of the organization, one group believes, feared increased popular participation because the nature of machine control depended upon personal arrangements behind closed doors, decisions that could hardly survive the test of popular ratification. The fewer people involved, the easier it was to maintain the type of control essential to the continued success of the organization. More fundamentally, another group has postulated that the machine's constituents exhibited little or no interest in democratizing the political process, thus making it easy for the bosses to oppose innovation. "The movement for direct popular democracy," according to Richard Hofstadter, "was, in effect, an attempt to realize Yankee-Protestant ideals of personal responsibility, and the Progressive notion of good citizenship was the culmination of the Yankee-Mugwump ethos of political participation without self-interest." Initiative and referendum have been singled out as being "unthinkable" outside the context of this ethos. George Mowry has echoed Hofstadter in concluding that such democratic measures as the direct primary left the urban ethnic masses "distinctly cold." [22]

Despite the wide acceptance of this interpretation, it fails to take into account some very salient factors. The contrary views of the good government associations notwithstanding, the success of the urban political machine was not due solely or even primarily to authoritarian methods and corruption. It rested instead on the fact that the machine filled certain basic needs for its constituents better than any viable alternative. To continue to receive allegiance, the boss and his lieutenants had to constantly adjust their methods or face extinction. Opposition to primaries and similar innovations was a tenable enough position in a quiet era, but when political

reform had become the watchword continued adherence to
the old methods could prove fatal. This adjustment proved
much easier because politicians soon discovered that, if
properly handled, democratic measures might even enhance
the organization's effectiveness. Direct legislation required
the gathering of signatures on petitions and no one was
better equipped to do that than the machine. In primaries the
candidate with organization backing had a profound advantage and there was a strong indication that primaries might
remove the need to assign so many places on the party ticket
to nonurban candidates. It soon became clear that urban
voters, especially when organized by the machine, turned out
in greater numbers for primaries than their rural counterparts; Democratic primaries in New York, for example, were
always decided from the Bronx on south. By the same token,
electing U.S. Senators by popular vote proved infinitely more
conducive to urban interests than selecting them by rural-
dominated legislatures. In short, the major components of
the popular strain of political reform served to enhance the
importance of the urban working class vote, and the machine
was better prepared than any other organization to take
advantage of that situation. All that innovations such as the
primary really did, as Henry Jones Ford observed in 1909,
was to alter "the conditions that govern political activity thus
determining its extent and quality." Politics, he realistically
concluded, would continue to be carried on by politicians
just as art is the business of artists and engineering of
engineers. Since the existing political order was the primary
means by which the small town–business coalition sought to
stave off the socioeconomic thrust of the urban masses, it was
necessary for urban lawmakers to first open up the system
before they could really accomplish anything significant in
that area.[23]

The stake of the urban working class in democratic reform,
then, determined the nature of the contest over the various
measures in the major industrial states. Some old stock
activists such as Pingree, Jones, Whitlock, and Tom Johnson
joined the urban masses in pressing for such reforms, either

out of a dedication to an open society or because they hoped
to reap political benefit for themselves. Many middle class
reformers, as in Massachusetts, were apprehensive "about
the ascendancy of so-called undesirable social elements, in
particular the non-Yankee wage earning classes; to broaden
popular participation through political innovations meant
only to facilitate that tendency." In Rhode Island, too, the
"Yankee oligarchy clung to limitations on the franchise as a
defense against alien invasion," leaving the urban Democrats
as the main sponsors of increased popular participation. The
situation in the other five states differed only in degree. The
basic division on nearly all popular political issues pitted
urban new stock lawmakers, aided by some old stock
liberals, against the representatives of the state's traditional,
small town populace. In any event, the urban lawmaker was
highly visible not only as an opponent of most aspects of the
patrician program but also as a supporter of the popular
one.[24]

Whatever position the urban political machine may once
have taken on many popular reform matters, it gradually
came to realize the advantages inherent in any political
adjustment that augmented the influence of the city in
general or of urban working people in particular. In practice
this meant vigorously championing an expansion of urban
leverage through such devices as home rule, legislative
reapportionment, and direct legislation, as well as accepting
such new wrinkles in the political process as the direct
primary, woman suffrage, and the popular election of U.S.
Senators and other officials. Coupled with this was a vigorous
defense of registration and voting procedures designed to
protect the wage earner in the exercise of his franchise.

The dedication of the urban lawmakers in the major
industrial states to effective city government was particularly
evident in their stand on home rule. Only four states in the
nation had been willing to grant their cities any authority
apart from the legislatures before 1900, and none of these
was in the industrial Northeast. The drive for greater urban
independence received much of its impetus from the need to

cope with worsening socioeconomic crises, and harmonized
with the urban politician's desire to disentangle himself from
the network of restrictions placed upon his activities in the
state capital. In New York the drive for home rule reached its
apex in 1913, when the city lawmakers were also at the height
of their statewide influence. In that year Democratic floor
leaders introduced a comprehensive home rule bill in their
respective houses. The measure aroused the ire of upstate
lawmakers and patrician reformers in the city by seeking to
vest power in the hands of the Board of Aldermen elected by
wards, thus protecting the machine's functionaries from
control either by upstate legislators or fusion mayors. The
measure empowered aldermen to grant franchises, fix salaries, and oversee the Civil Service and Public Service
Commissions and the Boards of Education and Estimate.
The *New York Times,* spokesman for the silk stocking
districts, lavishly denounced the proposal, and after its
passage accused the Tammany Hall Democrats of violating
the principle of home rule on numerous occasions. Most of
these alleged deviations involved the creation of state pension funds for city employees. In the 1915 constitutional
convention the Democratic delegates pressed hard for meaningful home rule for New York City but were frustrated by
upstate Republicans.[25]

Chicago's representatives were similarly anxious to release
that city from the control of the Illinois General Assembly,
but were stymied by the price demanded by the downstate
counties. The latter insisted that Cook County agree to a
fixed limit on the number of representatives at Springfield.
Since this was regarded by most Chicagoans as too dear an
exaction, the Windy City remained under state direction.
Many Chicagoans opposed a 1907 home rule proposal
because it opened the possibility of adopting Prohibition and
Sunday closing on a local option basis, extending even to
precinct choices. What they desired was home rule run from
city hall where all their prerogatives would be protected by
the ability to elect sympathetic mayors. Their counterparts in
Ohio were more successful. The 1911 constitutional conven-

tion adopted a proposal drafted by the Municipal Association of Cleveland and Mayor Newton Baker over the objections of Prohibitionists, utilities, and rural lawmakers. The measure was ratified on the referendum ballot and the Democrats pledged themselves to its implementation in 1912. Cleveland became the first city to adopt a new home rule charter in the spring of 1913. Rhode Island's urban Democrats sought to achieve greater city autonomy by degrees, favoring local option on tax matters, the ability of the city to condemn land, and the creation of municipal utility commissions. They also expended a great deal of effort resisting the attempts of the legislature to place even further restrictions on city officials. Aside from abortive efforts at a general home rule provision, Connecticut's urban legislators also sought piecemeal accretions of functions. In 1913 Democratic control of the senate, coupled with support from some urban Republicans in the lower house, led to the enactment of laws permitting cities to issue bonds and facilitating the revision of municipal charters. A general home rule bill introduced by a Hartford Democrat failed in 1917 on a 19–16 vote in the senate, with the entire minority delegation in support.[26]

Since the legislatures retained such a wide measure of authority over the cities, urban lawmakers pressed for apportionment that was more consistent with population distribution. Such efforts in New York were generally to no avail because of what Al Smith called a "more delicate reason": upstate distrust of the alien population of metropolitan New York. The battle came to a head in the constitutional convention where the Democrats and many New York City Republicans fought to reapportion the senate on the basis of population. The burden of the battle was borne by Democrats who insisted that since the city had 52 percent of the state's population and paid 73 percent of its taxes, it should be entitled to more than twenty-one of its fifty-two senators. The fight against reapportionment was led by Republicans, who prevailed in the end. In Illinois, downstate representatives tried to limit Chicago to one-third of the seats in the General Assembly, and several newspapers labeled its representatives selfish and power hungry when they failed to go along. One Republican senator from rural Cook County agreed to support the limitation, provided that it bind only the city and not the county. As previously noted, downstate lawmakers also tied the issue of apportionment to home rule, resulting in a Mexican standoff. The nearest the Chicago Democrats could come to achieving more equitable representation for their interests was by adhering to the practice of cumulative voting. Although undemocratic on the surface, the system did allow the minority party to elect single representatives in heavily Republican districts. Massachusetts urban spokesmen also pressed unsuccessfully for reapportionment in the constitutional convention.[27]

Urban Democratic attacks on the apportionment system in Connecticut and Rhode Island were even more intense, because of the greater magnitude of the inequities involved. In 1911 Connecticut's Democratic Governor Simeon Baldwin called for reapportionment of congressional and senate seats, and floor leader Spellacy introduced legislation providing for equal districts based upon population. The Roraback Republicans candidly objected on the grounds that such a plan would "give the cities all the Senators," and the Judiciary Committee accordingly substituted a much less drastic measure. The fight to resurrect the original version failed on a 16–10 vote, with one Hartford Republican joining the Democrats. In 1913 Spellacy's successor, John McDonough, was similarly unable to revive the matter. The situation in the lower house was so stacked against them that the urban Democrats sought to achieve their ends by creating new towns within the boundaries of the major cities, since each town meant two more seats. Rhode Island's urban Democrats were equally frustrated in all their attempts. Their clamoring for redistricting in the lower house pressured the Brayton combine to propose a reapportionment amendment in 1907 that supposedly would divide the state into 100 equal districts. The Republicans blunted its effect by stipulating that each town had to have at least one representative, that no city could have more than one-fourth the total, and that election would be by district. Newport would have one district "so black with Democrats that we could never elect a Republican," Brayton candidly acknowledged of his proposal to switch from at-large elections, "but we would pack all the Democrats into that district and the other three districts would always be Republican." Further Democratic pressure brought about the establishment of a redistricting commission for the state senate and congress, but the minority party opposed this because the senate would have the largest voice in selecting its membership. The body's proposals divided the state into three Congressional districts, all of which contained some portion of Providence County, thus diffusing the biggest bloc of Democratic votes in the state. Party chairman Frank Fitzsimmons and other officials testified vehemently against the bill without success. Democrats worked for several years to have the senate elected from thirty districts of nearly equal population rather than by towns, but without avail.[28]

Since home rule and reapportionment were so difficult to achieve, urban lawmakers sought to bypass the state legislature completely through initiative and referendum. Many saw the twin forms of direct legislation as means of forcing rural, business-oriented legislatures to meet urban working class needs. Some perhaps also regarded the measures as popular issues that could be milked for their political dividends, but whose actual impact on the legislative process might prove to be slight. For whatever reason the urban new stock lawmaker in the main rallied to the cause of direct legislation, contrary to the view that initiative and referendum were "intelligible only from the standpoint of the Anglo-Saxon ethos of popular political action." [29]

Only in Illinois was there overt evidence of urban new stock opposition to direct legislation, and even that arose from the introduction of factors outside the merits of the issue. Some Chicago lawmakers allegedly feared that downstate groups might use direct legislation to enact such odious measures as Prohibition, and that limitations would be placed upon the number of signatures and votes from Cook County. Governor Dunne himself, who was enthusiastic about the twin devices, regarded his election as a mandate in favor of their enactment, and recommended them to the General Assembly several times. The major arguments in favor of the measures came from Socialists, Progressives, urban Democrats, and organized labor, while the major voices against were those of downstate Republicans. All the Democrats fought the limitation on Cook County, but when it was adopted a split in their ranks developed. The Harrison-Dunne people supported the measure despite the restriction, but several Sullivanites refused to concur. After the senate adopted the proposed constitutional amendment, the house failed to reach the necessary two-thirds total by one vote when several Sullivan Democrats defected. The great majority of city lawmakers voted for direct legislation despite the restriction.[30]

Arguments over the percentage of votes needed to set the process in motion complicated the direct legislation debate in Ohio, but Cleveland lawmakers strongly favored the innovation. Opponents sought to weaken it by requiring the signatures of 30 percent of the registered voters on any petition. The Cleveland Democrats fought the amendment but gave the whole measure unanimous endorsement despite it. In 1913 they won a battle for municipal initiative and referendum upon the petition of only 10 percent of the electorate. The Cleveland lawmakers also insisted upon safeguards to protect the petitions against possible abuses, particularly when it was revealed that the conservative Equity Association had sought to use the new device to eradicate workmen's compensation and new tax laws. Recall of public officials was also popular with the city representatives, one of whom introduced a measure to that effect in 1911. All five Cuyahoga senators voted for the measure when it passed the upper house in 1913.[31]

Their corresponding numbers in Connecticut were eventually frustrated by the Roraback interests, but not without a strong effort on behalf of direct legislation. Arch McNiel of Bridgeport introduced two initiative and referendum measures in 1911, one binding and one advisory. The Republicans quickly killed the first in committee, but the minority party kept the advisory bill alive long enough to spark a spirited debate. McNiel and Spellacy argued vigorously in favor of the proposal, while GOP leader Stiles Judson contended that legislative issues were too complicated for the voters to understand. The bill passed the senate 27–6, with all the negative votes being cast by Republicans. In the lower house, however, the GOP majority overwhelmed the Democrats 95–37. The Democratic platform declared for initiative and referendum in 1912 but party efforts to enact it in the next session were again unsuccessful. Rhode Island Democrats also worked for adoption of a constitutional amendment permitting initiative and referendum, beginning with a resolution in 1910. In 1913 the Democrats and the legislature's few Progressives came very close to slipping two initiative and referendum measures past the Brayton Republicans in the lower house. The Progressive version was defeated 48–47, supported by all the chamber's Democrats, whose proposal in turn failed 52–45.[32]

Massachusetts was more successful in enacting direct legislation during the Progressive Era, and the state's urban Democrats were again instrumental in its adoption. In 1911 they voted for an advisory initiative and referendum proposal, but were not content with its nonbinding nature. In the same session a binding direct legislation bill passed the lower house by a two-to-one margin. Once again a Democratic–labor legislator coalition produced a legislative victory, but the same combination failed twice to pass the house version in the senate. In 1913 the urban coalition, petitioned by the state Federation of Labor, succeeded in proposing a constitutional amendment for direct legislation that was finally adopted by the voters. In the constitutional convention, urban and labor delegates prevailed in their attempts to keep initiative and referendum in the new document. The section was ratified by the voters and "generally secured a higher percentage of votes in districts dominated by Irish and New Immigrant people." [33]

For reasons already considered, urban machine lawmakers also eventually embraced the direct primary. The Tammany Democrats in New York had opposed the idea for several years, but did an about-face during the Smith-Wagner era, despite the infighting between Boss Murphy and Governor Sulzer. The administration bill aimed at abolishing the state convention and picking all candidates by the primary method, but it also required the signatures of only 1 percent of the eligible voters on a nomination petition. Murphy viewed this as undermining the party organization and fought it in the legislature. Sulzer allegedly pressured organization legislators who reacted by voting against the bill and causing its defeat. The Tammany forces then enacted a primary bill that provided for a higher percentage of signatures, but Sulzer vetoed it. This impasse over the primary law that the Democrats had pledged to enact was one of the prime factors in Sulzer's impeachment. At the special session in December 1913, Tammany Governor Martin Glynn pressed the legislature for a series of what the *New York Times* called "radical laws" including the primary, Massachusetts ballot, workmen's compensation, direct election of U.S. Senators, and a constitutional convention. The *Times* reported with horror that the Democrats were also committed to initiative, referendum, and recall as part of Murphy's plan to "give people what they want." At any rate, the assembly passed the measure within the week 109–0, with only one Democrat refusing to concur. The Democrats beat down a Progressive amendment to have a bipartisan commission supervise elections, and ignored a *Times* suggestion that independent Democrats have the same number of poll watchers and election judges as the organization was allowed. The senate quickly followed suit but only after GOP State Chairman William Barnes had damned the measure as being in the "revolutionary tradition of Robespierre and Theodore Roosevelt." The gallery reportedly roared with laughter when politicos "Big Tim" Sullivan and James

Edward F. Dunne of Illinois. (*Photograph from the Illinois State Historical Society*)

A TAIL OF TWO CITIES

Life June 18, 1914

The tail of the Tammany Tiger embraces Albany as well as New York City. In 1914 urban legislators effectively controlled the New York State Legislature and were able to pass a number of reform measures. (*Courtesy of the New York Public Library Picture Collection*)

OF COURSE

Charles F. Murphy paints stripes on the Tammany Tiger spelling out municipal ownership, which urban new stock politicians often supported as an alternative to public regulation of utilities. This 1905 cartoon implies that Murphy's motives were selfish. (*Courtesy of the New York Public Library Picture Collection*)

WAITING AT THE CHURCH

These three states were slow to ratify the Nineteenth Amendment that enfranchised women. Urban new stock politicians accepted woman suffrage reluctantly, only after it had become apparent that ratification of the amendment was inevitable. (*Courtesy of the New York Public Library Picture Collection*)

William Green of Ohio. (*Photograph from the Ohio Historical Society Library*)

TWO BIRDS -- ONE STONE

—Adapted from Ding, in Des Moines Register.

The Kaiser could make no shrewder move than to sub-
sidize every grog shop in America to keep on at full
blast ladling out the stuff that takes the stamina
out of this great people.

---DR. FRANK CRANE.

Support for Prohibition was often coupled with strong anti-Ger-
man prejudice, since brewers were most often German. World War
I fueled both sentiments, as this 1918 Prohibitionist poster shows.
(*Courtesy of the New York Public Library Picture Collection*)

Robert F. Wagner of New York. (*Photograph from Brown Brothers*)

"TWO LOVELY BERRIES MOLDED ON ONE STEM."

A 1917 cartoon illustrating the common
origins of support for Prohibition and
blue laws. (*Courtesy of the New York
Public Library Picture Collection*)

This cartoon, depicting Republican reluctance to abolish property
qualifications for voting, appeared in the *Sunday Tribune* (Providence, R.I.) in 1914. (*The Rhode Island Historical Society*)

Al Smith of New York. (*Photograph from Brown Brothers*)

THE ONLY ARGUMENT AGAINST IT

Democrats in Rhode Island proposed the creation of public markets during the depression preceding World War I. The cartoon illustrates one response. (*The Rhode Island Historical Society*)

Frawley voted for the primary law after opposing it for years, but the organization was now behind it. In both 1915 and 1917 the Democrats also helped resist attempts to repeal the primary law and go back to the convention system.[34]

New Jersey's Democratic bosses were slower to accept the direct primary, but many of their younger followers were instrumental in enacting the reform in 1911. As early as 1909 Jersey City Democrats voted for an abortive bill that was killed by a bipartisan coalition. South Jersey consistently opposed the primary because it was rural and underpopulated and feared that north Jersey candidates would have a decided advantage. The Wilson administration endorsed the so-called Geran Bill, introduced by a former student of the governor's at Princeton. The Smith-Nugent machine in Newark fought the bill behind the scenes, but Jersey City boss Bob Davis allowed his followers freedom of choice. When the bill passed the assembly by a close 34–25 tally, the votes of four Newark and nine Jersey City Democrats were crucial to its success. In Ohio the direct primary was enacted in 1913, during the period of Democratic rule, with the overwhelming support of the Cleveland delegation. Only two assemblymen and one senator from among the Cuyahoga lawmakers abstained on the final vote, and the twenty-three negative votes were all cast by rural, mostly Republican, legislators.[35]

Chicago Democrats were also in favor of the primary method, provided the party organization was able to function to its best advantage. Illinois's first primary law was enacted during the administration of Republican Governor Charles Deneen, but it needed a good deal of Democratic support since several leaders of the governor's own party, including the speaker of the house, were opposed. Republican Boss William Lorimer fought the measure because in his view, it worked against "representation of the different subdivisions, geographically or by the different nationalities." Even his enemies credited much of the primary's success to the efforts of Roger Sullivan, and several of his most faithful lieutenants voted in favor, as did future Chicago Mayor Anton Cermak.

In the senate, the vote was 40–1, with one Chicago Democrat abstaining. Ironically the first primary election in 1912 resulted in the nomination and election of Sullivan's rival Edward Dunne as governor; he won by virtue of an overwhelming triumph in the city of Chicago. The entire Dunne slate, all Irish-Americans, achieved victory primarily in Cook County, underscoring the advantage bestowed upon urban candidates by the primary system. Chicago Democrats also favored extending the law's coverage and preventing antiorganization forces from undermining the machine's ability to nominate its candidates. City lawmakers introduced primary bills for General Assembly candidates, judgeships, presidential preference, and Cook County offices. Pragmatically, they strongly opposed amendments to abolish precinct committeemen in the city of Chicago and have ward captains elected.[36]

Urban lawmakers in Massachusetts also favored primaries, providing that urban and party interests were served. Their support was possibly increased because factionalism between the Boston ward bosses made the convention a surefire breeder of strife and bitterness. In 1912 Boston Democrats voted for a presidential preference primary, but only after amending the bill to provide for at-large election of delegates to the national convention. In 1910 the Democrat–labor legislator coalition blocked passage of a Republican primary bill because it was to become operative only upon petition of 10 percent of the voters in each county. Three years later a Democratic attempt to establish a preferential primary for the U.S. Senate was killed by the majority party. At the same time, the Boston Irish insisted upon primaries being administered by the party machinery, and blocked attempts to permit crossovers or independent registration. Rhode Island Democrats pressed for the institution of primaries, with some Providence Republicans concurring, but the Brayton forces squelched all such attempts.[37]

In Connecticut both parties candidly admitted that primaries would result in enhanced influence for urban candidates and took their stands accordingly. Democratic leaders pledged themselves to the measure in 1911, except for New Haven Boss Davey Fitzgerald who warned the legislature that it would open the door for urban domination. Most rural lawmakers used the same argument in attacking it, while some urban Republicans endorsed the idea as a means of increasing their leverage within the rural-dominated party. In the senate where urban interests were fairly well reflected, the primary bill passed by a solid 22–5 margin with only Republicans in opposition. In the lower house, where the towns dominated, the proposal failed by more than two to one, amid general agreement that Hartford, New Haven, and New Britain would be the main beneficiaries if the method were adopted. Two years later a primary bill was again introduced and passed the senate 21–10 with only one Democrat opposed. The house killed the measure 75–150, after a debate that emphasized the urban-rural division anew.[38]

As a further indication of their desire to democratize the political process by maximizing the impact of the urban working class vote, city lawmakers sponsored a wide variety of alterations in the electoral process. Rearrangement of registration and voting procedures to make them more conducive to wage earners was an important consideration. Cleveland's representatives sought to have election days declared half-holidays and to keep the polls open longer. Cuyahoga lawmakers also strongly supported the proposal to prohibit employers from accompanying their employees to the polls in both 1913 and 1917. Connecticut Democrats tried unsuccessfully through several sessions to keep the polls open until late evening for the convenience of laborers. In Massachusetts, the Boston Irish coupled their concern for the urban voter with a strong desire to have party lines strictly observed. They pressed for extended registration time, but only if enrollment were by party; they opposed a totally open primary with no affiliation required. Martin Lomasney's chief lieutenant David Mancovitz also successfully amended the primary law to prevent crossovers. New York Democrats centered most of their attention on adoption of the so-called

Massachusetts ballot which required party affiliation, and
passed it over Republican objections during Governor
Glynn's famous "radical" special session in December 1913.
They also played a major role in blocking efforts of upstate
Republicans to limit the franchise by barring those who
could not read or write English. Rhode Island Democrats
directed their attention toward lengthening the registration
period and allowing canvassers to register people in their
homes, since immigrant stock people were not always aware
of the necessity to register. They also sponsored measures to
protect employees from retaliation by employers, to replace
the Board of Canvassers in Providence with an electoral
commission and to allow employees time off with pay in
order to vote.[39]

Much more crucial to augmenting the electoral power of
the urban worker in Rhode Island was the repeal of the
economic restrictions that still applied in local elections.
Despite general abolition elsewhere, Rhode Island still
stipulated a minimum property qualification for common
council elections. The situation often produced serious
deadlocks as new stock Democratic mayors, elected by
universal male suffrage, found their programs stymied by city
councils chosen by restricted franchise. The requirement of
property qualifications was so highly valued by the GOP that
Charles Wilson, Brayton's successor as party leader, acknowledged abolition to be "distinctly a Democratic measure" and that its implementation would mean a Republican
defeat. In each session of the General Assembly the Democrats introduced a constitutional amendment to abolish
property qualifications only to have their efforts frustrated by
the Republican majority. Occasionally a few urban Republicans or a handful of Progressives joined them, but the result
was still the same. In 1910 the Democrats mounted a massive
campaign of petitions from the cities and the Republicans
tried to counter by replacing property qualifications with
educational ones. The attempt failed and the abolition of
property qualifications itself was defeated in the house 52–39,
amid Democratic pleas to aid the workingman and Republi-

can arguments that a voter needed to have a stake in society to act responsibly. In 1912 there was an almost daily attempt by Democratic leaders in the house to pry the measure from committee, all of which were fruitless. In 1913 Democratic pressure forced the Republican leaders to declare the matter so important as to require consideration by a constitutional convention, a ploy that almost backfired when enough urban Republicans deserted to the Democratic-Progressive cause to pass the resolution for a convention in the house. The senate again saved the day for the Republicans, as it did in 1914, by blocking efforts to discharge the resolution from committee. By 1915 and 1916 the regular Republicans in the house had sufficiently regained their composure to bottle it in committee, although seven of their number voted to discharge it in the latter year. It took the Democrats until 1928 to abolish property qualifications by constitutional amendment, and by that time the union of the Irish and the newer immigrants in the Democratic party had been effected and the reign of the Yankee Republicans was ended.[40]

In addition to maximizing the urban working class vote, New England Democrats were also especially insistent upon having as many officials as possible stand for election as often as possible. Connecticut Democrats pressed hard for the election of county commissioners rather than their appointment by the legislature. The attempt failed in the senate in 1911. It was revived in 1913 when it passed the senate on a "strict party vote," but failed in the house despite its endorsement by the Democratic caucus. A similar bill perished in committee in 1917. City Democrats also worked for the election of judges in 1913, but the house again negated the favorable action of the senate. Concurrently, urban lawmakers consistently favored enlarging the powers of executive officers because they were elected at large and by universal male suffrage at the expense of the state legislature and common councils that were chosen by districts and by restricted suffrage. Thomas Spellacy began the drive to increase the governor's appointive power in 1911, but the Roraback organization caused its defeat in the senate. In 1912 a proposed constitutional amendment to free the governor from senate control over appointments and removals passed the Democratic upper house but failed in the lower one; a bill to allow the chief executive to appoint judges failed even to clear the senate in 1917. Similar Democratic attempts to increase the powers of mayors and lieutenant governors were also dispatched by the majority party.[41]

That same insistence upon frequent evaluation of public officials animated the efforts of Massachusetts urban lawmakers to resist biennial elections. Governor Foss opposed the Republican move in 1911 unless the GOP would agree to enact recall to balance the scales. The measure passed the house with the Republicans voting 98–18–11 in favor and the Democrats dividing 58–44–10; the senate killed the measure. The issue caused a rift between Governor Walsh and Martin Lomasney in 1915, with the Mahatma of Ward Eight engineering its defeat in both the legislature and the constitutional convention, where a proposal providing for popular election of judges also failed. In Rhode Island urban lawmakers failed in three different sessions to free the governor's appointive powers from senate control. They also tried to have the appointment of certain local officials such as police commissioners subject to popular referendum. The state's urban lawmakers also favored making the governor's veto more effective by raising the votes necessary to override it from the three-fifths established in 1909. Their concern for popular government led them also to oppose the change-over from annual to biennial elections, a reform dear to the hearts of the patrician reformers, and to insist that state commissions report every year.[42]

Rhode Island Democrats also concentrated their fire on the rules of the General Assembly in order to give the minority party more leverage. One of their primary aims was to secure greater membership on committees since the system of appointment by the leadership was so manifestly unfair that even one Republican asserted that "you cannot find any precedent for this procedure anywhere in Christendom." The legislature, charged Democratic leader Albert West of Providence, "was run like a gambling joint on Sunday. Nobody knows who is behind it." To further weaken the obstructive committee structure, they unsuccessfully fought to have all committees elected, to require only a two-fifths vote to discharge bills, and to stipulate that committees be made to report all bills to the floor. To hamper the Republican practice of jamming through legislation in the confusion attending the end of a session, the Democrats favored prohibiting the introduction of any new bill after the fifty-second day of the sixty-day session, and providing that no bill could be reported out of committee after the fifty-sixth day.[43]

The magnitude of the changes required to effect truly democratic government in their respective states eventually led most urban lawmakers to campaign for calling a constitutional convention. In New York the necessary resolution was passed despite Republican efforts during the frantic special session of December 1913, at Governor Glynn's insistence. The vote was 31–13 in the senate, with only one Republican joining in, and 86–21 in the assembly. Unfortunately for the hopes of urban New Yorkers, the election in 1914 produced a conservative Republican majority that stymied the aspirations of the original proponents of the convention. Al Smith and Samuel Gompers led the fight for provisions desired by the urban dweller and the workingman, but they were generally outvoted. Both Tammany and the state Federation of Labor eventually called for the charter's defeat because it failed to provide for home rule and legislative reapportionment and did not contain any of labor's demands. Ironically, upstate Republicans and conservatives also opposed ratification because they feared that the constitution centralized too much power in the governor. The proposal thus failed New York City by 245,000 votes and the state by 375,000. The Ohio convention was much more productive, providing for such innovations as initiative and referendum, woman suffrage, home rule, tax reform, a direct primary, judicial reform, and much socioeconomic legislation. The resolution

calling the convention passed both houses with heavy
majorities; only twenty-four rural and small town representatives refused agreement, while those of Cleveland, Cincinnati, Toledo, Dayton, and Columbus were all but unanimously in favor. The finished product received its biggest
margin of support in Cuyahoga County, a whopping 82
percent.[44]

In New Jersey the pressure for constitutional revision
came from populous, polyglot north Jersey. In 1911 the
enabling legislation failed to pass the assembly by a 23–27
vote. Essex and Hudson County Democrats comprised
eighteen of the twenty-three affirmative votes. Two years
later a proposal passed 40–17, with all but one of the
lawmakers from the six northeastern counties voting in favor,
but a coalition of Republicans and rural Democrats defeated
the measure in the senate. Small town intransigence, this time
in the lower house, also frustrated urban Democratic attempts for a constitutional convention in Connecticut in
1913. Democratic agitation in Rhode Island forced the
Brayton combine to propose the creation of a commission to
study the need for such a body by 1912. Democratic leaders
labeled the proposal a "lemon" designed to fool the people,
but voted for it "to test Republican sincerity." When the
committee report was finally ready in 1915, it advocated
many pet Democratic measures such as the abolition of
property qualifications, prohibition of dual officeholding,
and reapportionment. The Republicans therefore refused to
submit the report to popular referendum and stymied
Democratic efforts to discharge it from committee, a reversal
so flagrant that even the GOP governor deemed it a betrayal
of party pledges. The Democrats continued their unavailing
efforts to call a legitimate constitutional convention in nearly
every session.[45]

Chicago Democrats were a bit more hesitant on the subject
of constitutional revision because some apparently felt that
city interests might actually suffer reverses under a new
instrument. Some, including Governor Dunne, favored instead the adoption of a so-called gateway amendment that

would remove the restriction against having more than one constitutional amendment considered in any given election. This ambivalence led to split votes in the Chicago delegation in 1911, 1913, and 1915. When the proposal was finally adopted in 1917, most Chicagoans lent their support. The successful convention in Massachusetts was, according to its official historian, "a democratic bid for popular support at the expense of Republican conservatism." The Republicans steadfastly blocked all such attempts until the Walsh administration, when popular sentiment forced their hand. In 1914 a GOP bill passed the house after the Democrats failed to substitute their own system for choosing delegates, but it failed in the senate. The following year the Democrats again failed to enact their proposal and generally voted for the GOP version. The few votes cast against it were nearly all Republican and small town in origin. The referendum in favor received its highest vote total in metropolitan Boston, and such urban Democrats as Lomasney combined with labor representatives to push for a variety of socioeconomic and political changes of benefit to their constituents. The convention's official historian called the Mahatma the "most intense personal force in the convention," styling his actions fair, generous, sympathetic, and respected.[46]

Perhaps the most lasting contribution made by the urban new stock lawmaker to progressive political reform was his part in the ratification of the Seventeenth and Nineteenth Amendments to the U.S. Constitution, the only two political innovations to be adopted nationwide. Their support of the direct election of U.S. Senators, in preference to having them chosen by malapportioned legislatures, was highly consistent with their position on home rule, apportionment, direct legislation, and primary elections. As William Sulzer pointed out when he was a congressman supporting the proposed amendment in 1911, the apportionment system in New York was so weighted against the Democrats that they had to carry the state by over 100,000 votes to ever have a chance of choosing a Senator. The existing situation in the industrial states all but guaranteed the selection of solons who were old

stock, Protestant, small town, business oriented, and generally Republican, a process that had earned the senate the
reputation as a bastion of privilege and reaction. Election at
large could greatly enhance the chances of candidates who
were urban new stock, non-Protestant, sympathetic to labor
and welfare measures, and, above all, Democrats.[47] The
reasoning behind urban Democratic support of direct election became obvious from the first popular elections. The
first Massachusetts Democrat to run at large was John F
Fitzgerald and the next was David I. Walsh. Roger Sullivan
in Illinois, Thomas Taggart in Indiana, and Timothy Hogan
in Ohio all made the senatorial race. Only Walsh was
successful, but the potential for producing future Kennedys,
Wagners, and Ribicoffs was clearly demonstrated. In the
course of the debate over direct election numerous urban
Democratic leaders sought to define the issue as one of
democracy versus privilege. True democracy could only be
realized, Governor Dunne of Illinois asserted, when all
important state and national officials were elected by popular
vote, while Sulzer said that the only issue was that the people
"can and ought to be trusted." Assembly member Patrick
Dillon of Rhode Island insisted that the people and not the
corporations should select U.S. Senators, while Democratic
leader John Meany of Massachusetts opined that the people
had already demonstrated their capacity to act wisely by
selecting other public officials. Whether or not the adoption
of the Seventeenth Amendment accomplished these lofty
purposes is debatable, but it is certain that the upper
chamber has demonstrated much greater concern for urban,
industrial, minority group America than it ever did under the
old system of selection.[48]

In New York the lines were clearly drawn. The ratification
resolution in the senate was introduced by Wagner, and all
thirty-two Democratic members voted for it, including the
twenty-two representatives of metropolitan New York City;
the four dissenting votes were cast by upstate Republicans.
GOP opponents castigated the proposal as a "step toward
pure democracy," an "act of stultification," an admission

that the legislature was unworthy, and "an insidious advance against the foundations of the Republic." In the assembly thirty-two of New York County's thirty-five Democrats and seventeen of Brooklyn's twenty-three voted yes on the amendment as did all nine of Buffalo's. Democrats cast 70 percent of the votes in favor of ratification, and New York City contributed 70 percent of those. Four negative votes were cast by upstate Republicans, and six others abstained, including the minority leader. The other thirty-two Republicans voted for a popular measure despite the obvious distaste of the party leadership.[49]

The clash between urban Democrats and small town Republicans in Rhode Island was even more intense. After the amendment was introduced the Brayton organization quickly sent it to a committee on special legislation consisting of five Republicans, two Democrats, and one Progressive. Predictably the committee recommended rejection and a spirited debate ensued. Republican spokesmen argued that the existing system was devised by the founding fathers and that it had worked especially well in Rhode Island. In contrast, Assembly Member Dillon of Cumberland charged that the system was rigged to produce corporation spokesmen like Nelson Aldrich. In the end the house rejected the committee report 39–54 and ratified the amendment. Thirty-seven of the chamber's thirty-eight Democrats constituted the bulk of the proamendment votes. They were joined by the assembly's lone Socialist, a few Progressives, and about one-third of the Republicans, nearly all of whom were of urban new stock origin. The senate, as the last resort of the Brayton machine, sent the measure to committee, where the Republicans held a six-to-one advantage, from which it never emerged. Thus Rhode Island became the only northeastern state to deny ratification and the result represented another victory for the small town–business Brayton combine over the urban Democrats.[50]

A similar division took place in Connecticut, only in that state enough Republicans deserted the Roraback organization to effect ratification. The resolution in the lower house passed by a vote of 151–77. All 119 Democrats present voted for ratification, but only 32 of the 109 Republicans did, and they again were nearly all from urban areas. In the senate, where the Democrats had a three-to-two majority, the measure passed easily. Although it was adopted by a voice vote, the results in the lower house, the identity of its sponsors, and the Democratic control of the senate left no doubt as to the source of the primary impetus.[51]

In Massachusetts Democratic devotion to direct election prompted the party to seek enactment of the reform by the surest possible means. In a resolution prepared by Frank Donahue, the secretary of state, they moved to petition Congress to call a popular convention in order to bypass the state legislatures. The Republicans countered with a proposal by George Barnes of Norfolk County to amend the Donahue resolution so that it merely asked Congress to effect the change in any way it saw fit. That Barnes's amendment reflected something other than a conviction in favor of direct election became apparent upon questioning. He admitted that he had "grave doubts" about its wisdom, was skeptical that it would produce men of the same caliber as the existing system, and would support the reform only because it "reflects the sentiment of the people." The vote on the Barnes amendment was the nearest thing to a test of policy on the issue between the two parties, and the Democrats clearly established their claim as the staunchest supporters of direct election. All thirteen Democrats in the senate, joined by four labor legislators, opposed the amendment but the regular Republicans carried it. All but one of the Democrats then voted for the amended resolution, as did all but two Republicans who apparently refused to countenance any form of direct election proposal. In the lower house the Republicans failed in their attempts to qualify the Donahue resolution. A few Republicans expressed their distrust of popular election forthrightly but most sought to alter the language so that Congress was "requested" to call a convention, rather than ordered to do so. The resolution as drafted by Donahue passed by a whopping 162–37 vote, with all the negative votes being cast by Republicans. Since the senate refused to concur, the matter lay over until it was superseded by the Seventeenth Amendment itself. Both houses then ratified by voice vote, but the contest in 1912, plus the fact that the Democrats had carried the Bay State in the November elections, once again left no doubt as to who was more enthusiastic about direct election.[52]

The urgency for direct election seemed magnified in Illinois by two incidents involving selection of U.S. Senators by the General Assembly. In 1909 the election of Republican William Lorimer, the "Blond Boss" of Chicago's West Side, had been accomplished by the existence of a slush fund which allegedly resulted in the bribery of fifty-seven Democrats. Lorimer was subsequently expelled from the Senate and the necessity to choose two Senators in 1912 resulted in a deadlock that consumed four months of the legislature's time. As a result, support for the amendment was more bipartisan than on the east coast. The ratification resolutions were introduced by downstate Republicans in both houses and Governor Dunne urged the legislature to endorse "the greatest victory for popular government in fifty years." Even so, senate Republicans made an effort to sidetrack the measure by trying to table the motion to refer it to committee. The maneuver failed on a partisan vote and the measure was recommended favorably by the committee where the Democrats enjoyed a slim majority. The senate then approved ratification unanimously. In the lower house the vote was an equally decisive 146–1 with only one downstate Democrat opposed.[53]

The amendment enjoyed similarly strong backing from nearly all political factions in Ohio, but it was again the urban Democrats who pressed the issue. The ratification resolution in the senate was supported by the entire Cuyahoga and Cincinnati delegations, less one absentee. The lone negative vote was cast by a Xenia senator whose biography described him as an "uncompromising republican." In the lower house the measure received the votes of all thirteen Cleveland assemblymen and seven of the ten Cincinnati ones, the others being absent.[54] New Jersey's urban Democrats also pressed for the Seventeenth Amendment. Of the forty-two votes for the resolution in the lower house thirty-six were Democratic and six Republican. The Democrats who abstained were nearly all from the southern half of the state. Democrats in the senate provided ten of the eighteen affirmative votes while the lone negative ballot was cast by a downstate member of the majority party. Eight of the nine Republicans concurred. Thus urban new stock lawmakers were clearly one of the major forces behind the ratification of the Seventeenth Amendment.[55]

Their support for woman suffrage was much slower to evolve but it was, in some cases, a crucial factor in the success of the Nineteenth Amendment. Early urban new stock antipathy toward female voting proceeded from a variety of sources. Political bosses feared the possible impact that a group of idealistic females might have on their hardheaded operation. Men feared that women might vote in large numbers for a number of other undesirable measures, chiefly Prohibition. Their fears were reinforced by the *"kinder, kuchen, kirche"* attitude of their continental European constituents, for whom the idea of women working outside the home, going to school, or voting was repugnant. Foreign language newspapers were consistent in their denunciation of the women's rights movement, and many Catholic clergy warned of the possible dire consequences. The suffragettes themselves contributed mightily to this antagonism by their often unabashed nativism, asking aloud how the nation could deny the vote to old stock, Protestant females while conferring it freely upon males who "had neither understanding of American principles or a heritage which easily acquired it." Some likewise objected to the Fifteenth Amendment for enfranchising black males and leaving white females voteless.[56]

Accordingly, urban machine politicians contributed substantially to many of the defeats suffered by the advocates of statewide woman suffrage well into the second decade of the twentieth century. Referendum votes in such urban industrial states as Pennsylvania, New Jersey, Ohio, Massachusetts, Illinois, and New York regularly lost in the great metropolises; Al Smith cheerfully owned up to having defeated a suffrage statute while speaker of the house. Some prominent urban new stock political leaders never lost their distaste for females voting; one was Lomasney, who justified his position on the grounds that "you can't trust these women. They are apt to blab everything they know." Most of their counterparts, though, gradually made their peace with the movement in time to provide materially significant backing for the Nineteenth Amendment.[57]

The reasons for this adjustment are not too difficult to understand. The momentum of the suffragette movement was becoming irresistible and their demonstrations, lobbying, letters to the editor, and general arm-twisting were becoming nearly impossible to ignore. By resisting to the bitter end, the urban machine ran the risk of facing the wrath of the newly enfranchised half of the electorate. If women were going to get the vote anyway, then they had to be bound to the machine by ties of gratitude. Charles F. Murphy once remarked to Frances Perkins that he was opposed to woman suffrage but that if women ever did get the vote, she would make a very good Democrat. As numerous states enfranchised women at least on a limited basis, it became clear that none of the dire consequences feared by the politicians had come to pass. Women, it seemed, divided along the same general class, ethnic, and religious lines as did men; there was no such thing as the female vote. The major result of the change, as historian William Hesseltine once observed, was that it took twice as long to count the votes. When queried by a reporter about the significance of the 1913 Illinois statute granting limited suffrage to women, grizzled old "Bathhouse John" Coughlin opined that "it won't make very much difference at all." [58]

At the same time, the nature of the suffrage movement itself underwent a change in its attitude toward the foreign stock working class, led by such social workers as Frances Perkins, Jane Addams, Florence Kelley, and Sophonisba

Breckinridge. Working daily with immigrant stock people, these suffragette leaders were able to combat the stereotypes of their sisters, and to demonstrate that woman suffrage could be a powerful weapon to effect socioeconomic change. Hence they broadened their appeal, inserted propaganda in foreign-language papers, and involved themselves in the causes of the working class, which responded by altering its views of the suffragettes. Many new stock politicians eventually came to see the possibilities inherent in enfranchising their own females. With the political initiative shifting to the urban voter through the other innovations already discussed in this chapter, doubling the urban vote could only have a beneficial effect. Their opponents also became aware of this potential and intensified their opposition to woman suffrage. Opponents of the reform in Illinois emphasized that "slum women will predominate," while in Rhode Island General Brayton himself testified that female enfranchisement posed a possibly fatal threat to the continued dominance of his organization. As Andrew Sinclair has observed, the "hard core" of opposition to the Nineteenth Amendment in the Northeast lay in "its fear of immigrant female voters." As Barbara Solomon said, "those who thought 'Patrick' was bad enough did not want to add 'Bridget' to their problems." [59]

This change-over was especially evident in New York. The opposition of Smith and Murphy has already been noted, and the behind-the-scenes efforts of Tammany leaders contributed mightily to the defeat of a suffrage referendum in 1915. By 1917, though, the Hall maintained neutrality to test the wind and found that the measure carried metropolitan New York by an even more overwhelming margin than it had failed by two years earlier. Smith, by now governor, urged the legislature to ratify the Nineteenth Amendment, while one New York lawmaker boasted that the Democratic party had been "a consistent friend of woman suffrage" and another rejoiced that "it was in a Democratic year that suffrage was granted to the women." On the final vote on ratification, city Democrats were nearly unanimous in their support.[60]

The same pattern, with slight variation, occurred in Illinois. In 1913, although Governor Dunne endorsed a suffrage statute, the followers of Harrison and Sullivan refused to go along. Nine of Chicago's ten Democratic senators and twenty-two of its twenty-six assemblymen voted in the negative. Dunne later wrote that even after passage he was "importuned in many directions to use my veto power," presumably from his fellow Chicago Democrats since they were the only sizable bloc opposed. By the time the Nineteenth Amendment was considered six years later, though, only three Chicago Democratic senators and five representatives failed to vote for ratification.[61]

Some Cleveland Democrats advocated female suffrage as early as 1911, but many of their cohorts failed to agree. As late as 1917, five Cleveland representatives and two senators voted against a bill allowing women to vote in presidential elections, and even in 1919 one senator and six representatives refused to petition Ohio congressmen for support of the pending suffrage amendment. When the latter was considered, however, only one Cleveland Democrat voted no while three others abstained.[62]

Some Connecticut Democrats also favored female suffrage early in the decade, but measures to permit it in local elections in both 1913 and 1917 split their ranks almost literally down the middle. Two years later, though, nine of the eleven Democratic senators voted for the Nineteenth Amendment, while the other two abstained and every single party member in the lower house followed suit. Ten Republicans opposed ratification openly, while twenty-two others abstained.[63]

In Rhode Island, the issue was complicated by the debate over property qualifications. The president of the state suffrage association, Elizabeth Upham Yates, set the tone by arguing that adoption of woman suffrage, coupled with retention of property qualifications, would limit the privilege to "American women" and counteract the effects of the "foreign vote." The amendment itself was adopted with almost unanimous support but Democratic spokesmen then tried to amend the enabling legislation to provide for the abolition of property qualifications for women in the hope that this step would lead to "full male suffrage" as well. The Republicans skillfully adjourned, but the Democrats persisted for three months and the GOP was finally forced to kill the property qualifications revision 29–57, "party lines being strictly observed." Even so, several votes for the enabling legislation came from Democrats, who realized that the enfranchisement of even some of the large numbers of potential urban women voters would materially aid their cause.[64]

The Boston Irish, with the exception of czar Martin Lomasney, also made the adjustment to woman suffrage by 1919. In 1913 the Gaelic Democrats overwhelmingly opposed both a proposed constitutional amendment and an advisory vote on the subject, and two years later the advisory ballot lost heavily in the Boston area and the mill towns. Because of the opposition of such prominent Republicans as Henry Cabot Lodge and Calvin Coolidge, the measure received only 35.5 percent of the votes cast. By 1919, though, it was evident that the Democrats had adjusted much more rapidly than their opponents. Lodge voted against the amendment in the U.S. Senate; Coolidge, as governor, submitted it to the General Court without comment, while Republican lawmakers cast nearly all the fifty-two votes against ratification. Only the three representatives of Lomasney's home district marred the affirmative record of city Democrats. By the 1920 campaign Curley had taken to electioneering with his wife and proclaiming that female voters were "the conscience of America." [65]

What Lomasney was to the Boston Irish and woman suffrage, Jim Nugent was to the New Jersey Democrats. The Newark boss reportedly never forgave Woodrow Wilson for his "surrender" to the suffragettes and ran for the Democratic nomination for governor in 1919 to "stand four-square against prohibition and woman suffrage." The remaining north Jersey Democrats underwent the same transition as their counterparts in other states. In 1915 both Hudson and

Essex Counties returned sizable margins against a suffrage referendum, but by 1919 only the Nugent-led Essex contingent held out, in union with several Republicans from south Jersey. All twelve Jersey City assemblymen voted for ratification.[66]

The adjustment of most urban new stock legislators to the realities of woman suffrage epitomized their attitude toward political reform in general during the Progressive Era. So long as the enfranchisement of women appeared to be a device favored by old stock Americans to blunt the impact of the lower class vote and stymie attempts to alter the socioeconomic status quo, the urban machine and its constituents resisted it ferociously. Once it became apparent that the idea was politically popular, that its impact upon the machine's methods of operation would not be catastrophic, and, above all, that its enactment might actually add significantly to the growing power of the urban vote, most city politicians ceased their opposition and became open, if not avid, advocates of female voting. These three conditions —the popularity of the proposal, its actual impact upon the operations of the organization, and its effect upon urban voters—largely determined the attitude of politicians toward reform. With few exceptions, these criteria usually made them opponents or skeptics concerning such patrician reforms as civil service, the short ballot, or the city manager. Such innovations were not popular with their constituents, could seriously interfere with machine activities, and restricted rather than augmented the power of the urban lower and middle classes. Only where the small town–business coalition was in such complete control of state government as to shut off all urban aspirations for capturing the legislature and reaping the spoils was there much percentage in pressing for good government legislation. Even then the issues rarely assumed burning importance. The popular strain of progressive reform was quite another story. Despite all the rhetoric about using the direct primary and the like to break the power of the boss and the machine, those whose business it was to win elections realized, upon more sober reflection, that democratic reform put a new premium upon organization and technique. Regardless of speculations that enthusiasm for such measures could only have proceeded from the *Weltanschauung* of native, Protestant America, the evidence of referenda and legislative roll calls clearly reveals that the representatives of new stock, non-Protestant America contributed immensely to their enactment. For them the goal was not the realization of an abstract ideal, but rather political power—power that would provide sufficient leverage for the actualization of social and economic measures of even greater practical importance.

CHAPTER 5

~~~~~~

An American Kulturkampf:
The Birth Pangs
of Cultural Pluralism

There was one type of Progressive Era reform to which urban new stock lawmakers were almost uniformly opposed: attempts to legislate conformity to prevailing moral and cultural standards. In the context of the times, their attitude often marked them as hopeless reactionaries, for a growing number of reform-minded Americans had come to regard such measures as the ultimate solutions to the nation's problems. The reformed political and economic system, many felt, could only succeed if it were operated by those who shared the values of the dominant culture. The various subcultures would either have to be converted to that point of view or be excluded from further participation. In the broader perspective of history, however, the obstructionism of the representatives of the urban immigrant masses on such efforts squares both with the nation's traditional ideal of an open society and the emphasis of modern-day liberals on cultural pluralism.

The sources of that opposition were both apparent and subtle. Urban new stock lawmakers were certainly acting to protect vital elements of their own culture from nativist attack, a frequent theme in U.S. history. The cultural tone of the nation had been set during the colonial period by the

English Protestants who formed the bulk of its inhabitants. English was firmly established as the mother tongue and surnames and place names quickly became anglicized. British influence pervaded a wide variety of human activities such as style of dress, the size and operation of the family unit, the role and use of sex, the consumption of food and alcoholic beverages, and the types of recreational activities allowed. Standards for the observance of the Sabbath were also fixed, and the Puritan Ethic with its emphasis upon hard work, thrift, and individual moral responsibility for success or failure became the norm. White was the only acceptable skin color, and people of other hues were either enslaved or eliminated. Clashes over mores between English and non-English ethnic groups did occur, but the French Huguenots, Scotch and Scotch-Irish Presbyterians, German Pietists, and Dutch soon became part of the national consensus, with only a few minor alterations on either side. For the most part this dominant culture was unconsciously imbibed by succeeding generations, but it was also consciously inculcated through literature, the Protestant churches, and the public schools. From *Poor Richard's Almanack* through *McGuffey's Reader* to Horatio Alger, the message remained essentially undiluted.[1]

The first great challenge to the hegemony of the white, British, Protestant consensus was provided by the mass migrations of the two decades before the Civil War. The British immigrants and even many of the German and Scandinavian Protestants shared many cultural ties with the American majority and were readily assimilated. The Irish and German Catholics seemed to challenge the cultural consensus by their use of alcoholic beverages, their observance of Sunday, and the creation of a school system designed to perpetuate their own customs and values. The result was the rise of militant temperance and nativist groups that sought to fend off this invasion by propaganda, direct action, and political activity. Their concern was heightened by the crisis over slavery; many Americans embraced nativism in the hope that unity against a foreign menace might hold together the nation's crumbling institutions. When it did not, nativism and temperance were submerged during the Civil War and Reconstruction, and there followed an uneasy period of truce.[2]

This standoff persisted until the impact of the New Immigration began to be felt in the 1890s. The newcomers from southern and eastern Europe, French Canada, and the Orient brought with them a bewildering variety of customs and attitudes that differed substantially not only from those of the national consensus but even from those of the Old Immigrants. Some of the earliest clashes came between the two great subcultures of the Old and New Immigration. German Jews were often horrified at the behavior of Russian Jews and coined some of the worst epithets in the anti-Semitic lexicon. The Catholic majority of the newcomers resented the efforts of the Irish and German clergy to impose their peculiar brands of Catholicism upon them, while Irish laborers in San Francisco were only too glad to join in the persecution of Chinese and Japanese to take the burden of nativist attack off themselves.[3]

In time, the Old and New Immigrants found themselves thrust into a necessary alliance. The Irish politicians soon discovered that they needed to respect a man's cultural heritage if they hoped to get his vote. The Catholic church, with two millennia of experience harmonizing diverse human elements, began to exercise its healing influence. German and Russian Jews learned that 6,000 years of a common heritage transcended the experiences of a few centuries. Most importantly, the new waves of nativism that swept the United States did not distinguish between the Old and the New Immigrants to any great extent. By the time the first Irish Catholic ran for governor in New York in 1914, alarmists whispered, "If a Catholic is elected, perhaps a Jew is next." Bigotry, by its nature, is not given to fine distinctions.[4]

The New Nativism began in the 1890s with the formation of the American Protective Association and the Immigration Restriction League. It was fostered by a host of writers ranging from the respected academic sociologist E. A. Ross to the hack popularizer Madison Grant. The message was essentially the same: the rapidly multiplying minorities threatened the "great race" and its superior culture. The only real disagreement was between those who retained faith in the civilizing power of their culture to Americanize the newcomers and those who felt that the only solution was to end immigration altogether. Eventually the "uplifters" and the "excluders," as Oscar Handlin has sagely observed, developed a consensus on two major points: that there really was such a thing as a distinct American culture and that homogeneity, per se, was socially desirable. "To be cosmopolitan," the *Boston Transcript* theorized, "is to be badly governed." [5]

To a large degree, then, the urban Democratic lawmakers in the seven industrial states were motivated largely by an instinct for self-preservation in defending their own and their constituents' culture; they also recognized the political gains to be made among New Immigrant voters. Just as the native bosses of the urban political machines wooed the Irish and German voters by defending them during the pre–Civil War nativist hysteria, so did the Irish politicos of the Progressive Era court the New Immigrants. Years of sensitivity to the cultural peculiarities of their constituents and of playing "United Nations politics" had conditioned them to the political potential of such actions. In a deeper sense, however, the cultural struggle of the period was the result of the presence of two very different and almost incompatible world views, deeply rooted in religious background.

The older ritualistic tradition was the legacy of medieval Christianity. Its essence was the intellectual assent of the individual to a common body of doctrine, buttressed by an elaborate ritual and the sacraments, all presided over by a hierarchy with clearly defined authority. These characteristics separated their adherents from the rest of society and fostered the idea that "outside the Church there is no salvation." Although the world was filled with evil it was basically good because God made it and no mere man could question his ways. Consequently the ritualist was conditioned to accept the world as it was, but to keep himself apart from it and earn his salvation by clinging to the beliefs and practices of the church. Society and religion were two separate spheres of his life and the thought that government should ever supplant the church as the custodian of individual morality was anathema. Government might temper his physical condition by welfare or regulatory legislation, but it must refrain from directives affecting his immortal soul. The commandments of God and the church served as guides to moral conduct, but it was expected that individuals would fall from grace periodically and so provision was made for absolution. The key word in the use of all fleshly pleasure was moderation, and defect was as much condemned as excess (unless, of course, one chose to do so for a higher purpose, as in the case of clerical celibacy). The result was a tradition that left questions of morality to the individual conscience, with the church as the only guide.[6]

The pietistic tradition, on the other hand, almost completely eschewed any prescribed doctrine, liturgy, or ritual. Since there was also virtually no hierarchical organization, it mattered little with which pietistic sect one affiliated. The only important criterion was a "personal, vital and fervent faith in a transcendental God." One was not born into membership in the religious community as among the ritualists, but rather at some point in his life had to experience a personal conversion, his "decision for Christ." Baptism, consequently, was not administered soon after birth, but rather in adulthood. To promote this "change of heart," the pietists used revival meetings instead of the daily liturgy. The individual was much more on his own against the evil in the world and hence more anxious to eradicate all potential barriers to his own and his neighbor's salvation. The only way he could save himself was to save his neighbor and the only way he could do that was to purge the world of evil. "It was a matter of grave concern to the New England Puritan," one commentator has observed of that highly pietistic group, "that his neighbor's manners and morals be acceptable unto God." If this could be accomplished through moral suasion or good example, so much the better; but if that failed, the pietist felt a strong moral obligation to work for the passage of coercive legislation to save his neighbor from his own follies. Whether the evil was liquor, gambling, pornography, or slavery, it must be eradicated if man were to be saved. If "right belief" was the hallmark of the ritualist, "right behavior" was clearly that of the pietist.[7]

Although all American religious denominations were split to some degree between the ritualistic and pietistic traditions in the nineteenth century, one or the other generally emerged victorious. The pietistic approach captured virtually all the Calvinistic denominations. Most affected were the Congregationalists, Methodists, Disciples of Christ, and Quakers, the sects most involved in the antislavery movement. Although the Presbyterians and Baptists were fragmented, the pietists predominated. In fact, among the major Protestant denominations in the United States only the Episcopalians and the Lutherans failed to fall within the orbit of evangelical pietism. Both of these antedated Calvinism and had not carried their dispute with the medieval church nearly as far. Luther had vigorously debated with the Calvinists over the issues of Sunday observance and legislated morality. Unlike the other Protestant faiths, Lutheranism was an immigrant sect and reflected Old World attitudes more than American ones. Generally the German or Missouri Synod Lutherans were highly ritualistic and unkindly disposed toward moral legislation, while the Scandinavian Lutherans were more inclined toward pietism. The German Lutheran view of morality was that "it is the duty of the secular government to prevent vice with lawful means, but it is the duty of the Church to save men by faith in Christ from committing sin." [8]

The crusading spirit of the pietists sustained the abolitionists and provided much of the moral underpinnings for the Social Gospel, but it contained a darker side. "In lesser men," Will Herberg has observed, "excessive piety frequently degenerates into smug and nagging moralism." Faced with the challenge of industrialization, urbanization, and immigration, much of pietism "exhausted its crusading spirit in campaigns to improve individual morality, refusing to see that the genuinely moral problems of the time were social problems that could not be adequately dealt with merely from the standpoint of personal betterment."[9]

By far the largest liturgical denomination was the Roman Catholic church. Although its hierarchy and occasional lay groups issued periodic statements on temperance and proper Sunday behavior, these usually stressed moderation rather than abstinence. More importantly, few if any ever called for secular legislation to effect these ends, relying instead upon the moral authority of the church. Since individual failings were the result of original sin, purely natural efforts could hardly eliminate them. The eastern European Jews, who comprised the next most sizable portion of the New Immigration, closely resembled the ritualists in their attitudes and practices. Man, they held, was capable of descending to great depths of evil, but he was still not inherently bad. Moderation, not abstention, in the use of all worldly pleasures was the ideal, and the sinner had to be treated with tolerance and understanding. The ancient Jewish tradition did not even have a word for censorship, holding it to be "not a constructive force in character development." These attitudes were reinforced by centuries of persecution and a position as a permanent minority group. Believing that "tyranny is infectious," Jews insisted that "it is a primary tenet of Judaism to fight against the mistreatment of any human being, whatever his race, religion or ancestry may be." Together with the Christian ritualists, the Jewish immigrants were predisposed to resist legislated morality.[10]

The profound differences in outlook between pietists and ritualists were reinforced by consideration of class, residence, and political affiliation. The pietistic religions, in the main, were those of middle class America. Evangelical Protestantism had become "an institutional reflection of certain strata of middle-class America," for whom the individualism of their essentially frontier religious outlook "served as a means of ignoring and evading the social problems of urban,

industrial America." The adherents of these faiths, those
upon whom "the long religious hand of New England rested
heavily," were the ones mainly affected by the "status
revolution." Catholicism and Judaism were largely working
class denominations. Washington Gladden, the famous Social Gospeler, observed that only one-tenth of his Congregational church's membership came from the working class,
while a Pittsburgh census revealed that businessmen and
salaried and professional workers constituted almost two-
thirds of the membership of the city's Protestant churches,
and only 10 percent of its overall population. For the
workingman gambling and the saloon were among the few
diversions available, and Sunday was the sole day of
recreation. Condemned to a life of manual labor, there
seemed to be little reason to postpone gratification in
anticipation of future reward, a fundamental principle of the
middle class. Episcopalianism was generally at the other
end of the social scale where immediate gratification was
the product of abundance rather than scarcity. Among the
ritualists, only the German Lutherans could really be clas-
sified as predominantly middle class, but cultural issues like
Prohibition and Sunday observance usually detached them
from the rest of that class.[11]

The pietist-ritualist division was also reflected in the
nation's geography. The pietists were overwhelmingly pre-
ponderant in rural and small town America, in the South and
West. In the cities they occupied the middle class neighborhoods between the "gold coast" and the ghettos. Nearly all
those who have studied the vote distribution on referenda
dealing with moral legislation have observed that their
greatest source of strength lay in the rural and small town
areas and in the middle class sections of the city, while the
opposition was usually centered in the working class and
upper class districts of the cities. The upper classes sought to
keep the working class districts "wide-open" for "slumming"
trips, and thus joined with their inhabitants to resist the
drives of the urban and rural middle class to "clean up" the
city. The free and easy atmosphere of the city made it the

prime target for the moral reformer, while the agrarian myth reinforced the pietistic world view.[12]

The struggle over manners and morals during the Progressive Era became more and more a partisan one. The diverse coalition that formed the Republican party in the 1850s was held together not only by its opposition to slavery, but also by its devotion to pietistic ideals. It quickly absorbed the Prohibitionists and nativists, and its greatest voting strength lay in New England and in those areas of the West and Midwest settled by transplanted descendants of the Puritans. Its opposition to slavery seemed motivated at times by dislike of blacks, and one member of the 1860 convention pledged that the party would "take care of the Dutch and Irish after the nigger question is settled." The Evangelical Protestants remained the backbone of the GOP, although the party attracted Episcopalians on economic grounds and drew its share of German Lutherans and New Immigrants as long as cultural issues were kept submerged.[13]

In the logic of the two-party system, the ritualists were drawn inevitably toward the Democratic party. Being the party of "negative liberalism," it was much less likely to use the coercive power of government to interfere with "personal liberty." Being the minority party, it entertained fewer qualms about the social strata from which it recruited its following. During the generally bleak days from the Civil War to the advent of the New Deal, the northern wing of the party survived primarily by the ability of its Irish ward bosses to deliver the votes of the Catholic working class. The native Americans who adhered to the party outside the South were often described as "hedonists," those who entertained no aspirations toward middle class respectability and held a "live-and-let-live" attitude toward manners and morals. "The Democratic party," Indiana Democratic Senator John Kern explained in 1895, "has never posed as the great and only party of morality and temperance. The Republican party has." Not surprisingly, the Democrats soon came to reflect the attitudes of ritualists and hedonists while the Republicans gradually became the captive of the Anti-Saloon

League, the Women's Christian Temperance Union, the
Immigration Restriction League, and similar expressions of
militant pietism. In the South such groups had to be
Democratic, but since the issues were local they rarely
caused problems for national party unity. The national
Republican leadership, dominated by business leaders and
dependent to some degree upon the New Immigrant vote in
key states, managed for a long time to hold the pietistic
enthusiasm of its constituents in check, but eventually
capitulated. As early as 1887, the GOP platform in twenty-
seven states favored some form of Prohibition and opposed it
in only one. Even in the International Telephone and
Telegraph Company scandal of 1972, a sympathetic colum-
nist acknowledged that "Republicans always look worse
when they are charged with venality, probably because they
tend to piety." By the Progressive years, the GOP had
become the major political vehicle for moralistic reform,
leaving the urban new stock Democrats as its major opponents. Only those Republicans also courting the new stock
vote, some elements of the business community, hedonists,
and those few Americans really committed to cultural
pluralism were willing to stand with them.[14]

One of the most long-standing and bitter battles between
these two cultural traditions was over the proper way to
observe Sunday. Before the Reformation, European Chris-
tians had held the day to be a joint one of worship and
recreation, to be marked by feasting, dancing, and playing
once the religious ceremonies were over. This "continental
Sunday" tradition continued in Catholic and Lutheran
countries, but the advent of Calvinism produced a different
outlook. The masters of Geneva proposed a return to the
Hebraic Sabbath where the Pharisees had even limited the
number of steps to be taken. The members of the consistory
visited homes without prior notice to ensure that no work or
recreation was done. When the Puritans settled New England they established a similar set of rules, codifying them
into so-called "blue laws." The great wave of Catholic and
Lutheran immigrants in the 1850s meant the importation of

the more ancient continental Sunday tradition, and the native pietists tightened their restrictions to prevent desecration of the Lord's Day. The New Immigrants of the late nineteenth and early twentieth centuries were even more committed to the older traditions and with the necessity of working upwards of sixty hours or more a week in a factory, they were fortunate to have even Sunday for recreation. Sunday blue laws were also "seemingly constructed to despoil poor Sabbath-observant Jews" who had to close their shops two days a week. About the only sympathy for enforced Sunday observance among the immigrant working class was engendered when such laws were the only way they could have a day off. Especially as they applied to recreation, however, they and their representatives led efforts to repeal them.[15]

In Connecticut, the defense of the blue laws was a major goal of the Roraback Republicans, and repeal a fervent desire of the urban Democrats. The greater representation of urban new stock interests in the senate led to occasional victories there, but the malapportionment of the lower house served to defend the cultural status quo. The debate was often marked by inflated rhetoric and acrimonious personal invective but both sides felt that the issue involved nothing less than their way of life. In 1909 a proposal to allow Sunday recreation was introduced by a New Haven Democrat; it passed the senate by two votes, but failed to reach the house floor. Two years later Democratic floor leaders Spellacy and Murphy introduced similar measures in their respective houses and set off a furious exchange. Small town Republicans, charging that the measure "would tend to cripple the morals of the state," opposed "any invasion of the Puritan's heritage to the state." "The notion of abrogating one of the ten commandments was abhorrent" to them. One Republican senator, an old stock factory owner from Danbury, insisted that it "would be demoralizing to legalize Sunday sports," and that "as a manufacturer, I have learned that they [employees] were not ready for work on Monday after Sunday athletics." Democrats and a few urban Republicans countered by insisting that the working class needed a day of recreation and had to be able to shop on Sunday. Stratford Republican Stiles Judson supported the bill and accused his fellow party members of having been "in communication with the shade of old John Calvin." As Bridgeport Democrat Joshua Meltzer, a Russian Jewish immigrant, spoke in favor of passage, a Yankee lawmaker ridiculed him for his "sing song" manner of speech, and Meltzer retorted that he was "proud to be Hebrew and of foreign birth." The bill again passed the senate by two votes, but lost in the house 90–70. [16]

The intensity heightened in the following years. The Gaelic Association of Athletic Clubs of Connecticut, at its 1912 convention, announced its intention of having the Sunday laws so tightly enforced that even the Yankees would tire of them, but little came of it. The following year the same coalition of urban lawmakers pressed for the legalization of Sunday sales, movies, concerts, and sports. A prominent Wesleyan University economist, Willard Fisher, was fired for speaking in favor of the proposals before a Democratic meeting, and the Central Labor Union of Connecticut and State Federation of United Germany pressed for passage. The Lord's Day League and the Christian Endeavor Union lobbied equally hard against any change. The chancellor of the Roman Catholic diocese of Hartford announced his opposition to requiring men to work on Sunday, but endorsed the idea of permitting recreation. Once again all the bills failed. A proposal to permit Sunday movies passed the senate in 1919, but the house again came to the rescue of the state's Yankee culture.[17]

In Rhode Island the lines of division between the Brayton Republicans and city lawmakers were almost as clearly drawn. In 1910 the Democrats proposed that markets remain open on Sunday because the working class had no adequate refrigeration. The state's Protestant clergy protested, arguing that food would not perish that quickly, while the retail grocers, barbers, and the state Federation of Labor also expressed reservations about work on Sunday. Two years later the Democrats concentrated their attention on legaliz-

ing concerts and other amusements and drew fire from the
Anti-Saloon League, the United Ministers Association, the
Federation of Churches, and the New England Southern
Conference of the Methodist Episcopal Church. Opponents
conceded that concerts might be all right, but that the
amusements could "degenerate into low class entertainment
like vaudeville," while proponents insisted that the main
beneficiaries of legalization would be the "poor and foreign
born." [18]

In 1911 attempts to permit the sale of food and alcoholic
beverages were equally unsuccessful, even with the addition
of a local option provision. A Sunday concert bill got
through the lower house then, and again in 1914 by a vote of
44–42, backed by the Democrats and urban Republicans.
Supporters argued that it was a "working class bill" and one
favored by "minorities" who had not the opportunity for
recreation during the week. One Yankee Progressive countered that "Sunday was a fine institution as handed down to
us by our forefathers, but I see in this bill a move to
secularize the first day of the week." The senate rejected the
Sunday concert bill in both 1913 and 1915, and also killed a
Sunday sales proposal. In 1917 the Democrats concentrated
upon Sunday baseball, got it through the house on a 46–30
vote, but again met their downfall in the "packed" upper
house.[19]

The conflict over days with religious significance did not
end with Sunday in Rhode Island. In 1913 the principal of a
Providence elementary school refused to accept the excuses
of several Catholic children who missed classes to attend
Good Friday services. A Catholic priest resigned from the
school board in protest, and a few non-Catholic members
voted to reprimand the principal, but the majority upheld the
action. A measure was immediately introduced to make
Good Friday a legal holiday, and the struggle went on
through several sessions of the General Assembly. In 1914
house Democratic floor leader Albert West petitioned to
have saloons closed on Good Friday, but was checked by a
Providence Progressive who sought to close them on Memo-

rial Day. A French-Canadian Democrat from Woonsocket took up the fight for a Good Friday holiday in 1917, but again to no avail.[20]

In New York the Sunday issue generally revolved around baseball and saloons, with the same cultural and political divisions applying. In 1913 the Joint Committee on Revised Police Legislation, chaired by Robert Wagner and including Franklin D. Roosevelt, studied the Sunday question in New York City and concluded that the current blue laws had little public support, were openly flaunted, and led to police graft. The committee therefore proposed to give the city a greater measure of home rule, create a department of public welfare to oversee police activities in this area, and hold a referendum on Sunday liquor sales. Wagner introduced such a measure in the senate, arguing that the law was hypocritical since most saloons were open anyway and that its enactment would curtail police graft. Tammany Senator George McClellan, son of the Civil War general, supported the plan, chiding his colleagues that "the Legislature cannot attempt to legislate for original sin," and for once the *New York Times* agreed with the Democratic organization. Upstate Republicans, aided by a few old stock city senators, defeated the proposal by two votes, and their counterparts in the assembly shot down a compromise plan that would have closed saloons only during church hours.[21]

Attempts to allow Sunday movies were similarly unsuccessful until wartime austerity put the industry in a financial bind, giving proponents an economic argument. Even so, the debate in the assembly was along cultural lines and was long and bitter. A Cortland Republican set the tone by charging that passage would amount to "stamping God's word as of no effect," and "amending Moses' law," while several other upstate lawmakers criticized Sunday observance south of the Hudson. Democratic floor leader Charles Donahue replied that "Moses was an organization Democrat" and that he also wrote other commandments, such as "don't covet your neighbor's rights." The measures passed on a narrow 76–73 vote, with the body's Democrats and Socialists unanimously in favor. As in Rhode Island, the Democrats proposed to make Good Friday a legal holiday, with no greater success. City Democrats were also frustrated in their efforts to legalize Sunday baseball and other types of recreational activities on the Sabbath. Proposals by New York Democrats to allow Sunday ball games lost several times between 1913 and 1918, but were finally crowned with success in the latter year. The bill passed the senate 26–20 with the chamber's Democrats and all but two city Republicans in favor, over the opposition of upstate lawmakers. The assembly Rules Committee tried to bury the measure but finally had to report it to the floor where it passed. The issue of permitting Sunday baseball also produced ethnocultural splits in the legislatures of Massachusetts and Ohio.[22]

Closely related to the issue of Sunday baseball was the legalization of boxing. The native middle class often frowned upon athletic contests for profit, and professional athletes enjoyed a social status roughly the same as that of saloon-keepers, racketeers, and vaudevillians. The opponents of legalization argued that it would increase the amount of gambling and other illegal activities, while its proponents argued that legitimating sports would lessen criminal influence. The urban new stock working class saw professional athletics as a relatively cheap form of entertainment and one of the few available roads open to fame and fortune. To millions of young men trapped in tenements and facing a life of drudgery in a sweatshop, Horatio Alger was named John L. Sullivan, "Philadelphia Jack" O'Brien, "Battling" Levinsky, Ed Delehanty, Stanley Coveleski, or Heinie Zimmerman. All the social breeding or family influence in the world was no substitute for fleetness of foot, strength of arm, or quickness of hand. Professional athletes did not get rich but they earned a decent living, and the reputation and contacts made could be parlayed into a later career in business or politics. Many urban politicians had attracted their first following because of athletic prowess, and aimed to keep the door open for others to do the same.[23]

In Illinois Chicago Democrats tried through several sessions to effect legalization of boxing. In 1909 one of their number guided the measure through the house, but it was defeated in the senate with the vote divided largely along ethnic lines. The Ohio Boxing Commission Bill, introduced by a Cleveland Democrat, passed in 1911. Connecticut Democrats were unsuccessful with a similar proposal in 1913 and 1917, as were their counterparts in Rhode Island from 1912 to 1915. In every case the vote closely paralleled that on questions of Sunday observance, with Democrats and urban Republicans in favor and small town Yankees holding the line. The Tammany Democrats managed to legalize boxing and create a commission to oversee it during the 1911 session, but spent the next several years trying to defend their handiwork against repeal attempts. In 1914 they narrowly beat off repeal legislation introduced by a New York City Progressive and endorsed by the *New York Times*. In 1916 Governor Charles Whitman asked for repeal on the "grounds of public morals" and a Bronx Democrat tried to blunt criticism by introducing a bill to prevent fight promoters from controlling bouts. In 1918 Jimmy Walker sponsored an amended commission bill which had the backing of the armed services and limited bouts to fifteen rounds. In the senate all twenty-one Democrats, aided by ten urban Republicans, secured its passage and the same pattern prevailed in the assembly.[24]

The nation's ethnoreligious differences were most clearly visible in the school issue. To a degree only now beginning to be appreciated, the public schools had become agencies for the inculcation of the mores and values of the pietistic tradition. *McGuffey's Reader* taught generations of students to read English, but in the process they were expected to imbibe the values of thrift, self-reliance, rugged individualism, and personal piety. Students from other cultures were accounted failures unless the schools were able "to civilize, to Christianize and to Americanize" them. "We Americans," Walter Hines Page once insisted, "have got to . . . hang our Immigrant agitators and hang our hyphenates and bring up our children with reverence for English history and in awe of English literature." [25]

The tensions that built up in immigrant children as they found themselves torn between the culture of their parents and that of the public schools have been dealt with in many places, but nowhere more graphically or perceptively than by Oscar Handlin in *The Uprooted*, who observed of a reader used in public schools: "The whole book is false because nothing in it touches on the experience of its readers and no element in their experience creeps into its pages. Falsity runs through all their books, which all were written to be used by other pupils in other schools; even the arithmetic sets its problems in terms of the rural countryside. Falsity runs through all their education. They learn the songs their mothers never sang. They mouth the words of precepts with no meaning." Too often they were taught by native teachers insensitive to and contemptuous of their traditions and values who "could twist the knife of ridicule in the soreness of their sensibilities; there was so much in their accent, appearance and manners that was open to mocking." Long after he had become cardinal-archbishop of Boston, William O'Connell remembered of his public school days that Irish Catholics "were made to feel the slur against our faith and race, which hurt us to our very hearts' core." [26]

It was to combat this situation that the ritualistic groups developed their own school systems. Taught by teachers who understood both cultures, immigrant children were better able to acquire the tools and skills needed to make their way in the New World with a minimum of psychic damage due to social disorganization. The vast system of parochial schools, financed largely out of the meager earnings of immigrant workers, was one of the most remarkable educational achievements in human history. As early as the 1840s the conflict over the school system made a political impact, when Archbishop John J. Hughes of New York City began to lobby for state aid to parochial schools and the elimination of Bible reading in the public schools. Although Governor

William Seward, with his eye on the Catholic vote, was sympathetic, the resultant uproar contributed greatly to the nativist hysteria of the Know-Nothing Era. Hughes compounded his offense by helping to create a Catholic party in the city elections of 1841. Although the controversy in New York eventually subsided, it continued to flare up periodically in various forms. Catholic and Jewish clergy resurrected the issue of banning Bible reading in public schools in the twentieth century. New York City Democrats and Socialists also led the ineffectual opposition to a 1918 textbook censorship law. As the political scientist Charles Merriam observed of Illinois in the Progressive Era, the debate over the school system was usually fought between a "Catholic-labor-foreign complex" and a "Protestant-capitalist-native American complex." [27]

In Illinois the controversy revolved around the proposal to provide free and uniform textbooks for schoolchildren. Urban lawmakers favored the free part but insisted upon equal treatment for parochial schools and objected strenuously to the requirement of uniformity. Catholic and Lutheran clergymen and Catholic labor leaders were the major people who testified against the bill. Chicago Democrats were also the major opposition to a proposal to ensure "moral practices" in the public schools in 1909. By far the biggest controversy came in Massachusetts over the issue of state aid to private and parochial schools. Yankee Protestants tried to cut off money to Catholic schools and, after several unsuccessful efforts, a Progressive-Republican coalition introduced a constitutional amendment to that effect in 1914. Democratic leader Martin Lomasney countered with a bill prohibiting state aid to other private schools as well. Since Catholic schools received only about $49,000 in state aid and other private institutions such as Harvard received $18,000,000, Lomasney's intent was to place the Yankees on the horns of a dilemma. Republican speaker Grafton Cushing ruled that Lomasney's motion was not made seriously, but the Democrat–labor legislator coalition was able to kill off the proposed amendment.[28]

Lomasney was serious, however, and when the issue was raised in the constitutional convention the Mahatma reintroduced his amendment. Although Catholics in the convention objected, most went along while the majority of non-Catholics seemed willing to sacrifice the generous portion received by other private schools if that were the price of ending parochial aid. All but nine of the ninety-four Catholic delegates voted for the provision and it was ratified even though Cardinal O'Connell and the *Boston Pilot* conducted a vigorous campaign against it. When informed of the cardinal's opposition, Lomasney, a devout Catholic, snapped, "tell his eminence to mind his own business." The action cost the parochial school system financially, but the absence of state aid gave it a powerful argument for resisting Yankee attempts for closer supervision in the 1920s.[29]

The role played by urban new stock lawmakers as cultural brokers also dictated a strong stand against demands for immigration restriction. Spurred by racist literature, nativist groups, usually with the cooperation of organized labor, pressed for the enactment of a literacy test as a requirement for immigration. The urban political machines, dependent upon continuing immigration for fresh supplies of voters, were among the major institutions that resisted the proposals. Individual lawmakers also understood that demands for restriction constituted a negative evaluation of their way of life. As Tammany's "Big Tim" Sullivan confided to young Franklin Roosevelt, "The people who had come over in steerage . . . knew in their hearts and lives the difference between being despised and being accepted and liked." Their stand on immigration restriction for a long time put the urban politicians in alliance with big business against organized labor and thereby damaged the alignment that seemed to be building on economic issues, but the growing militancy of New Immigrant workers caused a gradual reshuffling of positions. At any rate, Presidents McKinley, Taft, and Wilson all vetoed literacy test bills before Congress was able to muster the necessary votes to override them in 1917.[30]

As state legislators, the urban Democrats were unable to

exercise direct influence over Congressional action on the literacy test, but they did attempt to apply what pressure they could through petitions and memorials. In 1914 Martin Lomasney introduced a resolution in the Massachusetts General Court calling upon Congress to reject the pending literacy test bill and requiring a roll call vote so that everyone's constituents could judge his stand. The resolution passed both houses with only thirty-five Yankee Republicans in the lower house willing to go on record in favor of restriction. In Rhode Island urban lawmakers of both parties kept the issue alive for several sessions. In 1913 the Republicans defeated a resolution asking President Taft to veto the literacy test bill, but several of their number abstained. The Brayton organization held the line against a similar measure, with only six Republicans from Providence, Newport, Pawtucket, and Woonsocket joining the Democratic minority. Two years later the Republicans again refused to concur on the issue, the committee chairman candidly admitting that it was "too hot to handle." [31]

The demand for conformity that developed out of World War I and the Red Scare put severe strains on the nation's committment to an open society, and urban lawmakers responded in varying ways. The attacks on German-American culture, language, and institutions were so intense that the "March King," John Phillip Sousa, composed a wedding march to replace those written by Wagner and Mendelssohn. Sauerkraut became "liberty cabbage" and hamburgers, "Salisbury steaks." Both Theodore Roosevelt and Woodrow Wilson warned "hyphenates" that America "does not consist of groups" and that anyone who thought of himself as belonging to a national group "has not yet become an American." The Red Scare of 1919 focused on suspected radicals such as the Industrial Workers of the World, but the fallout took in organized labor and "foreigners" in general. So intense was the nation's suspicion of anyone different from the traditional American norm that propaganda minister George Creel later boasted that "not a pin dropt in the home of anyone with a foreign name but that it rang like thunder on the inner ear of some listening sleuth." Those who defended the targets of the antiradical hysteria were often branded with the same labels.[32]

It was especially difficult for the representatives of new stock America to oppose demands for superpatriotism because their own loyalties were so easily called into question. There was also some satisfaction in being able to deflect the attacks of nativist groups to other minorities and to prove one's loyalty by joining in with the majority. The more farsighted saw that pressures for conformity, once set in motion, recognized no boundaries and could readily be turned against any minority. This ambivalence produced a mixed record in defending minority rights during the war and the Red Scare. In Rhode Island the urban Democrats were substantially swept up in the hysteria. Providence Democrat Addison P. Munroe sought to ban the IWW flag because it stood for "no God, no master," and "resistance to organized government." Senate Democratic leader William Troy of Providence made impassioned defenses of the state's minorities and proclaimed Rhode Island "an excellent example of a melting pot," but scrupulously refrained from praising German-Americans. He also urged the registration of aliens, and suggested that anyone who was not 100 percent loyal "be lined up against the wall." Providence Mayor Joseph Gainer, another Irish-American, proclaimed severe penalties for uttering any disloyal word against the United States.[33]

Cleveland's Democrats evidenced much more hesitation about superpatriotism but were reluctant to express it openly. About half the delegation withheld their votes from a bill that would create an Americanization program in the public schools, while the majority of their number refused to back a requirement that the flag be displayed. Several abstained from a proposal to prevent the dissemination of German "propaganda" and from the discontinuance of the publication of election notices in German. Three Clevelanders

joined the assembly's German-American members in opposing the prohibition of the German language in the elementary schools, and five others abstained.[34]

In New York the urban Democrats, under the leadership
of Smith and Wagner, openly opposed many of these same
measures. Upstate representatives sought to use the loyalty
issue to discredit the Democrat's labor, welfare, and regulatory measures and to break their political base of immigrant
votes. Wagner had a personal stake in this defense because
his own German birth was cited by nativists as proof that the
state's socioeconomic measures were a foreign plot. Tammany Democrats parried these attacks and pressed for
antidiscrimination legislation. In the banner year of 1913
Democratic floor leaders Aaron Levy and Wagner sponsored
an amendment to the state's civil rights bills to prohibit
discriminatory advertising by places of public accommoda-
tion. In the 1915 constitutional convention and after, they led
the fight against the enactment of a literacy test for voters.
The measure banned voters who could not read and write
English; Wagner attacked the proposal as one that "does not
belong in this day of toleration and liberal thought," when
"the only language that counts is that of liberty, fraternity
and equality." City Democrats also led the opposition to a
bill to limit officeholding to native-born Americans and to
require a ten-year waiting period after citizenship before
voting, while Al Smith, as governor, vetoed measures providing for teachers' loyalty oaths, approval of private school
curricula by the Board of Regents, and allowing the courts to
remove anyone from the ballot "who does not support the
ideals of the United States." [35]

Most significantly, since their own self-interest was not
directly involved, New York's Democrats came to the
defense of the Socialist lawmakers who were expelled by the
Lusk Committee in 1920 as an aftermath of the Red Scare.
Supported by the Citizens Union, the New York City Bar
Association, the Central Federated Union, Senator William
Borah, and Fiorello La Guardia, the Tammany Democrats
and eleven city Republicans voted against expulsion. Only

three of the assembly's Democrats joined sixty-eight Republicans in voting for banishment. Governor Smith disapproved of the legislature's action with a ringing message insisting that "law, in a democracy, means the protection of the rights and liberties of the minority. . . . It is a confession of the weakness of our own faith in the righteousness of our cause, when we attempt to suppress by law those who do not agree with us." Very few urban lawmakers apprehended the broad issues raised by Smith and not all were willing to risk the possible results of defending unpopular minorities, but those who did provided a blueprint for the future.[36]

Edward F. Dunne, as governor of Illinois, also styled himself the defender of the state's minorities. The grandson of a Fenian who founded the Emmett Guards, an all-Irish unit during the Civil War, Dunne was a staunch advocate of Irish home rule. In 1919 he led an Irish-American delegation to Versailles to press the cause upon Woodrow Wilson and the Allies. Even while many were beginning to question the loyalty of German-Americans, Dunne delivered paeans on their contributions to Illinois at the Belleville centennial, on the birthday of John Peter Altgeld, and at the unveiling of a statue of Goethe in Chicago. When a Chicago sailor named Samuel Meisenberg was killed in the Vera Cruz incident in 1914, Dunne eulogized him as "a descendant of a race whose virility has been attested to by its survival of and triumph over the persecution of ages and the proscriptions of centuries." He also pointed out that the majority of those who died in the incident were of recent foreign extraction, thus demonstrating the absolute loyalty of naturalized citizens.[37]

The cosmopolitan nature of American society was one of Dunne's favorite themes and he was fond of repeating the phrase that "Europe, not England, is the mother country of America." When a group calling itself the "American Committee to Celebrate One Hundred Years of Peace Between English Speaking People" asked him to aid in their cause, Dunne agreed to cooperate only if the name were changed to the Peace Centenary Commission and the group made to include "not only English but Irish, Welsh, Scotch, German, French, Norwegian, Swedish, Russian, Italian, and other bloods represented in this commonwealth." When the committee concurred, Dunne contacted Congressman John J. Fitzgerald of New York and helped secure federal funds for the project. On numerous occasions he lectured recent immigrants on their duty to support their adopted homeland, but was also quick to point out that naturalized citizens and their descendants had often demonstrated this fealty whether they were from the "banks of the Elbe, the Rhine, the Danube, the Loire, or the Shannon." [38]

By far the most spectacular cultural issue of the Progressive Era was Prohibition. The legislative struggle was partly along urban-rural lines; it often pitted the middle class against those above and below it, and generally saw the Republicans favoring Prohibition and the Democrats opposing it; but all these conditions were primarily the result of the geographical, social, and partisan distribution of the nation's ethnic groups. Basically the Prohibition fight was a "struggle for status between two divergent styles of life," engendered by efforts to achieve "public affirmation of the abstemious, ascetic qualities of American Protestantism." [39]

Pietistic Protestantism was clearly the backbone of the Prohibition movement. The Anti-Saloon League styled itself "the Protestant Church in action," while Frances Willard, founder of the Women's Christian Temperance Union, insisted that "I am first a Christian, then I am a Saxon, then I am an American, and when I get home to heaven I expect to register from Evanston." For many old stock, Evangelical Protestant Americans, Prohibition became a panacea that would remove nearly all the problems of urban industrial life; the saloon replaced the sweatshop, the tenement, the trust, and the political machine as the source of all evil. The Reverend Charles Sheldon, prominent Chicago Social Gospeler, argued that Prohibition would eliminate poverty and labor agitation, while the evangelist Billy Sunday assured his followers that "every crime against the grand old flag crept out of the grog shop." Industrial accidents would be virtually eliminated if workers remained sober, and productivity would increase. Closing the saloon would also sever one of the major ties between the political boss and the working class. Once World War I got under way, the need for conservation of grain harmonized nicely with appeals for patriotic sacrifice and the corresponding dislike for those German-Americans who predominated in the brewing and distilling business. All these arguments had great appeal for those whose pietistic penchant for remaking the social order had already been highly sensitized by other reform causes.[40]

The opponents of Prohibition delighted in pointing up the "dissimulation and hypocrisy" that was often mixed with the movement's zeal. While an Irishman or a German got drunk in public, a Catholic priest charged, the native American "pretending to be a total abstainer, takes his strong drink secretly and sleeps it off on a sofa or in a club room." Will Rogers observed that "the people of Oklahoma will continue to vote dry and drink wet as long as they can stagger to the polls," and Governor Dunne delighted in reminiscing that dry leaders attending gubernatorial receptions regularly partook of the "then lawful and exhilarating cocktails." The Prohibitionists' main target was the saloon, the habitat of the working class, and beer and light wines were proscribed on an equal footing with hard liquor. The urban working class was to be the big loser when Prohibition was adopted. "The farmer boys," charged a disgruntled Chicago Democratic senator, "will get drunk from the silo." [41]

The ritualistic religions were at one in their denunciation of Prohibition. Although some Catholic bishops worried over the high incidence of drinking among their communicants, few were willing to go beyond the church's traditional stand of personal temperance. Most agreed with the eminent economist Father John Ryan that legal Prohibition was "elegant, despotic and hypocritical domination." The Episcopal bishop of Iowa scored the "disappointments and disasters, the illiberal fanaticism and unwarranted license of the so-called temperance reform," while the Missouri Synod Lutherans charged that "prohibition does not discriminate between proper and improper use of a gift of God." Jewish spokesmen generally regarded it as "both superficial and ineffective," and insisted that "moderate indulgence in wine and other spirits is quite in keeping with the Jewish tradition." Occasionally the deep cultural gap surfaced in the debates on the floor of the state legislatures. Chicago Democrat John Boehm, a Bohemian Catholic immigrant, accused the Prohibitionists of trying to take away "his religion and his god," while Oak Park Republican Henry Austin, a Son of the American Revolution and a Baptist, retorted that his religion taught him that liquor was evil and that therefore he had never tasted it. In New York Tammany Democrat Martin McCue blamed the whole issue on the Evangelical Protestant clergy: "They have discarded the Ten Commandments," he charged, "and are now amending the Constitution. They need the Bible no more, and they are seeking to substitute the policeman's night stick for the Bible of Jesus Christ." [42]

The liquor interests naturally sought to channel the ritualistic outlook to their advantage by agreeing to bankroll the opposition cause in return for assurances that ethnics would not seek to save beer and light wines at the expense of hard liquor. Businessmen often feared Prohibition as a giant step toward the confiscation of property, the first shot in the Bolshevik revolution. Prohibitionists regarded the immigrant working class as tools of those business interests, but they failed to understand the deep cultural and religious roots that arrayed the urban lawmaker and his constituents against the proposal. Whatever sinister economic interests may have financed the resistance to Prohibition and notwithstanding those committed liberals who spoke out against it, the urban new stock Democrats acted from profound conviction to long-established principles. Although their greatest effort involved trying to prevent the ratification of the Eighteenth Amendment, the urban lawmakers had prepared themselves for their role by seeking to stave off Prohibition schemes on the state level for several previous years. In some cases, they sought to propose compromise solutions to accommodate the

Prohibitionists, but the situation had become too emotionally charged to negotiate. During the struggle over ratification, the opponents of Prohibition generally sought to have the matter submitted to a popular referendum on the theory that the malapportionment of the legislature worked greatly in favor of ratification. The ardent Prohibitionists knew they had the votes in the state house and refused to risk defeat by allowing the public to render a direct decision on the Eighteenth Amendment.[43]

The deep cultural division on Prohibition was long evident in Illinois. Evanston was the home of the WCTU and suburban and downstate sentiment was overwhelmingly in favor. Chicago, with its heavily new stock population, was the center of resistance, allied only with the Peoria distilleries and the German-American enclaves in the East St. Louis area. "Almost no known dry has been elected mayor, prosecuting attorney, or sheriff of Chicago or Cook County," Charles Merriam observed, "and many campaigns have turned chiefly upon the problem of comparative wetness." In a referendum just before the ratification of the Eighteenth Amendment, the city voted more than three to one against it, with the only notable support "found in higher rental areas where the native white of native parentage predominated." Eighty-eight percent of the New Immigrants voted no, as did 78 percent of the Old Immigrants, compared with 58 percent of the old stock vote. The Germans and Czechs voted over 90 percent against it, with Lithuanians, Italians, and Irish following close behind. Only the Swedish-Americans and the blacks showed any appreciable sentiment for the idea. "Prohibition was the greatest ethnic issue," the most thorough student of Chicago's nationality groups has concluded, "both for its precise aims and for the more general ethnic-Native American conflict which it epitomized." [44]

In the General Assembly the votes on statewide Prohibition in 1917 and on the Eighteenth Amendment in 1919 turned essentially on ethnic affiliation. In 1917 the senate approved statewide Prohibition 31–18, but the house defeated it 68–80. All ten Chicago senators, all Catholics, and

the entire twenty-seven-man assembly delegation, all but two
of new stock origins, voted no. The two Republican senators
and eighteen assemblymen who joined the opposition were
either of Irish, German, Swedish, Norwegian, Jewish, or
Negro extraction or represented such districts. The five
Republican senators and twelve assemblymen who voted yes
were all old stock Protestants who represented Yankee
districts. The downstate vote in both houses was overwhelmingly cast in favor of Prohibition, but the exceptions were
even more instructive. Four of the six downstate senators
who opposed were Irish or German-Americans from Peoria
or East St. Louis. Of the thirty-five downstate assembly votes
against, seventeen were Catholics, fifteen were Irish-Americans, and ten were German-Americans, while the few old
stock legislators who joined them primarily represented
Peoria and heavily Teutonic Madison and St. Clair counties.
One of their number, Lee O'Niel Browne, was an attorney
for the Liquor Dealers Protective Association.[45]

The 1918 election and the building pressure for national
Prohibition cost the wet forces several key downstate seats
and ensured the ratification of the Eighteenth Amendment,
but the ethnic divisions were just as pronounced. The
Chicago senatorial delegation split perfectly along ethnic
lines with the three new stock Republicans joining the
Democrats in opposition and the five old stock GOP senators
favoring ratification. All twenty-six city Democrats and
fifteen Republicans formed the most solid opposition bloc in
the lower house and all but one were of Irish, German,
Czech, Polish, Italian, Jewish, Norwegian, Swedish, or black
derivation. Nearly all the city Republicans who supported
ratification were old stock Protestants. The downstate senate
vote was exactly the same as in 1917 except that an old stock
Republican from La Salle who had replaced an Irish
Catholic Democrat voted for ratification. Of the fifty-seven
Republicans and twenty-two downstate Democrats who
voted in favor of the Eighteenth Amendment, all but two
were old stock Protestants. Seventeen of the twenty-five

downstate representatives who opposed ratification were of Irish, German, or Swedish descent. A giant rally in the First Methodist church of Springfield marked the victory; the minister, with a clenched fist, proclaimed a campaign for worldwide Prohibition, "by God's help." [46]

The pattern was much the same in the other six states. In New York in 1916 Republican Governor Charles Whitman came out in favor of an optional Prohibition referendum measure that gained the support of the Anti-Saloon League and several of the state's Protestant clergymen. The opposition was headed by the Brewers Association, the Hotelmen's Association, the State Federation of Labor, and the pastor of the Emmanuel Lutheran church. The highlight of the committee hearings was a debate between the president of the Anti-Saloon League and the counsel for the Brewers Association. The Tammany Democrats and conservative Republicans united to defeat the effort. By the time of the Eighteenth Amendment, Republican National Chairman Will Hays had committed state chairman George Arlidge of Rochester to ratification and the Tammany forces were unable to stem the tide alone. Republican caucuses in both houses stamped it a party measure and only a handful of GOP members refused to concur. Tammany Democrats desperately sought to strike the enacting clause or submit the issue to a referendum, but the Republican ranks held firm. The senate passed the measure by a narrow 27–24 vote with only two Republicans from Albany and Buffalo joining the Democrats in opposition. The assembly followed suit 81–66, as eleven Republicans lined up with the Democrats and Socialists against ratification. All eleven were from greater New York City, Buffalo, or Albany, and over half were of Irish, Jewish, or German derivation. The Democrats and Socialists were almost all representatives of those ethnic groups. Even after it was over, Tammany floor leader Martin McCue made a last effort to exempt beer and light wines from the enforcement law, but failed because of the opposition of the WCTU, the Anti-Saloon League, and several clergymen. When a joint committee killed the proposal, its ten old stock Republican members voted against beer and light wines, while its six Irish and Italian Democratic members voted for them.[47]

A coalition of the representatives of New Jersey's six northern counties and the resort areas in Atlantic County managed to postpone ratification in that state until 1922 but were finally defeated. The New Idea Republicans generally joined with Prohibition forces by the second decade of the century and their position "played an important role in enabling north Jersey urban Democrats to seize control of the reform movement." The key to the Prohibition victory in 1922 was the capture of populous Essex County by old stock Republicans who broke the north Jersey bloc against ratification. The senate vote was 12–4 and cut across party lines with a Jersey City Democrat and three Republicans from Paterson, Atlantic City, and Morristown forming the opposition. South Jersey voted overwhelmingly in favor. In the house the vote was 33–24 with the eleven Essex County Republican votes providing the margin of victory. All eleven Jersey City assemblymen, mostly new stock Democrats, voted no, as did the entire Passaic and Atlantic County delegations. Spokesmen for the Methodist church hailed ratification as a "victory for every Christian force in the state." [48]

Prohibition in Ohio, the home of the Anti-Saloon League, was a victory for the "small towns and the natives who had migrated to the city" over the "patrons of the saloons." The urban new stock representatives of both parties led the fight against it. When the Democrats controlled the legislature in 1913, Danish-American Senator William Greenlund of Cleveland proposed a state liquor-licensing law which passed both houses with solid urban support. When the Republicans regained power in 1915, they repealed the measure, returning to the concept of local option. The entire Cleveland and Cincinnati delegations in both houses voted against the change, but the rural and small town areas prevailed. By 1919 the Republicans controlled the General Assembly and ratification of the federal amendment was achieved with little difficulty. The representatives of Cleveland, Cincinnati, and Toledo cast three-fourths of the senate votes against it after a futile attempt to submit the proposal to a referendum. Twenty-four of the twenty-nine negative votes in the lower house were cast by predominantly new stock assemblymen from Cleveland, Toldeo, Dayton, and Cincinnati; the other five were Irish or German-Americans from smaller towns. Even after ratification, several new stock lawmakers from Cleveland and Cincinnati voted against the creation of enforcement machinery.[49]

Democrats and labor legislators in Massachusetts tried as early as 1910 to enact a state liquor-licensing bill to quiet the agitation for Prohibition but were unsuccessful. In a 1918 Boston referendum the Irish, Italian, Jewish, and Negro wards combined with the blue-blood Back Bay districts to defeat Prohibition. On the day that the General Court met to vote on the Eighteenth Amendment the house chaplain broke a precedent of his forty-one-year career by praying for ratification, while the state's Congregational, Unitarian, Presbyterian, and Christian Science churches developed an elaborate bell-ringing signal system to tabulate the vote of each lawmaker. After the Democrats failed to attach a referendum provision the senate ratified by a 27–12 count, with the representatives from heavily new stock Boston, Holyoke, New Bedford, Fall River, Cambridge, and Lawrence forming the opposition. During the house debate John L. Donovan, a representative of Martin Lomasney's district, insisted that the amendment would fail on a secret ballot vote but was unable to get the house to agree to that procedure. The vote was an almost perfect ethnic split, with Yankee Republicans from both urban and rural settings in favor, while Irish Democrats and their ethnic allies of both parties were opposed. From among the Yankee Republicans only the Back Bay representatives refused to go along with ratification.[50]

This cultural split among the Yankees was also visible in Rhode Island where the Methodists and other pietist churches favored Prohibition, but the Episcopalians refused to do so. It was the unanimous opposition of the new stock representatives of both parties that caused the defeat of the Eighteenth Amendment. In both 1918 and 1919 the Democrats and urban Republicans succeeded in postponing the amendment on very close votes. In the latter year a resolution to instruct the attorney general to bring suit against Congress's power to propose the amendment passed both houses by voice vote, to avoid having names recorded on the explosive issue. The same Democratic–urban Republican coalition frustrated the efforts of small town Yankee Republicans to revive the amendment in 1920.[51]

Connecticut, the only other state to refuse ratification, accomplished the feat by much the same means. The small town Yankee–dominated house voted in favor of ratification, but the senate refused to concur. The amendment passed the house 153–96 after a bitter exchange between Irish Democrats and Yankee Republicans. The former charged the Republicans with hypocrisy, insisted that Prohibition would not work, and pressed for a referendum. A Waterbury Democrat demanded a popular vote because he was "one of the less than twenty members who represented collectively more than one half the population of Connecticut." Although the Yankees carried the measure through the lower house, the senate defeated the amendment 14–20 with Democrats and urban Republicans joining forces.[52]

The resistance of the urban new stock lawmakers to Prohibition was the capstone of their efforts to prevent the channeling of the reform impulse of the Progressive Era into a crusade for the cultural reupholstering of the nation's minorities. They also opposed attempts to restrict normal activities on Sunday, unless such practices entailed compulsory labor for their constituents. They resisted efforts to use the public school system as an instrument for the acculturation of minorities, and sought to legalize boxing and professional athletics. They fought against immigration restriction and limitations on the right of immigrants to vote and hold office. Although their primary concern was defense of the rights of their own constituents and the political power they represented, the more advanced of their number, like Al Smith, even undertook to defend other unpopular minorities. Governors Dunne and Walsh and Mayor Fitzgerald of Boston, for example, worked to ban the showing of *Birth of a Nation* because it was a slur on the state's black citizens.[53]

Where these stances on cultural reform placed the urban new stock Democrats and their allies on the political spectrum is still a debatable question, most of which centers on where the reforms themselves fit into an era that has been defined as "progressive." Subsequent generations of liberal scholars, committed to cultural pluralism, have judged immigration restriction, Sunday blue laws, and Prohibition, like black disfranchisement and segregation, to be improper goals for progressives to pursue. It is tempting to see them as conservative measures, but the identity of their sponsors makes that very difficult. Many of the same native stock Americans who have been identified as supporters of much of the era's political and socioeconomic reforms have also emerged as proponents of Prohibition. Richard Hofstadter sought to explain the problem by styling such efforts "a ludicrous caricature of the reforming impulse, of the Yankee-Protestant notion that it is both possible and desirable to moralize private life through public action." In the most recent and thorough study on Prohibition, James Timberlake argues convincingly that moral regeneration reforms were "an integral part of the Progressive Movement," drawing on "the same moral idealism" and seeking "to deal with the same basic problems." He is quick to point out that their appeal lay largely with the old stock middle class, and that "other progressives, especially those identified with urban-labor-immigrant elements, disliked the reform and fought it." The understanding that there was more than one "progressive movement" provides the key to evaluating the actions of the urban Democrats.[54]

Both the old stock, middle class reformers and the urban-labor-immigrant ones were able to cooperate effectively on labor and welfare measures, business regulation, and other socioeconomic measures, although their motives were not always the same and they differed in how far they should go. Both groups were often able to work together to broaden political participation, since the middle class reformer's ideological commitment to democracy harmonized with the new stock lawmaker's need for political power. It was the cooperation of these two groups that accounted for most of the success of the Progressive Era in the major industrial states. The disagreement, as Huthmacher has observed of Massachusetts, flowed from the fact that the native middle class reformers aimed at "uplifting others" while the immigrant stock representatives were striving for political and socioeconomic "self-improvement." A large segment of the old stock middle class concluded that none of the other changes would have the proper effect unless the foreign stock working class shed its alien culture and became touched by "the long religious hand of New England." Since cooperation on political or socioeconomic matters is difficult with allies who are denigrating one's life style, the reform coalition eventually strained and broke over these issues. "One of the strongest human cravings," Martin Lomasney once explained, "is to be left alone and the uplifter is never liked." Much of the key to the decline of the progressive impulse is to be found in the increasing fixation of the Yankee, Protestant segment of the reform coalition on moral regeneration and the corresponding resentment aroused in the new stock working class portion.[55]

If anything, the intensity and significance of such issues was even greater in the decade that followed the Progressive Era. Arguments over the enforcement of Prohibition proved even more acrimonious than debates over its original adoption. Widespread flaunting of the law made its pietistic proponents even more determined to retain it. Immigration restrictionists stopped fencing with halfway measures like the literacy test and rammed through a quota system that all but eliminated immigration from southern and eastern Europe. Several states sought to close their parochial schools and beefed up Americanization campaigns in the public schools. In 1924 and 1928, clashes between candidates who represented the ritualist and pietist traditions almost ripped apart first the Democratic party and then the nation. These clashes so immobilized the country that meaningful reform was not possible until the Great Depression ended the "politics of provincialism." The struggle over moral regeneration during the Progressive Era cast a long shadow, but the conflicts demonstrated, both to the urban new stock politicians and to many native reformers, that a true liberal had to be committed to the right of minorities to live according to their own lights. One of the first important acts of the New Deal Congress was the repeal of Prohibition.[56]

CHAPTER 6

The Dimensions
of Urban Liberalism

Until recently most accounts of the Progressive Era, either explicitly or by implication, have excluded the urban immigrant–descended working class from participation. Some have done so by dealing with this numerically significant segment of the population as a "social problem," debating the issue of whether it was "progressive" to favor or oppose such measures as immigration restriction and forced "Americanization." [1] Generally this debate has focused on the attitudes of native middle class reformers with little or no consideration being given to the feelings of the immigrants themselves. Those who have sought to characterize the activities of the urban new stock masses and their representatives during this volatile reform era have usually concluded that they were either indifferent or hostile toward meaningful change.

Much of this consensus has resulted from interpretations regarding the origins of the reform impulse which have excluded urban new stock groups almost by definition. The field was once dominated by an agrarian interpretation that viewed progressivism as the logical outgrowth of the Granges, Alliances, and Populists. Although acknowledging that the Populist party itself was dead by the turn of the century, the most influential proponent of the agrarian school, John D. Hicks, nevertheless insisted that there were a number of prominent progressives "whose escutcheons should bear the bend sinister of Populism," and that "populistic doctrines showed an amazing vitality." Hicks stopped short of crediting rural lawmakers with the enactment of the Progressive Era's hallmark measures, but stressed their similarity with those advocated by the Populists and their predecessors and left no doubt as to the cause and effect relationship. Even though most accounts of the Progressive Era written since World War II have examined urban settings, the notion of agrarian origins still strongly persists. As late as the mid-1960s, Wayne E. Fuller, writing in *Agricultural History*, could still insist that "the majority of those who did become reform leaders came from the farms and small towns of rural America." Even though most reformers may have been city dwellers by the Progressive years, Fuller expressed the conviction that "in thought and feeling the majority of them belonged to rural America where they had their roots." [2]

The shift to an investigation of the urban roots of progressivism did not really enhance the role of the urban new stock working class because historians generally concentrated upon other segments of city society. Most favored has been the old stock middle class of professionals, intellectuals, and independent businessmen whose progressivism has been established by constructing leadership profiles, collective biographies that provide a composite portrait of the socioeconomic characteristics of prominent members of acknowledged reform organizations. The technique was first developed by George Mowry in his study of California progressivism where he found the typical reformer to be young, college educated, of old American stock, reared in the tradition of New England Protestantism, and "well-fixed." Most of his reformers were attorneys, journalists, independent businessmen, physicians, or bankers. Alfred D. Chandler studied 260 officials of the 1912 Progressive party and arrived at substantially the same conclusions, finding them generally to be old stock businessmen, lawyers, editors, professors, authors, and social workers. Their evidence set the tone for discussions of progressivism for over a decade, with the only noticeable disagreement arising over the question of motivation.[3]

One segment of scholars has been willing to credit the middle class reformers with motives of idealism and altruism. Speaking of Boston's "Yankee reformers," Arthur Mann called them part of "the long line of men and women in Western civilization who have fixed their eyes on what ought-to-be." Others found such a view too unsophisticated and looked to psychology and sociology for their explanations. Robert H. Wiebe, in *The Search for Order*, has argued that the key lay in the acceptance by the middle class of the values of the bureaucracy: systematization, rationalization, and efficiency. This common outlook bound them together in opposition to all those forces that represented unpredictability or instability in society, whether these emanated from capital or labor. More influential with respect to the motivation of the native middle class was the concept of the status revolution as developed by Mowry and Hofstadter. For them the key to the reformist impulse lay in the fear of established professionals and intellectuals of declining status engendered by the rise of big business and the urban masses. So threatened, they turned to reform to resolve their status anxieties and recoup their waning prestige. "Progressivism," Hofstadter concluded, "was to a very considerable extent led by men who suffered from the events of their time, not through a shrinkage in their means but through the changed pattern in the distribution of deference to power." Despite disagreements over motivation, the bulk of the Progressive Era's scholars have centered their attention on the native middle class, loosely defined, and ignored the urban new stock masses.[4]

Most of those who have deviated from this consensus have emphasized the contributions of groups even farther removed from the inhabitants of the cities' polyglot slums. Focusing on municipal reform, Samuel P. Hays has located the reformist impulse in the urban upper classes, the directors of the largest corporations and those who were listed in the social registers. Their primary purpose was to create an elitist government in which the urban working class would have little or no voice. Wiebe, in *Businessmen and Reform*, while acknowledging that the nation's commercial and industrial leaders opposed many of the reforms widely associated with the Progressive Era, has noted that they did favor others, particularly the regulation of business activity. Gabriel Kolko has carried this suggestion several steps further and interpreted the entire era as being motivated "by the needs of interested businessmen." The reform agitation of the period, Kolko charges, "was initially a movement for the political rationalization of business and industrial conditions, a movement that operated on the assumption that the general welfare of the community could best be served by satisfying the concrete needs of business." Like those that focus on the middle class, such definitions leave little room for participation by urban new stock Americans.[5]

It remained for Hofstadter to make explicit what the others usually only implied. In his brilliant and provocative *Age of Reform* he "singled out, as a phenomenon of the Progressive Era, the antipathy between the ethos of the boss-machine-immigrant complex and that of the reformer-individualist-Anglo-Saxon complex." Although Hofstadter often criticizes the reformers for harboring nativist prejudices and utopian goals and often sympathizes with the plight of the immigrants, he leaves little doubt that the "boss-machine-immigrant complex" acted primarily as a barrier to reform. Progressivism's key words, he insisted, were "patriotism, citizen, democracy, law, character, conscience, . . . terms redolent of the sturdy Protestant Anglo-Saxon moral and intellectual roots of the Progressive uprising." The immigrant, on the other hand, looked to politics not for the realization of high principles, but for concrete and personal gains. Under the circumstances immigrant stock Americans made little or no contribution to the era's success. "In politics, then," Hofstadter insisted, "the immigrant was usually at odds with the reform aspirations of the American Progressive. Together with the native conservative and the politically indifferent, the immigrants formed a potent mass that limited the range and achievements of the American Progressive." [6]

So well received was Hofstadter's critique of the "boss-machine-immigrant complex" that its general outlines and spirit infused even the standard works on American immigration. It was so widely held that those scholars who inadvertently discovered evidence of urban immigrant stock support for Progressive reform often felt compelled to explain it as aberrational or embryonic. Hofstadter himself acknowledged that "on some issues, to be sure, especially those like workmen's compensation, that bore directly on the welfare of the working population, the bosses themselves saw some areas of agreement with the reformer," but he dismissed it as of little consequence. Such cooperation "was of slow development in the Progressive Era itself, was uneasy and partial but occasionally effective," and "foreshadowed only vaguely a development that was to reach its peak under Franklin D. Roosevelt." Frank Freidel, in the first volume of his biography of FDR, noted Tammany Hall support for welfare legislation but deemed it "something rather different from the Progressive movement: workingmen's support of welfare legislation through the urban machine." In his study of Massachusetts Richard Abrams also acknowledged that the really serious demands for far-reaching political and socioeconomic change came "primarily from the large Irish-American segment of the population, who purported to represent the newer Americans generally; and, to a lesser extent, from the growing class of trade unionists." In spite of all that, Abrams reserves the designation "progressive" for the old stock middle class reformer and styles the others as "insurgents." Samuel Hays notes that urban Democrats in New Jersey and elsewhere seized control of the reform movement, but concludes that "the roots of the Democratic revival remain an enigma." [7]

Other scholars have presented evidence that reform relied

on the legislative support of urban new stock delegations but failed to suggest that the fact has any significance for current interpretations. Hoyt Warner begins *Progressivism in Ohio* by stating that he plans to test out the status revolution theory, but even though heavily polyglot Cleveland is time and again acknowledged as the bulwark of progressivism he takes no issue with the Hofstadter-Mowry view. Arthur Link states in several places that the Jersey City delegation was Woodrow Wilson's most reliable support as governor, but again makes little of it. James L. Crooks discusses in several places the reform efforts of Baltimore Democratic Boss John J. ("Sunny") Mahon, but draws no conclusion. The list could be extended, but it would only serve to belabor the point that scholars of the era have underestimated the reform contributions of the urban foreign-stock masses.[8]

Only within the last decade has any serious question been raised regarding this consensus on the negative attitude of the urban masses toward Progressive Era reform. J. Joseph Huthmacher provided the first, and still most sweeping, refutation in his landmark article "Urban Liberalism and the Age of Reform" in 1962. He raised a series of questions that were unanswerable if prevailing interpretations were correct. How did reform achieve so much in states with heavily polyglot populations? How could one explain the careers of Al Smith, Robert Wagner, David I. Walsh, and other prominent supporters of progressive legislation? How could progressive measures have succeeded in legislatures dominated by urban new stock lower class representatives? The answer, he insisted flatly, was that the "urban lower class provided an active, numerically strong, and politically necessary force for reform—and that this class was perhaps as important in determining the course of American liberalism as the urban, middle-class, about which so much has been written." He was careful not to credit the urban lower classes with the sole responsibility for the triumph of reform. "Effective social reform during the Progressive Era, and in later periods," he argued, "seems to have depended upon constructive collaboration, on specific issues, between reformers from both the urban lower class and the urban middle class (with the further cooperation, at times, of organized labor)." At the same time, Huthmacher did suggest that the major outlines of his "urban liberalism" were perhaps "more in line with what has become the predominant liberal faith in modern America" than that of the middle class. He concluded with a plea to fellow historians of the Progressive Era to "modify the 'middle-class' emphasis which has come to dominate the field and devote more attention to hitherto neglected elements of the American social structure." [9]

In the ensuing ten years a few scholars heeded this suggestion and produced some significant findings. Huthmacher himself, in another article and in the early chapters of his biography of Senator Robert F. Wagner, documented the central role played by Tammany Democrats in the triumph of progressive reform in New York. Nancy Joan Weiss pursued the situation in the Empire State still further, focusing her attention on the efforts of Tammany Boss Charles F. Murphy to achieve "responsibility and respectability" through the support of reform. Melvin Holli demonstrated that the acknowledged successes of Detroit's reform mayor, Hazen Pingree, were based primarily upon the political support he received from the city's ethnic working class. Charles Glaab and A. Theodore Brown in their *History of Urban America* all but wiped out the distinction between boss and reformer and demonstrated how Pingree, Tom Johnson, "Golden Rule" Jones, and other successful social reformers built "reform machines" based on the support of the urban masses. Using sophisticated methods of election data analysis, Michael Paul Rogin and John L. Shover illustrated the degree to which Hiram Johnson and the California progressives came to depend upon foreign stock workers for support. Both John M. Blum and Rudolph Vecoli described the reform contributions of the new Americans who inhabited New Jersey's northern counties.[10]

Despite these and other efforts the essentially negative view of the urban new stock masses and progressive reform still predominates since it is possible to regard these state and local studies as isolated phenomena. Together with the present study, however, they provide sufficient evidence to conclude that urban new stock lower class support for reforms commonly accepted as characterizing the Progressive Era was nationwide in scope and consistent enough in its general dimensions to justify labeling it with a common designation. Urban liberalism was a major force everywhere that the new stock working class formed a significant portion of the population, whether in a Pacific Coast state like California, a midwestern one like Illinois, Ohio, or Michigan, a New England one like Massachusetts, Connecticut, or Rhode Island, a Middle Atlantic one like New York or New Jersey, and even in a semisouthern state like Maryland. In some cases its practitioners were the most important reformist force in the state; in others, they played a supporting role; and in the case of Connecticut and Rhode Island, they fought a frustrating battle against insurmountable odds.

Allowing for local variations, the parameters of urban liberalism were strikingly similar in all the major industrial states. First and foremost was their support for welfare legislation of all types, whether factory laws, workmen's compensation, pensions, or the control of child and female labor. The regulation of the rates and services of a wide variety of businesses, particularly those vital to the interests of their constituents, was also a common denominator. So too was their general sympathy for a tax system that threw the burden on those able to pay, a view that caused them to play a key role in the ratification of the federal income tax amendment. Politically, urban new stock lawmakers were distinguished primarily by their support for any measure that enhanced the vote of their constituents—primaries, initiative and referendum, home rule, annual elections, and the popular election of U.S. Senators. Their efforts on behalf of the Seventeenth and Nineteenth Amendments were instrumental in achieving ratification in the key industrial states. They normally opposed other political innovations such as civil service, the short ballot, and the commissioner and city

manager forms of government, but many modern scholars
have raised serious doubts about the "progressiveness" of
such measures. Finally, urban lawmakers as a rule resisted
attempts at legislated conformity in the form of Prohibition,
Sunday blue laws, or Americanization. Although they were
not always quick to jump to the defense of other beleaguered
minorities, their record in that respect could stand comparison with most other identifiable groups of the era. These
positions, as Huthmacher argued, are broadly consistent with
what has been designated "liberalism" by twentieth-century
Americans.[11]

Urban liberalism was not the result of a systematic
program or a coordinated movement. A few of its leaders like
Dunne, Walsh, Smith, and Wagner occasionally articulated
some theory behind their actions, but urban liberalism was
mostly the sum of countless positions taken by thousands of
legislators with similar backgrounds in response to similar
problems. It was shaped by the cross-pressures of social
change, partisan politics, and legislative infighting. It was
born, at least partly, out of political necessity, of the need for
machine politicians to "give the people what they want" in
order to ensure their organization's survival. Part of it flowed,
at least vaguely, from their own cultural traditions, European
Social Democracy, guilds, Catholic social doctrine, or the
Jewish concept of charity. Some of it was nothing more than
a natural reaction against the attacks of nativists. Mostly,
urban liberalism was a product of the American urban
experience in an industrial age, a growing realization that the
power of government could be used to ameliorate the kind of
conditions every urban lawmaker had encountered firsthand.
Unlike the native middle class reformer, most of the urban
new stock lawmakers or their families had actually lived in a
tenement, worked in a sweatshop or factory, seen the victims
of industrial accidents, experienced prejudice, and known the
frustration of trying to push remedial legislation through a
hostile legislature dominated by old stock, rural, and business interests. These experiences did not necessarily make all
of them ideological liberals, but they did cause even the most

hard-bitten to throw their support behind at least some pieces of forward-looking legislation. One of the most poignant recollections of Frances Perkins's career in New York progressive politics was that of "Big Tim" Sullivan, the boss of the Bowery, rushing breathlessly up the hill in Albany to save a fifty-four-hour-per-week bill for women because he "had seen me sister go out to work when she was only fourteen and I know we ought to help these gals by giving 'em a law which will prevent 'em from being broken down while they're still young." The story illustrates not that "Big Tim" belongs in the pantheon of great American reformers but that even such "undoubtedly corrupt politicians" as he made their contributions to progressive reform.[12]

Given the weight of evidence in support of the existence of urban new stock progressivism, it is fair to ask why its presence has been denied for so long. The answer is as complex as the Progressive Era itself. Part of it results from the understandable preoccupation of historians with personalities and events on the national scene in preference to those on the state and local levels. This focus has distorted the whole fabric of American history, particularly unfortunately in the Progressive Era because, unlike the New Deal, it began in the cities and states and retained a dynamism all its own apart from national developments. It is much safer to rehearse the exploits of nationally known figures, no matter how often they have been studied before. Then, too, there are so many states and cities it is difficult to know which ones to study and what significance to place upon the results. Fortunately there have been several excellent state and local studies of the Progressive Era in recent years, but the problems still prevail.

This concentration on the national scene has been especially detrimental to the cause of urban liberalism because the states and the cities were its main stamping grounds during the Progressive Era. There were a few who achieved national influence or office during the period such as Joe Tumulty, James O'Gorman, David I. Walsh, or Senator Billy Hughes, the New Jersey Democrat who began life as an Irish immigrant machinist in Paterson and rose to become, by the Wilson years, "a close friend of the President who has been referred to respectfully as the President's spokesman in the Senate." It is likely, too, that a thorough investigation might reveal that the sizable bloc of urban Democrats in the House were second in importance to the success of the New Freedom only to their southern counterparts. For the most part, however, men like Smith, Wagner, Walsh, Stephen Young, Barratt O'Hara, and others who were to burst later onto the national scene were laboring in the less visible arenas of the state legislatures during the Progressive Era. Hundreds of their cohorts spent their entire public lives there and only attention to state developments can assess the importance of their contributions.[13]

Equally unfortunate is the fact that so few of the practitioners of urban liberalism left any accounts of their activities in the form of memoirs or papers. Most of them were workers, small businessmen, or officeholders, not inclined to see much value in chronicling what they did. As Oscar Handlin observed of Al Smith, "The written word did not come as easily . . . as the spoken word. Never a great reader of books, he was always more at ease before an audience than before blank paper. His important communications were face to face." The Happy Warrior's biographer found that "no significant body of Smith's correspondence or collection of his private papers seems to have survived," but that ample evidence was available in "published sources." [14] The professional politicians were undoubtedly mindful of the dictum of the sage of Ward Eight, Martin Lomasney: Never write anything down when you can say it, never say anything when you can nod your head. The evidence of their contributions rests mainly in the public record, in their votes, in the journals of the state legislatures, in committee reports, in newspaper accounts of legislative debates, and in the analyses of votes on referenda. As Rogin and Shover have demonstrated graphically in California, the use of small-unit election analysis may completely alter the prevailing view of which social segments provided the necessary mass support for progressive candidates.[15]

What other records of the Progressive Era exist, in the form of memoirs, analyses, and the minutes of good government associations, citizens unions, women's organizations, consumer groups, and the like, are thoroughly suffused with the old stock middle class view of the reform impulse. They were written by the editors, professors, journalists, social workers, businessmen, lawyers, and physicians who peopled the groups that most scholars have accordingly identified as the nucleus of the period's reform surge. By the very nature of their occupations and backgrounds, these reformers were far more apt to record what they did and to evaluate its effects than were the representatives of the urban masses. It is not surprising that the predominant view of the Progressive Era's ideals and aims has been that of the old stock middle class; nor is it surprising that it has been their view of the urban new stock masses that has prevailed. The welfare and prolabor measures that formed the most important reform goals for the latter group were viewed as vital only by the more advanced groups of middle class progressives; the majority were lukewarm toward them at best and increasingly hostile as time went on. Middle class enthusiasm for "power to the people" also lessened noticeably when it became clear who commanded the people's allegiance. The urban new stock working class—the political machine—also formed the major source of opposition to the structural political reforms and the cultural restrictions that so much of the middle class viewed as the main business of reform. Historians have all too often been willing to accept the middle class's negative evaluations of the urban new stock lawmaker at face value, without analyzing very carefully the value judgments behind them.

Scholars of the Progressive Era have often failed to appreciate the significance of the positive evaluation of machine politicians given by some highly regarded old stock middle class reformers. As noted in the first chapter, Robert S. Binkerd, head of New York's prestigious Citizens Union, acknowledged the reform efforts of Tammany Democrats in his oral reminiscences, noting that it was something that he had never seen referred to very much. Frances Perkins, whose contributions to reform spanned three decades, expressed in several places in *The Roosevelt I Knew* her conviction that the Tammany Democrats were a major reform force, and that they were more progressive than FDR at that stage in his career. She notes that in her fight for the fifty-four-hour week for women she had the support of Boss Murphy and his cohorts and that they did better "in this, which I thought a test" than did Roosevelt. She chronicles her close working relationship with Smith and Wagner who "became firm and unshakeable sponsors of political and legislative measures designed to overcome conditions unfavorable to human life." She dubbed the factory legislation they sponsored a "turning point," a "change in American political attitudes and policies toward social responsibility [that] can scarcely be overrated." Although acknowledging the political potential of their actions, Miss Perkins nevertheless was "convinced that the pull of social forces rather than vote-getting considerations moved the politicians in that direction." [16]

The same theme was struck by Frederic C. Howe in his memoirs. A university-trained expert, Howe began public life as the secretary of a good government association with a patrician's attitude toward urban reform. Elected to the Cleveland city council as a Republican, he soon fell under the spell of Tom Johnson and turned his interest more toward social reform. When he did, he left no doubt as to where his support lay. "But my friends," he recounted, "did not rally to such [reform] measures." They denounced measures to aid the poor as "socialistic" and "uneconomical." His support rather "came from the old gang," his measures "were passed with the aid of the men whom I had previously denounced." Unless they were bribed, Howe insisted, "the bad men . . . voted right; while representatives from the east-end wards often voted wrong." Later, on the major issues of public ownership of utilities and the three-cent streetcar fare, the same lines of division continued. "On the one side," Howe noted again, "were men of property and influence; on the other the politicians, immigrants, workers, and persons of small means." Howe's fellow Ohioan, Brand Whitlock of Toledo, also expressed a strong preference for the urban working class view over that of the middle class reformers. Whitlock's *Forty Years of It* becomes progressively a diatribe against the latter, whom he held to be "not only without humor, without pity, without mercy, but . . . without knowledge of life or human nature, and without very much of any sort of sweetness and light." Unimpressed with "the long religious hand of New England," Whitlock discoursed at length on the pernicious effects of Puritanism: "The good we had from Puritanism has been immensely overstated and exaggerated and it is not one whit better or greater in quantity or influence than that we had from the Cavaliers, or for that matter from the latest immigrant in Ellis Island. They themselves appreciated their own goodness and we have always taken their words for granted." By contrast Whitlock found even the most notorious Chicago ward bosses Coughlin and Kenna to have a more salubrious effect: "Perhaps Bath House John and Hinky Dink were more nearly right after all than the cold and formal and precise gentlemen who denounced their records in the council. For they were human and the great problem is to make the government of a city human." Such expressions of confidence in urban new stock politicians on the part of native middle class reformers were admittedly rare, but they were sufficiently frequent to raise significant doubts about the prevailing historical consensus.[17]

Historians have not recognized this, however, at least partly because they have identified much more readily with the old stock middle class of professionals, intellectuals, and businessmen than with any other segment of society. "The historian," a noted English critic once observed of Edward Gibbon, "must have some conception of how men who are not historians behave." To accurately reconstruct the total past, he should, in the words of the late Marcus Lee Hansen, "get around to the 'forgotten man,' and mentally move down into the slums and out into the fields." Historians are essentially middle class professionals and intellectuals and as such share to a large degree the ideals, values, world view, and life style of their counterparts in the past. Sociologist Milton M. Gordon, in his study of assimilation, argues that intellectuals are themselves a social subgroup, with the same tendency to identify with "their own kind" in the past as ethnic groups. When a member of an ethnic minority becomes an intellectual, Gordon argues, he increasingly relates more to members of his new subgroup than he does to the old. Our history has been largely written by old stock Protestants, and even those who have come from other traditions have generally imbibed their *Weltanschauung* through the educational system.[18]

Historians who are liberal activists sincerely involved in the social and political events of their own day have tended to concentrate on those from similar backgrounds pursuing similar objectives in the past. Perhaps this has led them to exaggerate the practical impact that such groups have had on the world around them. At any rate, U.S. history, until very recently, has been almost exclusively the story of the native, Protestant middle class. Only in response to minority group agitation and with the rise of significant numbers of non–British-American historians, have the sagas of blacks, Indians, Chicanos, and others been investigated to any degree. Even then, the greatest problem has been integrating their experiences into the entire fabric of American history, because they square so little with prevailing interpretations. What is true of U.S. history in general is especially true of the Progressive Era, for as Edwin Rozwenc has insisted, "preoccupation with the syndromes of middle-class anxieties and prejudices has served to distract attention from the content of progressive policies and the complex relations that comprised the political process during the Progressive Era." [19]

Even though historians have taken a somewhat broader view of the role of other minorities of late, they have been

THE DIMENSIONS OF URBAN LIBERALISM 213

reluctant to do the same for the immigrant stock working class. Liberals and intellectuals, as Michael Novak has argued in his highly controversial book on the "unmeltable ethnics," "empathize more with nearly any group in the United States than the lower-middle-class white or the ethnic voters." It is precisely this lack of mutual understanding that caused millions of blue-collar ethnics to flirt with George Wallace and to applaud Spiro Agnew's gratuitous shots at "effete intellectual snobs." Perhaps the antagonism stems from the fact that, unlike the blacks, Indians, and Chicanos, the European immigrants of the Great Migration arrived with a fully developed culture of very long standing in sufficient numbers and in advantageous enough circumstances to permit a separation based more on choice than discrimination. In particular, they alone were able to develop a political style and substance that allowed them to build an independent power base.[20]

The differences between the native reformist and the machine traditions were real enough and highly significant, but historians have often erred in assuming the automatic moral superiority of the former, while assigning all the evil effects of American politics to the latter. The native reformist tradition "assumed and demanded the constant disinterested activity in public affairs, argued that political life ought to be run, to a greater degree than it was, in accordance with general principles and abstract laws apart from and superior to personal needs, and expressed common feeling that government should be in good part an effort to moralize the lives of individuals while economic life should be related to the stimulation and development of individual character." The machine tradition, on the other hand, was "founded upon the European backgrounds of the immigrants, upon their unfamiliarity with independent political action, their familiarity with hierarchy and authority, and upon the urgent needs that so often grew out of their migration, took for granted that the political life of the individual would arise out of family needs, interpreted political and civic relations chiefly in terms of personal obligations, and placed strong personal loyalties above allegiance to abstract codes of laws or morals." For the native reformer politics was a matter of justice, reason, equality, conscience, fairness, and civic duty; for the machine politician it was a matter of compassion, forgiveness, mutual help, and loyalty. The individualist, rationalist philosophy of the liberal intellectual ill prepares him to grasp the value of the machine tradition, to "cope with group actions in politics." Most often he has simply concluded that good government is a function of the "middle class ethos" because it preaches that politics is for public rather than private good.[21]

Even conceding the essential differences, however, it is still clear that the dichotomy is too overdrawn and the comparison too invidious. Even though Richard Hofstadter did more to popularize the two-traditions argument than anyone else, he strongly implies throughout his analysis that the moral superiority of the reformers was often more apparent than real, and that "it is still possible to wonder whether the devices that are replacing them (i.e. the machines) are superior as instruments of government." The two-traditions argument seems vulnerable on several fronts. Most obviously the rhetoric of the reform tradition has too often been used to rationalize positions taken out of self-interest. Politics was used to advance self-interest long before the era of mass immigration, and machine politicians never reaped the benefits from government-business cooperation that native captains of industry did. Municipal reformers used reformist rhetoric to wrest political power from the masses and to cut needed social services, while business leaders embraced the notion of social responsibility to use the federal government to eliminate competition. Even one of the foremost advocates of the two-traditions theory has acknowledged ironically that "real self-interest might be closer to the interest of the community as a whole than to a man's narrower, and perhaps more apparent, interests." The more you have, the more you have to lose. "Civic mindedness," Michael Novak asserts, "is enlightened self-interest for the established. For the unestablished, it is unreal." [22]

The urban masses instinctively grasped the self-interest and potential letdown inherent in the reformers' arguments and rejected them in favor of more concrete and realizable goals. It should be clear that much that has been deemed constructive by future generations is closer to the machine-immigrant ideal than to the native-reformist one. The myriad of welfare legislation is most obvious, but so too is the acceptance of cultural pluralism and the realization of the need for personal contact between governed and government. When reform met the ideals of the machine tradition, its followers supported it; when it did not, they refused to go along. The fruits of the reform tradition have not been judged to be entirely positive—the alienation of urban government from the electorate, Prohibition, immigration restriction, and the like. Our two political traditions have spawned a mixed litter of progeny and a realization of that fact would better prepare historians to accept a constructive role for machine politicians in progressive reform.[23]

Finally, urban liberalism has been neglected for so long because interpretations of the reform efforts of the period have been so dominated by the concept of the "progressive movement." Ever since the publication of Benjamin Parke De Witt's *The Progressive Movement* in 1915, historians have sought, with little success, to attribute the positive results of this reform era to a single concerted effort by people having common backgrounds, pursuing a united program, and holding similar values. De Witt's own criteria for membership were general; he insisted only upon adherence to three ideals: the removal of special interests in political and economic affairs, the purification and extension of democracy, and the use of government to redress social inequities. Later generations of interpreters have made membership much more exclusive. Informed by native middle class values and limiting their investigations largely to the activities of native middle class organizations and individuals, they have arrived, naturally enough, at the conclusion that the achievements of the era were the result of a native middle class movement. Leadership profiles or collective biographies of prominent members of the Progressive party or similar organizations have established conclusively that such groups were clearly dominated by the old stock middle class, but they have failed to show any necessary causal connection between their activities and the positive legislative results that have earned the era the designation "progressive." In California, at least, "the electoral evidence questions whether the Progressive Party was typically progressive." Despite that fact, fidelity to the concept of the "progressive movement" has made it mandatory to deny the appellation "progressive" to any individuals or groups that did not possess the prescribed socioeconomic or ethnic background or that did not profess the agreed-upon set of values.[24]

Upon more intensive investigation, the concept of a singular progressive movement has proved impossible to maintain. Attempts to define a fairly clear-cut set of values that might characterize such a movement have proved to be totally unrewarding. The resulting ideas have either been so general as to include virtually everyone alive at the time or so ambiguous, and even contradictory, as to foreclose the possibility that members of the same movement could hold them simultaneously. The same fate has befallen those who have tried to discern a common program that might prove the existence of such a movement. Virtually every significant issue of the era—the regulation of business, the recognition of organized labor, welfare legislation, woman suffrage, Prohibition, immigration restriction, and a host of others—drove deep fissures into the ranks of those old stock middle class businessmen, professionals, and intellectuals who were supposed to constitute the heart of the progressive movement.[25]

Even more disconcertingly, the construction of "progressive profiles" in such representative states as Massachusetts, Ohio, Iowa, Wisconsin, and Washington have failed to verify the contention, central to the concept of a cohesive movement, that "progressives" were readily distinguishable by their socioeconomic or ethnoreligious backgrounds. Some have shown that people of widely varying backgrounds

claimed to be progressives, while most have demonstrated
that the backgrounds of those native middle class Americans
who joined "progressive" organizations were virtually indis-
tinguishable from those who affiliated themselves with acknowledged conservative groups. Recent studies have revealed considerable reformist activity among groups outside
the pale of any native middle class movement. Besides those
scholars who have focused on the urban ethnic working
class, others have chronicled the contributions of German-
American Catholics in the Midwest, Socialists, organized
labor, upper class socialites, big business, and agrarians. The
net result of all these findings has been to discredit rather
thoroughly the notion that the Progressive Era's achievements can be attributed to any single movement; but the
notion dies hard.[26]

Many have even tried to resuscitate it by positing the
existence of two or more movements, all of which retain the
basic native middle class character, but which seek to
account for some of the apparent discrepancies in programs
and values. Thus there have been analyses of political versus
social progressives, uncompromising versus middle-of-the-
road progressives, traditionalists versus modernists, New
Freedom versus New Nationalism, and eastern versus mid-
western-southern progressivism. All these are essentially
intramural distinctions, and fail to answer any of the
fundamental objections that have been raised to the concept
of a native middle class movement. "When historical evidence resists the historian so resolutely," Peter Filene has
argued persuasively, "one must question the categories being
used." When Filene produced his "Obituary for the 'Progressive Movement,'" virtually no one rushed forward to insist
that the reports of its death had been in any way exaggerated.[27]

In place of the concept of a progressive movement, more
and more historians have turned to the notion of a series of
loose, shifting coalitions to account for the legislative
achievements of the Progressive Era. Concentrating on the
actual mechanics of how reform candidates got elected and

how reform measures got adopted, they have uncovered a rich diversity present in political progressivism. Arthur S. Link first suggested that approach in his famous essay "What Happened to the Progressive Movement in the 1920's?" Departing from his own title, Link argued that there were really "many 'progressive' movements on many levels seeking sometimes contradictory objectives." Huthmacher used much the same language in his 1962 article when he suggested that social reform, at least, "seems thus to have depended upon constructive collaboration, on specific issues, from both the urban middle-class and the urban lower class (with the further cooperation, at times, of organized labor)." Insisting that "the basic riddle in progressivism is not what drove groups apart, but what made them seek common cause," David P. Thelen has carefully detailed the emergence of a reform coalition in Wisconsin spurred by the depression of the 1890s. "By 1898, if not 1896," he concluded, "the progressive coalition combined workers and businessmen, foreign born and native born, Populists and Republicans, drinkers and abstainers, Catholics and Protestants." Sheldon Hackney has attributed the triumph of progressive reform in Alabama to the interaction of "planters, populists, bosses and progressives," the latter consisting of the Hofstadter-Mowry middle class. Carl Chrislock has demonstrated that the initial impetus for progressive reform in Minnesota came from a coalition of the nonurban middle class, urban businessmen, and professionals and trade unionists, but that the initiative gradually passed to miners, Non-Partisan League farmers, and Socialists. Other examples of the coalescing of disparate groups could be cited, but it is clear enough from those already mentioned that the concept of reform coalitions is gaining wide currency.[28]

The central focus for the coalition theory is the assumption, first articulated by Samuel Hays, that the Progressive Era was fundamentally the response of Americans from nearly all walks of life to the conditions wrought by industrialization, urbanization, and immigration. These vast, impersonal forces profoundly and permanently altered the lives of every single American by producing fundamental redistributions of wealth, power, and status and by creating vast cleavages based upon geography, ethnicity, and religion. Industrialization produced, among other things, concentration of control in the production and distribution of goods and services, great extremes of wealth and poverty, a boom and bust cycle that threatened nearly everyone with periodic unemployment or business failure, declining farm income, child and female labor, unsafe and unsanitary working and living conditions, and insecurity in the face of old age or industrial accident. Urbanization exacerbated these problems, provided a seemingly insatiable need for social service that city governments were unable to meet, fostered political corruption, and engendered an urban-rural split that had serious consequences both politically and culturally. Immigration not only added millions of bewildered people who were affected by the impact of industrialization and urbanization, but also destroyed the cultural homogeneity that had previously prevailed and led to bitter clashes between old stock and new over economic security, political power, and life style.[29]

Ultimately, nearly everyone began to perceive that the only way to cope with his problems and to advance or protect his interests was to organize, for the new environment put a premium on large-scale enterprise. For most people, as Hays so effectively put it, it was a case of "organize or perish." Many organizations at first chose to work in the private sector, without requiring government action; hence the origins of labor unions, trade associations, farmer cooperatives, consumers unions, settlement houses, Social Gospelers, immigrant benevolent societies, and the like. Most, however, soon discovered that the realization of their aims required leverage and resources that only government could provide. At the very least, political action was necessary to prevent groups with rival interests from setting up legal roadblocks. The problems and divisions that plagued the nation in the real world finally came to be mirrored in the political world as well, a vital change that distinguishes the politics of the Progressive Era from the unreality of the Gilded Age.[30]

Success in political activity, however, dictates compromise and cooperation between groups and individuals of similar, though not necessarily identical, interest. To achieve passage, a piece of legislation must usually be constructed broadly enough to advance the aims of more than one segment of society. A child labor law, for example, might be acceptable to intellectuals and social workers for humanitarian reasons, to the urban working class because it would protect their children, and to labor unions because it would remove an unfair source of competition. All that is necessary is that they concur in that specific piece of legislation, not that they adhere to any broad set of principles or values. "To make a coalition," as Michael Novak has observed, "mutual love is not prerequisite. Mutual respect, or even mutual need will do." Such coalitions were by definition transitory. Allies on a socioeconomic measure such as child labor legislation might well become adversaries if the issue at stake were a cultural one such as Prohibition or Sunday observance. Competing urban interests might be temporarily united around such issues as home rule or legislative reapportionment. Some coalitions may have achieved relative permanence on certain categories of issues, but it is unlikely that any spanned the entire period or the whole legislative spectrum so as to justify labeling it "the progressive movement." It is only through an appreciation of this complex process of constantly shifting alignments on concrete measures that historians can hope to reconcile all the apparent contradictions that have emerged in interpreting the Progressive Era. Logic, as well as the mounting weight of evidence, virtually impels compliance with Peter Filene's contention that "the Progressive Era seems to have been characterized by shifting coalitions around different issues, with the specific nature of those coalitions varying on federal, state, and local levels, from region to region, and from the first to the second decade of the century." [31]

In this context of the Progressive movement as a series of

interacting and shifting coalitions rather than a monolithic one, it becomes possible to posit a vital and effective role for the urban new stock working class. Urban new stock liberalism was not "the progressive movement" any more than native middle class reform was. Many states obviously had viable reform periods without the presence of any significant urban new stock population. In those states where they did play a vital role, urban new stock lawmakers were subject to the same requirements to cooperate, compromise, and coalesce as any other segment of society. Some measures were obviously enacted over their active opposition; those very circumstances, however, underscore the essential similarity of their experience to that of the rest of society during the Progressive Era. Beset by the problems caused by immigration into a strange, urban, industrial world, they turned to the only form of effective political organization available—the urban machine—and sought through it to achieve some measure of the prosperity, security, and status that America had previously denied them. In so doing, they earned as much right to call themselves progressives as did any other identifiable social segment.

The significance of accepting the contributions of urban new stock working class liberalism to progressive reform has been stated clearly and succinctly by Michael Paul Rogin and John L. Shover in their excellent study on California voting behavior:

A reinterpretation that credits the urban laboring population with a central political role in the Progressive movement will restore a sense of continuity to the study of American reform. Hence, the upsurge of working-class and immigrant power that dominated American politics during the depression, and at least a decade thereafter, would no longer appear as a sudden phenomenon that burst forth in an Al Smith revolution in 1928. In California the political upheaval of the 1930's marked the augmenting and coming to power of the same groups that had sustained Johnson, Wilson and La Follette, buttressed the Progressive reforms two decades earlier, and kept what remained of reform politics alive through the 1920's.[32]

Acknowledgment of the importance of urban liberalism clarifies a number of issues about the Progressive Era itself. It explains why the reform impulse could sustain itself so well and so long in such key industrial states as New York, New Jersey, Massachusetts, California, Ohio, and Illinois that had such heavily new stock populations. If progressivism had been only a native middle class movement, or if the urban masses had been so apathetic or hostile toward reform as their detractors have alleged, then clearly such states could not have achieved the records they did. It also helps to show that outstanding individuals like Smith, Wagner, or Walsh, men whom even the advocates of native middle class progressivism have had to acknowledge as effective reformers, were not aberrations or lonely visionaries. The Progressive Era abounded with men from similar backgrounds pursuing the same objectives whom fate, ambition, or ability simply failed to single out for future fame.

Urban liberalism also provides much of the explanation for the resurgence of the Democratic party in the northeastern industrial states. From the low point of the 1904 election, the Democrats steadily improved their position until by 1916 they were able to elect a president in a two-party race, albeit by the slimmest of margins. By 1913 the party had captured both houses of Congress, mostly because of unprecedented gains in the Northeast, increasing their percentage of House seats in that region by 74.6 percent in 1910 and 54.6 percent in 1912. Beginning in Ohio in 1908, the Democrats also captured the governors' mansions in Illinois, New Jersey, New York, Massachusetts, Connecticut, Indiana, and even Maine and New Hampshire during most of the next eight years and dominated the state legislatures as well. As stated in the first chapter, the high point of progressive reform in most of the major northeastern industrial states came in these years under Democratic administrations backed by Democratic legislatures. The Progressive party, by contrast, lasted but two brief years, elected one governor, one U.S. Senator, twelve Congressmen, and a relative handful of

state legislators. Many of the leading Congressional Insurgents such as La Follette and Norris refused to join it, and
many politicians ran as Progressives strictly because the
regular Republican organization denied them renomina-
tion.[33]

The gains of the Democratic party are enigmatic only if
one is wedded to the concept of progressivism as a native
middle class movement and insists upon the conservatism of
the urban political machine. Everyone acknowledges that the
Democratic party in the northeastern industrial states was
dominated by urban machines that culled their votes largely
from the new stock working class, and its resurgence during
the height of the Progressive Era is intelligible only if one
also grants that these organizations had become vehicles for
reform. There is no way that a political party could enjoy the
kind of electoral success the Democrats did during an era
when an incumbent president received only 23 percent of the
vote because he was cast as a conservative unless the
electorate perceived that party as progressive.[34]

This Democratic upsurge in the Northeast suggests
strongly that the trends that were to lure the urban new stock
masses under its umbrella and help make the party dominant
from the 1930s on were already well established by the
second decade of the century. Unfortunately for the Democrats, Woodrow Wilson was not the man to preside over such
a development. His earlier academic writings contained
many damaging statements of Anglo-Saxon supremacy that
local Republicans could easily use against him. Not even his
veto of the immigration literacy test or his opposition to
Prohibition could wipe that out. Wilson also offended the
city bosses with his "ingratitude" toward "Big Jim" Smith
and further alienated them by assigning patronage to old
stock politicians, bypassing the regular, Irish-dominated
party organizations. The squabble over the peace treaty and
the League of Nations alienated millions of ethnic voters
from the party. In 1924 the national Democrats compounded
the error by denying the nomination to Al Smith, and by

refusing to denounce Prohibition and the Klan. John W. Davis got only 9 percent of the vote in Cleveland, 20 percent in Chicago, 40 in New York, and 35 in Boston.[35]

Even so, the massive outpouring of urban ethnic voters known as the Al Smith revolution was clearly not a sudden upheaval. Democratic Congressional candidates received 70 percent of the vote in New York in 1924, those in Boston, 57 percent, and those in Cleveland, 42 percent, all from 25 to 30 percent better than Davis. "In the majority of these urban areas Democratic strength in the 1920's was significantly greater than was indicated by the presidential vote in 1920 and 1924. Several of the areas tended to be predominantly Democratic during much of the 1920's, at least so far as the vote in elections to lesser offices was concerned. In Boston and Jersey City and in counties of New York City, the Democratic Party was apparently the majority party in elections after 1920, and in most areas Democratic candidates for these lesser offices ran well ahead of the Democratic contenders for the presidency in both 1920 and 1924." Smith himself was reelected governor of New York by ever-increasing margins in the 1920s, topping Davis by over a million votes in 1924. David I. Walsh and Robert Wagner were both elected to the U.S. Senate in 1926, indicating that candidates with urban new stock backgrounds and progressive records were a strong Democratic drawing card in the polyglot industrial states and that Smith's presidential performance in 1928 was more the culmination of a trend than a sudden revolution. Perhaps if the issues of war and peace had not intervened and someone other than Wilson had headed the party, the Democratic resurgence of the Progressive Era might have come to fruition at the beginning of the decade rather than the end.[36]

The acknowledgment of urban liberalism as a vital part of the Progressive Era might also serve to reestablish the period as a time of meaningful reform. It is a healthy development that scholars have corrected the millennial and simplistic view of the era popularized by such early interpreters as William Allen White and Vernon Parrington. They have demonstrated effectively that the period did not just pit the "people" against the "interests"; some of the "people" have been shown to be anything but disinterested and the effects of their efforts have been correctly perceived as being against the welfare of the great mass of people, whether through ineptitude or conscious conspiracy. Because they have been chasing the phantom of a monolithic movement, however, many scholars have been prone to generalize from these specific circumstances and to brand the results of the whole period as either ineffectual or malodorous. It might even be argued that the unflattering portrait of progressive reformers that has appeared in the last two decades is in itself an argument for investigating the attitudes of other social groups, since it is difficult to see how the era's positive achievements, especially in the area of labor and welfare legislation, could have flowed from such a questionable base.

The status revolution thesis, if carried to its logical conclusion, tends to reduce the reformist agitation of the era to an attempt to relieve psychological anxieties by seeking a relief from tension, a "necessary and (as they would have said) wholesome catharsis." In that view, the middle class reformer embraced reform, above all, because it made him feel better, not because it provided any meaningful change. Small wonder that Hofstadter found in certain of their efforts "much that was retrograde and delusive, a little that was vicious, and a good deal that was comic." The urban new stock liberal had little need of such symbolic absolution. He was seeking real solutions to concrete problems, and if the program did not have the desired effect he was not willing to take solace in having made a nice try. The labor and welfare measures that were the heart of his reform program have proven to be the period's most enduring legacy, and the political measures he espoused were meant to effect real transfers of power. Whatever else the period may prove to be, the perspective of the urban new stock liberal at least helps to remove it from the realm of psychology and into that of history.[37]

In the same vein, the acceptance of a role for urban

liberalism should prove a caution light for those who have been willing to relabel the entire era "a triumph of conservatism." The trouble is that this view deals only with issues on the national level and even there only with questions involving government regulation of business. In the major industrial states the business community fought tooth and nail against the labor, welfare, taxation, and regulatory laws that urban lawmakers and their middle class allies were pressing. In those states such as Connecticut and Rhode Island where the business-oriented Republicans held power throughout the era, such measures were effectively blocked. Every important business interest in New York was arrayed against the ratification of the income tax amendment, but it was accomplished. The same was true of the Triangle factory legislation. The political measures supported by urban lawmakers admittedly did not end business influence in their respective legislatures, but they certainly opened the way for other groups to compete on a more equitable basis. The cultural issues that formed such an integral part of the period in the major industrial states provoked divisions that have little or no relevance to conservatism. None of this is to say that it is necessarily wrong to conclude that the attempts at regulation of business on the federal level aided rather than retarded concentrations of political and economic power or even to hold that this was part of a conscious design. The efforts of the urban liberals operating within the context of a fluid, pluralistic reform surge, however, make it very difficult to understand how the failure of business regulation at the federal level could possibly serve as a basis for an adverse judgment on an entire period that produced so many other results.

The twin concepts of urban liberalism and coalition politics also shed some light on the circumstances that led to the decline of the progressive impulse in the twenties. Acknowledging the impact of the war and other factors, Arthur Link put the major blame on the fact that the progressive coalition that elected Woodrow Wilson in 1916 "was so wracked by inner tensions that it could not survive, and destruction came inexorably, it seemed systematically, from 1917 to 1920." Although he is referring to one specific coalition, it is fair to say that his analysis could be expanded to cover the coalition politics of the era in general. So much of reform's success in the major industrial states depended on the partnership of the native middle class, the urban working class, and organized labor. In the early part of the second decade of the century, this coalition was successful, since the humanitarian concerns of the middle class and their distaste for big business apparently outweighed their fear of the potential power that lay beneath them in the social scale. Later, they became uneasy and then frightened by the forces that their democratic rhetoric had unleashed.[38]

The increasing demands of the urban working class for welfare legislation and the growing influence of organized labor caused a dramatic shift of middle class support away from reform, if the cases of Hazen Pingree and Tom and Hiram Johnson are at all typical. The enthusiasm of the native middle class for political changes that resulted in "power to the people" declined precipitously as it became clear who the people were and what they would do with their new power. Above all, it seems clear that the progressive coalition in state after state cracked on the rocks of cultural reform. As the native middle class grew more and more militant in its desire to "Americanize" the foreign stock working class, the latter grew more and more defensive. The issues struck both groups in the innermost depths of their sensibility, touching on the worthiness of the standards by which they lived. It is hard to see how anything as fragile as the progressive coalitions were could have survived the superheated rhetoric of the debates over Prohibition and immigration restriction. The ire of the Wilsonian liberals at the "betrayal" of the president's foreign policy by the Irish and other ethnics of his own party was matched only by the latter's anger at Wilson's "betrayal" of the interests of their motherlands. The bitterly divisive issues of the twenties—the Red Scare, the Klan, Prohibition, immigration restriction, aid to parochial schools, the candidacy of Al Smith—kept the pot boiling. By 1928 William Allen White, the prototype of the status revolution progressive, was denouncing Al Smith, the prototype of the urban new stock progressive, as "a representative of the saloon, prostitution and gambling" and of "a group who have back of them only physical appetite and no regard for law or reform." Not until the trauma of the Great Depression was either side willing to seek any reconciliation. Under the circumstances cooperation between these two very vital elements of the progressive coalition on virtually any issue was effectively foreclosed.[39]

The rise of urban liberalism during the Progressive Era also squares very nicely with the revised picture of the urban political machine that is emerging from the works of sociologists, political scientists, and historians. The traditional view of the political machine stressed the notion of unscrupulous politicians manipulating masses of unthinking voters and reaping great bundles of graft and corruption. The picture contained a goodly measure of truth, but it was largely divorced from any appreciation of the conditions that produced the machine and was rooted in value systems that stressed individual political independence. Many critics of the machine were tinged with nativism, held up standards of political morality that probably never prevailed anywhere in the real world, and demanded a level of voter performance that could have only been the product of education, experience, and economic security that the urban masses had no way of acquiring.[40]

Without in any way denying or excusing the darker side of the urban political machine, many scholars have lately developed what might be called a functional approach to understanding its operation. They have asked such questions as: What were the forces that produced the machine? What kinds of services did it provide and to whom? What were the viable alternatives to having the machine provide them? What was the cost, both social and financial, compared with having the services provided by the viable alternatives? In answering these questions they have provided a substantially different picture of this very significant urban institution.

They have found its origins not in the conspiracy of evil men, but in such impersonal forces as the need of the city for social services, the fragmentation of urban government, the hamstringing of city government by rural-dominated state legislatures, universal manhood suffrage, the rise of professional politicians, and mass immigration. They have discovered that the machine performed a number of vital services for a variety of constituencies, that it constituted the necessary centralized authority to expedite the building of transportation and communication facilities and utilities. Several authorities have argued that there were virtually no viable alternatives to accomplish these ends and at least one has argued that bosses were "unspecialized professionals" who possessed a broader developmental viewpoint than today's specialized city planners. He has even argued that the graft level of 10 to 15 percent extracted by the machine was a tolerable one that still left the cost of construction cheaper than any available alternative.[41]

Other scholars have contended that the machine not only provided the immigrant working class with welfare benefits that would otherwise probably have been nonexistent, but that they often did so with less red tape and more concern for the dignity of the individual than professionally administered programs. They have also argued that the machine provided personal contact with government, facilitated naturalization and voter registration, and provided a career ladder for capable individuals as well as for the rise of entire minority groups. In short, recent scholars of the machine have portrayed it as a dynamic social and political institution that arose naturally out of existing conditions and that survived so well primarily because it met the needs of the time. Such an institution could hardly have reacted to the grass roots agitation for reform in the totally negative manner alleged by its detractors. Institutions that fail to be attuned to the felt needs of the time wither and die, and the urban machines thrived and prospered during the Progressive Era to the point where they could secure the presidential nomination for one of their own less than a decade later. That the urban political machine as perceived by Thomas Nast, Lord Bryce, and the National Municipal League could sponsor progressive reform seems admittedly farfetched; that the institution analyzed by Robert Merton, Elmer Cornwell, Eric McKitrick, Seymour Mandelbaum, Alexander Callow, and Monte Calvert could do so seems highly plausible.[42]

The acceptance of urban liberalism as part of the Progressive Era might also serve to shed some much needed light on two other areas: the possible survival of the period's reform surge in the 1920s and the relationship between the Progressive Era and the New Deal. Until the publication of Arthur Link's article in 1959, the prevailing view had always been that the 1920s was a decade of unrelieved reaction, an arid valley between two peaks of social progress. Link argued that "progressivism survived into the 1920s because several important elements of the movement remained either in full vigor or in only slightly diminished strength." Specifically he singled out farmers, organized labor, "independent radicals, social workers, social gospel writers and preachers," public power advocates, and "the Democratic organizations in the large cities, usually vitally concerned with the welfare of the so-called lower classes." There is a great deal to indicate that the latter group did indeed continue to play a highly constructive role in the decade after World War I, even though conditions severely limited their achievements. New York, for example, "an island of progress and reform," pressed forward new frontiers in labor and welfare legislation, education, housing, and public power. It did so, one hardly needs reminding, under the executive leadership of Tammany Hall's most illustrious son. In Massachusetts, too, the Irish Democrats and New Immigrants continued to fight for the same goals as they had during the Progressive Era, but without the necessary middle class backing, even though they were somewhat fearful of government intervention in their daily lives. Rhode Island's urban Democrats also kept up the pressure for revamping the political system, finally abolishing property qualifications and reapportioning the senate in 1928, as well as for more effective welfare laws, such as the creation of a workmen's compensation commission in 1921.[43]

Despite the decade's reputation for reaction, it saw great advances in most states in the realm of welfare legislation, and there is no reason to believe that urban new stock lawmakers were not a major force in its enactment. Hiram Johnson continued to receive ethnic working class support in the 1920s as solidly as he had before. On the national scene such urban new stock lawmakers as Wagner, Walsh, Fiorello La Guardia, Adolph Sabath, Emmanuel Celler, and Robert Bulkley played prominent roles in opposing the Mellon tax proposals, defending public power, protecting the rights of organized labor, urging federal aid for the unemployed, aged, and victims of industrial accidents, opposing immigration restriction, and even favoring federal antilynching legislation. When the depression hit, theirs were the loudest voices demanding federal action to aid the unemployed and promote recovery. William Leuchtenburg, noting these developments, has styled the 1920s "a time of transition within progressivism from the old-style evangelical reformism, under leaders like La Follette and Bryan, to a new style urban progressivism, which would call itself liberalism," a political force that "would be centered in the urban masses, often the 'new' immigrant workers of the great cities." The subject of the sponsorship of progressive action during the 1920s in both the states and the nation is one that deserves more careful investigation, but what is known thus far suggests strongly that the urban liberalism generated during the Progressive Era continued to be a major constructive force after World War I.[44]

An understanding of urban new stock progressivism also raises serious questions about those accounts that "contrast middle-class, Anglo-Saxon progressivism with the working-class, immigrant-based New Deal." [45] The proponents of the native middle class interpretation of progressive reform freely acknowledge that the New Deal had a heavy, if not predominant, immigrant working class cast. The evidence is overwhelming, and the point is central to their adverse judgment on the limited achievements of the earlier period. The "insulation" of the "Progressive" from the immigrant working class "was one of the factors that, for all his humanitarianism, courage, and vision, reduced the social range and radical drive of his program and kept him genteel, proper and safe." The New Deal, on the other hand, was a "drastic new departure" that contained a "social-democratic tinge that had never before been present in American reform movements," precisely because it dealt so centrally with the enactment of social welfare measures, the recognition of organized labor, and the integration of the urban ethnic working class into the political process. As a result, the latter gave the New Deal the overwhelming electoral support it had denied the middle class progressives. Roosevelt even "worked with the bosses wherever they would work with him." [46]

Many of those who had been active in progressivism, by contrast, "found in the New Deal an outrageous departure from everything they had known and valued." In his extensively researched *Encore for Reform,* Otis Graham studied the attitudes of 168 individuals who have been designated "progressive" by historians and contemporaries toward the New Deal and found that only 45 supported it or wished it to go further. The remainder either actively opposed it or refrained from comment. Those who did work with the New Deal, Graham concluded, "should be regarded, however, as the exception to the rule, outnumbered by those who saw in Roosevelt's work those same fatal tendencies they had long contested against." His sample was drawn mostly from national politics and included presidential advisers, Progressive party officials, members of the National Progressive League, Congressional Insurgents, muckrakers, professors, writers, Social Gospelers, social justice groups, municipal reform associations, and consumer groups. All these were primarily expressions of native middle class progressivism, but it seems fair to ask if they are representative of the wide variety of reform efforts of the era.[47]

This perceived dichotomy between the Progressive Era and the New Deal presents two major problems. First of all, it seems to require a belief that urban working class involvement in reform sprang fully grown from the brain of Buddha, as it were, in 1932. The traumatic impact of the Great Depression might have turned them around 180 degrees, but it seems highly unlikely. Recognition of machine efforts on behalf of progressive legislation and candidates during the Progressive Era and their continued efforts during the 1920s makes urban working class support for the New Deal much more understandable. Even more importantly, it is obvious that these judgments about the incompatibility of the Progressive Era and the New Deal are based on a comparison of the latter with native middle class organizations during the earlier era. Similar comparisons between urban liberalism and the New Deal in the areas of personnel, electoral support, and programs are likely to indicate a significantly higher degree of compatibility between the two reform periods.

With respect to personnel, it is true that Al Smith, one of the shining lights of statewide urban liberalism, became a powerful opponent of the New Deal, but his opposition was inspired mostly by bitter resentment against the man who had deprived him of the chance to gain retribution for his 1928 defeat. Several urban machines held out against FDR in the 1932 convention, but nearly all were reconciled by the time of the election. Martin Lomasney was a rabid partisan of Al Smith at the convention, but his home ward gave Roosevelt 84.3 percent in the election. Edward F. Dunne, leader of urban progressivism in Illinois, was a Roosevelt delegate in 1932 and was appointed by the president to some honorary positions. Ed Flynn, the boss of the Bronx and Roosevelt's most powerful political ally in New York, was a Tammany Hall senator following the lead of Smith and Wagner during the Progressive Era. More importantly, both houses of Congress contained many urban new stock legislators who had advanced from statewide positions in the Progressive Era and who were supporters of the New Deal, such as Robert Wagner, Stephen Young, Barratt O'Hara, Adolph Sabath, Mary Norton, Robert Crosser, Martin Sweeney, Edward Kenney, Anthony Griffin, James Shanley, Christopher Sullivan, and Samuel Dickstein. Wagner, of course, was much more than a supporter of the New Deal; he was the sponsor of several of its major pieces of legislation and was, as he had been at Albany, well ahead of FDR on most matters. A study of the caliber of Graham's is necessary before the point can be proved beyond dispute, but there is strong reason to believe that the outcome of such an investigation would be to establish that urban working class progressives found the New Deal much easier to accept than did middle class reformers.[48]

The question of urban foreign stock working class electoral support for the New Deal is nowhere at issue. It is universally acknowledged that FDR received almost unprecedented majorities in such districts throughout the entire nation, especially in 1936. These were mainly the same districts that for years had provided the mass base that kept the urban political machines in power. Roosevelt's margins generally became smaller and finally disappeared the higher up the socioeconomic ladder one went in any major city. Such a split is exactly the opposite one that allegedly prevailed during the Progressive Era when "reform drew its greatest support from the more discontented of the native Americans, and on some issues from the rural and small town constituencies that surrounded the great cities." Unfortunately there are precious few electoral analyses of the Progressive Era available for comparison. The one that specifically makes such a comparison, that of Rogin and Shover in California, demonstrates strong similarity between Hiram Johnson's support and Roosevelt's, with both scoring highest in the foreign stock working class districts of California. Similar studies in other states seem likely to indicate a high continuity of mass support for reform from one era to the other, if such investigations measure backing for Progressive Era candidates attuned to meaningful social reform.[49]

Programmatically there can be no doubt as to the New Deal's basic nonconformity to that of the status revolution progressives. The middle class progressives gave first priority to structural political reform, guaranteeing equality of economic opportunity, breaking the power of such collectivities as political machines and trusts, and uplifting the lower classes through conformist legislation. Clearly, such was neither the style nor the substance of the New Deal. Comparisons of the New Deal with the goals of the urban new stock progressives, however, reveals many more basic similarities. Both devoted primary attention to social welfare measures that would guarantee some measure of prosperity and security. Both sought to build the power of organized labor. Both sought to regulate the activities of American business, not in the interests of promoting competition or equality of opportunity, but of producing goods and services at reasonable prices. Both favored tax policies that set the burden according to ability to pay. Both approached political reform pragmatically and sought not to change the rules so much as to guarantee that each ethnic and socioeconomic group have access to the process. Finally both recognized to some degree the need for a culturally pluralistic society. Although both the New Deal and progressivism were bewildering mixtures, the urban liberal strain was a vital part of both and is much easier to identify in the New Deal than are the goals that have generally been seen as those of native middle class progressives.[50]

The recognition of the importance of urban liberalism during the Progressive Era, then, has the potential to serve several useful functions. It can operate as a corrective to the tendency of historians to focus their attention too exclusively on one segment of society. It can buttress the case of those scholars who have been urging their fellows to abandon the confining concept of a movement and to view the Progressive Era as the efforts of a wide variety of groups to coalesce around specific issues. It can help to refurbish the somewhat declining reputation from which the Progressive Era has suffered in recent years. It can provide vital clues for the reasons behind the breakup of the era's reform impulse. It can perhaps restore some greater degree of continuity to the evolution of twentieth-century reform movements.

It is even possible that the discovery of urban liberalism may provide some valuable clues for resolving the current estrangement between the ethnic working class and the urban middle class of intellectuals, professionals, managers, and bureaucrats. It is this gap that is threatening to destroy the New Deal coalition that has dominated politics for most of the past four decades. Conservative spokesmen gleefully point to the ethnic working class as a vital part of the "emerging Republican majority." Centrist Democrats warn of the dire consequences of ethnic working class defections if the Democrats keep pressing too hard on "the social issue" at the expense of "the economic issue." Advanced liberals speculate on replacing the ethnic working class with such new elements as the young and nonwhite minorities. George Wallace and Spiro Agnew have built their political strategies upon driving a wedge between the two groups by stressing the elitism and radicalism of the liberal establishment. Michael Novak has called for the creation of an "Ethnic Democratic Party" that would essentially be a coalition of old and new minorities with a lessened role for intellectuals, and has provided a list of suggestions for appealing to the progressive tendencies of white ethnics. All agree that the attitude of the ethnic working class will be crucial to the success of any efforts to provide workable solutions to the myriad of problems that still confront the nation.[51]

A survey taken just before the 1972 election at the behest of the *Washington Post* revealed that Catholic ethnic voters, numerically the largest descendants of the lawmakers considered in this study, were contemplating a massive shift to the Republican side, at least in the presidential race. Whereas 78 percent had voted for John F. Kennedy, 76 percent for Lyndon B. Johnson, and 59 percent for Hubert Humphrey, only 31 to 40 percent were committed to support George McGovern. Although issues of war and peace were partly the reason, the survey indicated that the two major causes were a feeling that the Democratic party had been captured by an elite minority, and that it was espousing radical social changes reminiscent of Prohibition. Although two-thirds of them, a higher percentage than among any other ethnic group, felt that the nation was "on the wrong track," they seemed more apt to regard Senator McGovern as representing those responsible for the country's malaise. Even his revelations of corruption in the Nixon administration and the Watergate affair were written off as extravagant moralizing. His handling of the Eagleton issue and the expulsion of Mayor Daley from the Democratic convention seemed to many Catholics to violate a cardinal rule of their political tradition, namely, loyalty and decency of treatment to individual politicians. All the reminders that one of their own products, Robert Kennedy, had once called McGovern the most decent man in the U.S. Senate were to no avail. In short, Catholic voters appeared to detect in George McGovern, rightly or wrongly, those same qualities of militant pietism that their ancestors had feared in William Jennings Bryan and Woodrow Wilson, and they were prepared to reject him in the same manner. The election returns suggest strongly that they carried out their intention.[52]

Yet there is still much evidence that ethnic voters were rejecting Senator McGovern and what they perceived as his brand of liberalism rather than the Democratic party and urban liberalism. Three out of four Catholic voters surveyed in the *Post*'s sample still regarded themselves as Democrats, and apparently voted for the party's candidates in Congressional and state races with about the same frequency as ever, even for those identified with many of the same positions as McGovern and with voting records as liberal, or more so, than his own. When paired against Edmund Muskie in the survey, President Nixon's margin dropped to 9 percentage points and against Hubert Humphrey it shrank to 4. Against Edward Kennedy, Nixon lost by 15 percentage points. One observer for the *New Republic* marveled at how Kennedy could say most of the same things about the Vietnam War or amnesty that McGovern did to ethnic

audiences and yet receive their approbation where McGovern did not. Large majorities still saw the Democrats as the
party of the workingman, poor people, minorities, older
people, and "people like yourself," while the Republicans
were heavily regarded as the party of big business and
wealthy people. Although the GOP received an edge on
handling issues of war, peace, and drug abuse, significant
majorities of those sampled felt that the Democrats were best
equipped to deal with tax reform, aid to parochial schools,
controlling inflation, abortion, and crime in the streets. The
ethnic voter seems clearly to be at a crossroads and the
historical alliance between him and the urban middle class
that has been the Democratic party for the past forty years is
in serious jeopardy, but not necessarily in danger of dissolu-
tion if lines of communication can be reestablished.

In this highly volatile situation, the experience of the
Progressive Era may offer a great deal to both the middle
class liberal and the ethnic American. It might help to instill
in the latter an appreciation that his progress toward
prosperity, security, and respect was largely the result of
supporting political programs that aimed at producing a
more open society politically, economically, and socially. It
might also help to produce in him a greater empathy for the
plight of other minorities and for their efforts to achieve
prosperity, security, and respect by the same methods. To the
middle class liberal the discovery of urban ethnic liberalism
might demonstrate that there is much in that tradition of
value, particularly that government must be personalized to
be worthwhile and that minorities have a right to live life
according to their own lights. It can perhaps inspire respect
for the values and traditions of ethnics and prevent the
cultural crusades that destroyed the coalitions of the Progressive Era. It may also help the urban middle class to
understand that ethnic working class concern over the
integration of schools, jobs, and neighborhoods is often
motivated by a sincere desire to preserve cultural traditions,
not necessarily by racism. Above all, middle class liberals
might learn to treat the ethnic working class as full partici-

pants in the political process with goals and methods of their own, as members of a diverse reform coalition rather than a monolithic movement suffused by only one set of values. Disagreement on some goals or methods, as the Progressive Era experience clearly demonstrates, does not have to preclude effective cooperation on others. If the middle class liberals and the ethnic working class can at long last come to the mutual understanding that was only partly and temporarily achieved in the reform efforts of the past, then maybe the gap between the ideals and the reality of American life can be significantly narrowed. Perhaps the real significance of urban liberalism and of the American experience was cogently stated by Darrett Rutman in *The Morning of America*:

In the years beyond 1789, governments drawn from but one of America's people—the White, Anglo-Saxon Protestant and propertied—would claim that being of the people and elected by the people, they ruled for the people. One after another of America's peoples—the propertyless, laboring man, the immigrant, the Catholic, the Jew, the non-white, the impoverished, would rise to claim it was not so.[53]

Notes

As a general rule references are grouped together at the end of each paragraph in the order in which the material to which they refer appears. Those referring to material in legislative journals are listed in the order they appear within the two general works *Senate Journal* or *House Journal*, or their equivalents. References to newspapers, the only source for following the debates in most state legislatures, are listed in the order in which they occur in the text. In most cases the year of the measure is mentioned in the text, providing a guide to the proper source.

CHAPTER 1

1. U.S. Bureau of the Census, *Abstract of the Thirteenth Census of the United States, 1910*, 195–218; Maldwyn A. Jones, *American Immigration* (Chicago, 1965), 92–207; Warren Thompson and P. K. Whelpton, *Population Trends in the United States* (New York, 1933), 41–106.

2. *Thirteenth Census, 1910*, 199–218; Jones, *American Immigration*, 210–216; Thompson and Whelpton, *Population Trends*, 65–66.

3. Jones, *American Immigration*, 207–278; John Higham, *Strangers in the Land: Patterns of American Nativism, 1860–1925* (New York, 1970), 68–194; Oscar Handlin, *The Uprooted* (New York, 1951), 144–210.

4. Alexander B. Callow, Jr., *The Tweed Ring* (New York, 1966), 48–90; Charles Glaab and A. Theodore Brown, *A History of Urban America* (New York, 1967), 207–223; Seymour Mandelbaum, *Boss Tweed's New York* (New York, 1965), 46–58; Elmer E. Cornwell, "Bosses, Machines and Ethnic Groups," *Annals of the American Academy of Political and Social Science* 353 (May, 1964): 24–30; Robert K. Merton, *Social Theory and Social Structure* (New York, 1967), 71–82; Richard Hofstadter, *The Age of Reform* (New York, 1955), 257–271; Eric McKitrick, "The Study of Corruption," *Political Science Quarterly* 72 (December, 1957): 502–514.

5. Handlin, *Uprooted*, 201–227; Merton, *Social Theory*, 71–82; Cornwell, "Bosses, Machines and Ethnic Groups," 24–30; Glaab and Brown, *Urban America*, 205–207; Harold Zink, *City Bosses in the United States* (Durham, N.C., 1931), 69–85, 218–230.

6. E. Digby Baltzell, *The Protestant Establishment* (New York, 1964), 49–52; Raymond Wolfinger, "The Development and Persistence of Ethnic Voting," in *American Ethnic Politics*, Lawrence H. Fuchs, ed. (New York, 1968), 163–193; Zink, *City Bosses*, 4–5, 40–46; Robert E. Lane, *Political Life: Why People Get Involved in Politics* (New York, 1959), 95–102. See also August Hollingshead and Frederich C. Redlich, *Social Class and Mental Illness* (New York, 1958), 68–79; Elmer E. Cornwell, "Party Absorption of Ethnic Groups: The Case of Providence, Rhode Island," *Social Forces* 38 (March, 1960): 205–210; Sonya Forthal, *Cogwheels of Democracy: A Study of the Precinct Captain* (New York, 1946), 19–45.

7. Zink, *City Bosses*, 74–75; Lyle Dorsett, *The Pendergast Machine* (New York, 1968), 3–41; Samuel P. Orth, *The Boss and the Machine* (New York, 1919); John T. Salter, *The American Politician* (Chapel Hill, N.C., 1938), 375–396; Charles Garrett, *The La Guardia Years* (New Brunswick, N.J., 1961), 15–16; Forthal, *Cogwheels of Democracy*, 31–32; Louis Eisenstein and Elliot Rosenberg, *A Stripe of Tammany's Tiger* (New York, 1966); James Michael Curley, *I'd Do It Again* (Englewood Cliffs, N.J., 1957), 61; Edward Flynn, *You're the Boss* (New York, 1947), 219–239; John H. Fenton, *Politics in the Border States* (New Orleans, 1957), 132–146; Merton, *Social Theory*, 71–82; Cornwell, "Bosses, Machines and Ethnic Groups," 201–205; McKitrick, "Study of Corruption," 506–507; Henry Jones Ford, *Rise and Growth of American Politics* (New York, 1911), 306.

8. Edward M. Levine, *The Irish and Irish Politicians* (Notre Dame, Ind., 1966), 3–47, 114–116; David Burner, *The Politics of Provincialism: The Democratic Party in Transition, 1918–1932* (New York, 1968), 15–16; Callow, *Tweed Ring*, 67; Nathan Glazer and Daniel P. Moynihan, *Beyond the Melting Pot* (Cambridge, Mass., 1970), 223–225; Fuchs, *American Ethnic Politics*, 13.

9. Burner, *Politics of Provincialism*, 15–16; Duane Lockard, *New England State Politics* (Princeton, 1959), 305–319; J. Joseph Huthmacher, *Massachusetts People and Politics, 1919–1933* (New York, 1969), 1–19; Milton Viorst, *Fall from Grace: The Republican Party and the Puritan Ethic* (New York, 1968), 120–123; Baltzell, *Protestant Establishment*, 49; Cornwell, "Party Absorption," 205–210; Kevin Phillips, *The Emerging Republican Majority* (New Rochelle, N.Y., 1969), 52.

10. Fuchs, *American Ethnic Politics*, 14–16; Joseph Schaeffer, "Who Elected Lincoln?" *The American Historical Review* 47 (October, 1941), 51–63; Paul Kleppner, *The Cross of Culture* (New York, 1970), 316–377; Huthmacher, *Massachusetts People*, 1–19; Samuel Lubell, *The Future of American Politics* (New York, 1965), 86–92; Joel A. Tarr, *A Study in Boss Politics: William Lorimer of Chicago* (Urbana, Ill., 1971), 3–24; Moses Rischin, *The Promised City: New York's Jews, 1870–1914* (Cambridge, Mass., 1962), 13.

11. Phillips, *Emerging Republican Majority*, 22, 52; Cornwell, "Bosses, Machines and Ethnic Groups," 202; Cornwell, "Party Absorption," 205–210; Wolfinger, "Persistence of Ethnic Voting," 173–175; John Allswang, *A House for All Peoples: Chicago's Ethnic Groups and Their Politics, 1890–1936* (Lexington, Ky., 1971), 152–153; Lockard, *New England Politics*, 308–314; Huthmacher, *Massachusetts People*, 1–19; Levine, *Irish Politicians*, 90–100; Viorst, *Fall from Grace*, 126–127.

12. Jones, *American Immigration*, 235–239; Phillips, *Emerging Republican Majority*, 50–51; Walton Bean, *Boss Ruef's San Francisco* (Berkeley, 1952), 1–40; Melvin G. Holli, *Reform in Detroit* (New York, 1969), 125–127; Wolfinger, "Persistence of Ethnic Voting," 173–175; Joseph L. Lieberman, *The Power Broker* (Boston, 1966), 19–30; Robert A. Dahl, *Who Governs? Democracy and Power in an American City* (New Haven, 1961), 32–51; Lockard, *New England Politics*, 305–320; Richard M. Abrams, *Conservatism in a Progressive Era* (Cambridge, Mass., 1964), 50–52; Zink, *City Bosses*, 194–291.

13. Milton Barron, ed., *Minorities in a Changing World* (New York, 1967), 258; Thompson and Whelpton, *Population Trends*, 64–65; Carey McWilliams, *Brothers under the Skin* (Boston, 1964), 333–335; Alex Gottfried, *Boss Cermak of Chicago: A Study of Political Leadership* (Seattle, 1962); Allswang, *House for All Peoples*, 6–10, 152–153; Lockard, *New England Politics*, 305–320; Huthmacher, *Massachusetts People*, 1–9; Lubell, *Future of American Politics*, 212–214; Viorst, *Fall from Grace*, 126–127.

14. Humbert S. Nelli, *The Italians in Chicago, 1880–1930* (New York, 1970), 88–125; John D. Buenker, "Edward F. Dunne: The Urban New Stock Democrat as Progressive," *Mid-America* 50 (January, 1968): 4–9; Zink, *City Bosses*, 80; Reinhard H. Luthin, *American Demagogues: Twentieth Century* (Gloucester, Mass., 1959), 22; Phillips, *Emerging Republican Majority*, 112–113; Rischin, *Promised City*, 222, 262–266; Nancy Joan Weiss, *Charles Francis Murphy, 1858–1924: Respectability and Responsibility in Tammany Politics* (Northampton, Mass., 1968), 13; Oscar Handlin, *The American People in the Twentieth Century* (Cambridge, Mass., 1966), 93–94.

15. Cornwell, "Bosses, Machines and Ethnic Groups," 28–30; Harold F. Gosnell, *Boss Platt and His New York Machine* (New York, 1933), 2–73, 262–290; Viorst, *Fall from Grace*, 1–41, 118–140; Lieberman, *Power Broker*, 18–21.

16. Higham, *Strangers in the Land*, 131–331; James H. Timberlake, *Prohibition and the Progressive Movement, 1900–1920* (New York, 1970), 125–184; Andrew Sinclair, *The Era of Excess: A Social History of the Prohibition Movement* (Boston, 1962), 83–106.

17. Chester Jones, "The Rotten Boroughs of New England," *North American Review* 97 (April, 1913): 485–490; Lockard, *New England Politics*, 272–275; Lieberman, *Power Broker*, 19–21.

18. Jones, "Rotten Boroughs," 488; Lockard, *New England Politics*, 178; *Providence Journal*, February 28, 1910. Erwin Levine, *Theodore Francis Green: The Rhode Island Years, 1906–1936* (Providence, 1963), 1–63, provides an excellent summary of Rhode Island politics in the era.

19. John M. Blum, *Joe Tumulty and the Wilson Era* (Boston, 1951), 11–14, 34–38; Warren Moscow, *What Have You Done for Me Lately?* (Englewood Cliffs, N.J., 1967), 7–55; *Illinois State Register* (Springfield), May 11, 1911.

20. William Riordon, *Plunkitt of Tammany Hall* (New York, 1948), 28; Clifford Patton, *The Battle for Municipal Reform* (Washington, D.C., 1940), 17, 70; Ransom E. Noble, *New Jersey Progressivism before Wilson* (Princeton, 1946), 22; Lincoln Steffens, *The Autobiography of Lincoln Steffens* (New York, 1931), 443.

21. Steffens, *Autobiography*, 467; Cornwell, "Party Absorption," 205–210; Lockard, *New England Politics*, 174–190; *Providence Evening Bulletin*, January 24, 1911; January 5, March 21, 1912; April 15, 1916; Murray S. Stedman and Susan W. Stedman, "The Rise of the Democratic Party of Rhode Island," *New England Quarterly* 24 (September, 1951): 329–339.

22. Lockard, *New England Politics*, 245–250; Lieberman, *Power Broker*, 27–30.

23. Lockard, *New England Politics*, 45–69, 94–101; Abrams, *Conservatism*, 25–53; Huthmacher, *Massachusetts People*, 1–19; Richard B. Sherman, "The Status Revolution and Massachusetts Progressive Leadership," *Political Science Quarterly* 78 (March, 1963): 60–63; Luthin, *American Demagogues*, 29.

24. Cornwell, "Bosses, Machines and Ethnic Groups," 28–30; Orth, *Boss and Machine*, 124–125; Gosnell, *Boss Platt*, 2–9, 262–290; J. Joseph Huthmacher, *Senator Robert F. Wagner and the Rise of Urban Liberalism* (New York, 1968), 40.

25. Noble, *New Jersey Progressivism*, 1–25; Wayland Dunaway, *History of Pennsylvania* (Englewood Cliffs, N.J., 1945), 478–481; Robert Bowden, *Boies Penrose* (New York, 1937), 37; J. Roffe Wike, *The Pennsylvania Manufacturers' Association* (Philadelphia, 1960), 10–20.

26. Hoyt L. Warner, *Progressivism in Ohio, 1897–1917* (Columbus, 1964), 1–22; Kleppner, *Cross of Culture*, 124–126; Viorst, *Fall from Grace*, 84–85.

27. Holli, *Reform in Detroit*, 13–14; Willis Frederick Dunbar, *Michigan: A History of the Wolverine State* (Grand Rapids, 1965), 524–544; M. M. Quaife and Sidney Glazer, *Michigan* (New York, 1948), 267–283; Stephen B. Sarasohn and Vera H. Sarasohn, *Political Party Patterns in Michigan* (Detroit, 1957), 3–15; Zink, *City Bosses*, 297–298; *Illinois State Register*, November 7, 1912; *Chicago Tribune*, November 6, 7, 8, 1912; November 18, 1914; Harold E. Gosnell, *Machine Politics: Chicago Model* (Chicago, 1968), 148; W. B. Phillips, *Chicago and the Down State, 1870–1927* (New York, 1929), 45–137. Kleppner, *Cross of Culture*, shows a definite affinity toward the GOP on the part of the "pietistic" Protestants, such as Methodists, Presbyterians, and Congregationalists, in five midwestern states including Ohio and Illinois. There was a corresponding tendency toward the Democrats on the part of Catholics and other "ritualistic" faiths.

28. Abrams, *Conservatism*, 182–183, 231–258; New York, Legislature, *Assembly Journal, 1910*, 1786, 2392; *1911*, 3725; *1913*, 74–75; New York, Legislature, *Senate Journal, 1910*, 1563; *1911*, 618; *1913*, 58; Holli, *Reform in Detroit*, 185–219; Warner, *Progressivism in Ohio*, 26–41.

29. Zink, *City Bosses*, 60, 204–243; William S. Vare, *My Forty Years in Politics* (Philadelphia, 1933), 116–133; Edward F. Cooke and G. Edward Janosik, *Guide to Pennsylvania Politics* (New York, 1957), 8–12; *Harrisburg Patriot*, January 5, 6, 20, 1915; January 6, 7, 8, February 1, April 15, 16, 17, 1913.

30. James K. Mercer, *Ohio Legislative History, 1909–1913* (Columbus, 1913), 519–646; *1913–1917*, 467–640; *1919–1920*, 451–639; Edgar J. Murlin, *The New York Red Book* (Albany, 1913), 85–190; New Jersey, Legislature, *Legislative Manual of New Jersey, 1913* (Trenton, 1913), 342–353.

31. The Commonwealth of Massachusetts, *Manual for the Use of the General Court, 1910*, 420–481; *1911*, 420–480; *1912*, 417–478; *1913*, 425–485; Connecticut, General Assembly, *Register and Manual, 1911*, 84–96; *1913*, 81–93; *1915*, 84, 96; J. Fred Parker, comp., *Manual with Rules and Orders, for the Use of the General Assembly of the State of Rhode Island* (Providence, 1913), 380–410.

32. Illinois, Secretary of State, *Blue Book of the State of Illinois, 1911* (Danville, 1911), 250–350; *1913* (Danville, 1913), 240–340; Tarr, *Boss Politics*, 21–22.

33. Hofstadter, *Age of Reform*, 178; Holli, *Reform in Detroit*, 172–173; Callow, *Tweed Ring*, 65, 263–264; Mandelbaum, *Boss Tweed*, 68; Eisenstein and Rosenberg, *Stripe of Tammany Tiger*, 20; Brand Whitlock, *Forty Years of It* (New York, 1968), 180–201; Frederic C. Howe, *Confessions of a Reformer* (New York, 1925), 91–140; John T. Salter, *Boss Rule: Portraits in City Politics* (New York, 1935), 69.

34. Whitlock, *Forty Years*, 195–197, 212–213. See also Callow, *Tweed Ring*, 299–300; Hofstadter, *Age of Reform*, 180–181; Timberlake, *Prohibition*, 153–154; Holli, *Reform in Detroit*, 170; Viorst, *Fall from Grace*, 124–125.

35. Holli, *Reform in Detroit*, 179; Salter, *Boss Rule*, 23; Callow, *Tweed Ring*, 4, 71; Levine, *Irish Politicians*, 93; Patton, *Municipal Reform*, 25–27; Glaab and Brown, *Urban America*, 211–213.

36. John Porter East, *Council-Manager Government: The Political Thought of Its Founder, Richard S. Childs* (Chapel Hill, N.C., 1965), 30; Holli, *Reform in Detroit*, 167–179; Glaab and Brown, *Urban America*, 217–219; Whitlock, *Forty Years*, 163–164; McKitrick, *Study of Corruption*, 508; Mandelbaum, *Boss Tweed*, 140; Merton, *Social Theory*, 298–300; Glazer and Moynihan, *Melting Pot*, lxiii.

37. See especially Glaab and Brown, *Urban America*, 201–229; and Holli, *Reform in Detroit*, 157–184. Ethnic minorities also supported reform movements in Cincinnati and Baltimore. See Zane L. Miller, *Boss Cox's Cincinnati: Urban Politics in the Progressive Era* (New York, 1968); and James L. Crooks, *Politics and Progress: The Rise of Urban Progressivism in Baltimore, 1895–1911* (Baton Rouge, 1968). The growing realization of these realities among genteel reformers is evident in Jane Addams, "Why the Ward Boss Rules," *The Outlook* 58 (April 2, 1898): 879–882.

38. The terms were coined by Glaab and Brown, *Urban America*, 213; Holli, *Reform in Detroit*, concurs on p. 156.

39. Holli, *Reform in Detroit*, 143–157.

40. Glaab and Brown, *Urban America*, 213–214; Jean L. Stinchcombe, *Reform and Reaction: City Politics in Toledo* (Belmont, Calif., 1968), 29–35; Patton, *Municipal Reform*, 57; Warner, *Progressivism in Ohio*, 24–35; Whitlock, *Forty Years*, 202–205, 296–297; Howe, *Confessions of a Reformer*, 91–104; Wellington G. Fordyce, "Nationality Groups in Cleveland Politics," *The Ohio State Archaeological and Historical Quarterly* 46 (1937): 125.

41. Michael P. Rogin and John L. Shover, *Political Change in California* (Westport, Conn., 1969), 55–85; Noble, *New Jersey Progressivism*, 14, 93–97; Lincoln Steffens, *The Upbuilders* (New York, 1909), xii–xiii, 25–27; Carter Harrison, Jr., *Stormy Years* (Indianapolis, 1935), 108, 118, 156, 190–191, 245, 267–268, 312–313, 319, 332–333; Tarr, *Boss Politics*, 21–22.

42. Noble, *New Jersey Progressivism*, 61, 98, 148–149; Huthmacher, *Senator Wagner*, 18–24; Frances Perkins, *The Roosevelt I Knew* (New York, 1946), 9–27; Warner, *Progressivism in Ohio*, 40–41; Abrams, *Conservatism*, 151–169; Burner, *Politics of Provincialism*, 19. Rischin, *Promised City*, 261–265, describes the political awakening of New York City Jews.

43. Riordan, *Plunkitt of Tammany*; Mandelbaum, *Boss Tweed*, 94–95; Huthmacher, *Senator Wagner*, 12–37; Oscar Handlin, *Al Smith and His America* (Boston, 1958), 39–44; Huthmacher, *Massachusetts People*, 63–64; Perkins, *Roosevelt*, 14–15; Blum, *Joe Tumulty*, 1–25; Buenker, "Edward F. Dunne," 3–5. See especially Wagner's 1918 campaign speech reprinted in J. Joseph Huthmacher, *Twentieth Century America* (Boston, 1966), 83–85.

44. Huthmacher, *Senator Wagner*, 12–37. See also his "Charles Evans Hughes and Charles Francis Murphy: The Metamorphosis of Progressivism," *New York History* 46 (January, 1965): 25–40; Blum, *Joe Tumulty*, 1–46; Arthur S. Link, *Wilson: The New Freedom* (Princeton, 1956), 1–37; Crooks, *Politics and Progress*, 77, 121.

45. *Chicago Tribune*, April 15, 1920; Zink, *City Bosses*, 61, 298; Huthmacher, *Senator Wagner*, 28; McKitrick, "Study of Corruption," 509–511.

46. Warner, *Progressivism in Ohio*, 199–428; Mercer, *Ohio Legislative History, 1909–1913*, 442–635; *1913–1917*, 467–640.

47. Noble, *New Jersey Progressivism*, 98–153; Blum, *Joe Tumulty*, 1–37; Arthur S. Link, *Wilson: The Road to the White House* (Princeton, 1947),

287; Link, *New Freedom*, 53; Rudolph Vecoli, *The People of New Jersey* (Princeton, 1965), 168. Samuel Hays, *Response to Industrialism, 1885–1914* (Chicago, 1957), 149, also notes that north Jersey urban Democrats seized control of the state's reform movement, partly because of the issue of Prohibition.

48. Richard B. Sherman, "Charles Sumner Bird and the Progressive Party in Massachusetts," *New England Quarterly* 33 (September, 1960): 330–344, and "Foss of Massachusetts: Demagogue vs. Progressive," *Mid-America* 43 (April, 1961): 75–94, Abrams, *Conservatism*, 132–133; Murray B. Levin and G. Blackwood, *The Compleat Politician* (Indianapolis, 1962), 15–72; Zink, *City Bosses*, 72–81; Huthmacher, *Massachusetts People*, 61–69.

49. Buenker, "Edward F. Dunne," 10–21.

50. Huthmacher, *Senator Wagner*, 24–37, and "Hughes and Murphy," 25–40; Weiss, *Charles Francis Murphy*, 69–91; David M. Ellis, James A. Frost, Harold C. Syrett, and Harry J. Carman, *A Short History of New York State* (Ithaca, 1957), 376–389; James MacGregor Burns, *Roosevelt: The Lion and the Fox* (New York, 1956), 37.

51. Lockard, *New England Politics*, 192, 239–250; Lieberman, *Power Broker*, 25–48; Cornwell, "Party Absorption," 205–210.

52. The best discussion of the development of reform coalitions is David P. Thelen, *The New Citizenship: Origins of Progressivism in Wisconsin, 1885–1900* (Columbia, Mo., 1972).

CHAPTER 2

1. See especially Clarke A. Chambers, *Seedtime of Reform: American Social Service and Social Action, 1918–1933* (Minneapolis, 1963), 1–27; Sidney Fine, *Laissez-Faire and the General-Welfare State: A Study of Conflict in American Thought* (Ann Arbor, 1966), 167–403; Roy Lubove, *The Struggle for Social Security, 1900–1935* (Cambridge, Mass., 1968), passim; Irwin Yellowitz, *Labor and the Progressive Movement in New York State, 1897–1916* (Ithaca, 1968), 1–88.

2. Handlin, *Uprooted*, 7–20; Marcus Lee Hansen, *The Atlantic Migration, 1607–1860* (New York, 1961), 280–306; Oscar Handlin, ed., *Immigration as a Factor in American History* (Englewood Cliffs, N.J., 1959), 20–41; Viorst, *Fall from Grace*, 5–12.

3. R. W. Green, ed., *Protestantism and Capitalism: The Weber Thesis and Its Critics* (New York, 1959); Lillian Parker Wallace, *Leo XIII and the Rise of Socialism* (Durham, N.C., 1966), 410–412; Joseph N. Moody, ed., *Catholic Social and Political Thought and Movements, 1789–1950* (New York, 1953), 325–583; Edward T. Gargan, *Leo XIII and the Modern World* (New York, 1961), 68–88.

4. Mordecai M. Kaplan, *Judaism as a Civilization: Toward a Reconstruction of American Jewish Life* (New York, 1967), 472–478; Rischin, *Promised City*, 30–43.

5. Lubell, *Future of American Politics*, 47.

6. Handlin, *Uprooted*, 117–144, 170–201; Jones, *American Immigration*, 223–239; Oscar Handlin, *Immigration as a Factor*, 76–93; Moody, *Catholic Social and Political Thought*, 843–904; Robert D. Cross, *The Emergence of Liberal Catholicism in America* (Cambridge, Mass., 1967), 108–115, 218–220; Philip Gleason, *Catholicism in America* (New York, 1970); Philip Gleason, *The Conservative Reformers: German-American Catholics and the Social Order* (South Bend, Ind., 1968); John Tracy Ellis, *American Catholicism* (Chicago, 1969), 144–146; Andrew Greeley, *The Catholic Experience: An Interpretation of the History of American Catholicism* (New York, 1969), 220–230; Aaron I. Abell, ed., *American Catholic Thought on Social Questions* (Indianapolis, 1968), 143–264.

7. Rischin, *Promised City*, 98–111, 149–161; Nathan Glazer, *American Judaism* (Chicago, 1957), 65–66, 136–139; Louis Finkelstein, ed., *The Jews: Their Religion and Culture* (New York, 1971), 295–307, 526–527; Handlin, *Uprooted*, 221–225.

8. Huthmacher, "Hughes and Murphy," 25–40; Weiss, *Charles Francis Murphy*, 69–99; Handlin, *Al Smith*, 52–61; Burns, *Lion and Fox*, 35–49; Perkins, *Roosevelt*, 12–14; Ellis et al., *Short History*, 376–389; Frank Freidel, *Franklin D. Roosevelt: The Apprenticeship* (Boston, 1952), 120.

9. Weiss, *Charles Francis Murphy*, 81–82; Huthmacher, *Senator Wagner*, 3–11; Handlin, *Al Smith*, 52–58; Ellis et al., *Short History*, 389–390.

10. Weiss, *Charles Francis Murphy*, 89–90; Huthmacher, *Senator Wag-*

ner, 29–31; Huthmacher, "Hughes and Murphy," 31–32; *Albany Evening Journal*, March 15, 1913; February 18, 1914.

11. Weiss, *Charles Francis Murphy*, 82–90; Huthmacher, *Senator Wagner*, 29–31; *New York Times*, March 15, April 5, May 11, July 24, 1913; Handlin, *Al Smith*, 58–60.

12. Handlin, *Al Smith*, 59; Weiss, *Charles Francis Murphy*, 85; Huthmacher, *Senator Wagner*, 29–31; *New York Times*, May 4, 18, 1913.

13. Weiss, *Charles Francis Murphy*, 83; Huthmacher, *Senator Wagner*, 5–10, 29–30; Handlin, *Al Smith*, 57–60; *Albany Evening Journal*, May 3, 1910; May 4, 11, 18, 1913; February 28, March 1, 27, 1914.

14. Weiss, *Charles Francis Murphy*, 85; Handlin, *Al Smith*, 59–61; Huthmacher, *Senator Wagner*, 30–31; *New York Times*, April 23, December 9, 10, 11, 12, 13, 1913.

15. Handlin, *Al Smith*, 103–109; *New York Times*, May 14, 27, 29, June 3, 17, July 22, August 10, 13, 17, 1915; April 25, May 2, 10, June 4, 1917.

16. Blum, *Joe Tumulty*, 14. Portions of the material on New Jersey in this book first appeared in John D. Buenker, "Urban, New Stock Liberalism and Progressive Reform in New Jersey," *New Jersey History* 87 (Summer, 1969): 79–104.

17. Noble, *New Jersey Progressivism*, 126–127; New Jersey, Legislature, *Assembly Minutes*, *1909*, 68, 636–637, 948–949, 976–977, 1308.

18. New Jersey, *Assembly Minutes*, *1911*, 52, 68, 637, 903, 1309; Link, *Road to the White House*, 263–265.

19. New Jersey, *Assembly Minutes*, *1911*, 321; *1912*, 320–321; *1911*, 249; *1912*, 687, 797; *1911*, 932, 353, 326, 817–818, 1096.

20. New Jersey, *Assembly Minutes*, *1911*, 52, 175, 249; *1912*, 755, 394.

21. New Jersey, *Assembly Minutes*, *1911*, 590, 213–214, 499, 320–321.

22. New Jersey, *Assembly Minutes*, *1909*, 514; *1911*, 898; *1912*, 35, 1512.

23. New Jersey, *Assembly Minutes*, *1911*, 320.

24. New Jersey, *Assembly Minutes*, *1911*, 329; *1912*, 1226; *1911*, 53; *1912*, 803; *1910*, 311; *1911*, 464.

25. New Jersey, *Assembly Minutes, 1912*, 884, 997–998, 1267; *1909*, 519; Noble, *New Jersey Progressivism*, 129.

26. Noble, *New Jersey Progressivism*, 122–125; New Jersey, *Assembly Minutes, 1907*, 324; *1908*, 247; *1909*, 650; *1910*, 369.

27. Ohio, General Assembly, *Senate Journal, 1913*, 467; *1915*, 896; Ohio, General Assembly, *House Journal, 1913*, 909; *1915*, 1173–1174; Warner, *Progressivism in Ohio*, 487. Portions of the Ohio material in this book first appeared in John D. Buenker, "Cleveland's New Stock Lawmakers and Progressive Reform," *Ohio History* 78 (Spring, 1969): 116–137.

28. Warner, *Progressivism in Ohio*, 402; Ohio, *Senate Journal, 1911*, 288; *1913*, 113; *1917*, 106; Ohio, *House Journal, 1911*, 852; *1913*, 423; *1917*, 132–133.

29. Ohio, *Senate Journal, 1911*, 218; *1913*, 800; *1917*, 473; *1913*, 834; Ohio, *House Journal, 1911*, 1067; *1913*, 879–880; *1917*, 680; *1913*, 204.

30. Ohio, *Senate Journal, 1911*, 226; *1913*, 446, 716, 755; *1913*, 281; Ohio, *House Journal, 1911*, 586; *1913*, 900–909, 1185; *1913*, 601; Warner, *Progressivism in Ohio*, 418, note 43, 426.

31. Ohio, *Senate Journal, 1913*, 271; *1911*, 164; *1915*, 365; Ohio, *House Journal, 1913*, 680; *1911*, 1122; *1915*, 820; Warner, *Progressivism in Ohio*, 335–336; Yellowitz, *Labor and Progressive Movement*, 130–138; Marc Karson, *American Labor Unions and Politics, 1900–1918* (Carbondale, Ill., 1958), 29–41, 129–136; Thomas R. Brooks, *Toil and Trouble* (New York, 1964), 108–112.

32. Ohio, *Senate Journal, 1911*, 295; *1914*, 149, 84; *1913*, 85, 481; *1914*, 147; *1913*, 258, 740; *1911*, 213; Ohio, *House Journal, 1911*, 1032; *1914*, 90, 140; *1913*, 1212; *1914*, 35; *1913*, 184, 896; *1911*, 1131; Warner, *Progressivism in Ohio*, 283, 294, note 82, 403, 418, note 46.

33. Ohio, *Senate Journal, 1913*, 771, 272, 449; *1919*, 465; *1917*, 326; *1913*, 447; Ohio, *House Journal, 1913*, 266, 506, 875; *1919*, 953; *1917*, 385; *1913*, 244.

34. Ohio, *Senate Journal, 1913*, 743, 682; Ohio, *House Journal, 1913*, 981–982, 226.

35. Buenker, "Edward F. Dunne," 9–11; William Sullivan, *Dunne: Judge, Mayor, Governor* (Chicago, 1916), 573–576. Portions of the material

on Illinois in this book first appeared in John D. Buenker, "Urban Immigrant Lawmakers and Progressive Reform in Illinois," in *Essays in Illinois History*, Donald F. Tingley, ed. (Carbondale, Ill., 1967), 52–74.

36. Illinois, General Assembly, *House Journal, 1915,* 169; *1909,* 243, 1263; *1915,* 1285, 657–659, 1287, 663, 1054; *1913,* 461, 916; Illinois, General Assembly, *Senate Journal, 1915,* 94–95, 674; *1913,* 1300, 1294.

37. Illinois, *House Journal, 1913,* 242; *Illinois State Journal* (Springfield), March 20, 1915; Sullivan, *Dunne,* 391; *Chicago Journal,* May 21, June 6, 1913; Illinois, *Senate Journal, 1913,* 1422, 170; *Illinois State Journal,* March 13, 1913; Illinois, *House Journal, 1913,* 791; Eugene Staley, *History of the Illinois State Federation of Labor* (Chicago, 1930), 264.

38. *Illinois State Register* (Springfield), May 12, 1909; Illinois, *Senate Journal, 1909,* 1003; *1913,* 1731; Illinois, *House Journal, 1911,* 343, 565; Sullivan, *Dunne,* 576, 647; Earl Beckner, *A History of Illinois Labor Legislation* (Chicago, 1929), 210; Staley, *Illinois Federation of Labor,* 272; *Illinois State Register,* May 12, 28, 1915.

39. Illinois, *House Journal, 1915,* 828; *Illinois State Journal,* June 3, 1915; Staley, *Illinois Federation of Labor,* 271; Beckner, *Illinois Labor Legislation,* 71, 171.

40. Edward F. Dunne, *History of Illinois,* Vol. 2 (Chicago, 1933), 335–336; Sullivan, *Dunne,* 528; Illinois, *House Journal, 1915,* 151, 194, 662; Illinois, *Senate Journal, 1915,* 1315.

41. Staley, *Illinois Federation of Labor,* 264, 554; Dunne, *History,* 226–227; Illinois, *House Journal, 1909,* 243, 273, 958, 1015; *1913,* 1436, 740–741, 1852, 1052, 1850, 1051, 1436; *1915,* 1161, 1129, 1168, 1162, 1142, 1554, 1161, 1143; Illinois, *Senate Journal, 1915,* 1028–1029, 1554; *Illinois State Journal,* May 19, June 10, 1915; *Illinois State Register,* June 10, 1915.

42. Dunne, *History,* 334–335; Illinois, *House Journal, 1915,* 854; *1913,* 743–745; Illinois, *Senate Journal, 1915,* 718; *1913,* 1082; *1915,* 91, 839, 1335; Sullivan, *Dunne,* 653.

43. Staley, *Illinois Federation of Labor,* 247–261; Beckner, *Illinois Labor Legislation,* 263; Illinois, *House Journal, 1909,* 769, 908; *1911,* 161; *1909,* 219, 674; *1910,* 318; Illinois, *Senate Journal, 1910,* 247; *1911,* 1117, 161, 536; *1915,* 45, 754, 1218; Sullivan, *Dunne,* 385.

44. Richard Abrams, "Paradox of Progressivism: Massachusetts on the

Eve of Insurgency," *Political Science Quarterly* (September, 1960): 382–388; David I. Walsh, "Labor in Politics: Its Political Influence in New England," *Forum* (August, 1915): 216.

45. H. La Rue Brown, "Massachusetts and the Minium Wage," *Annals of the American Academy of Political and Social Science* 48 (July, 1913): 13–21; Raymond L. Bridgman, *The Massachusetts Constitutional Convention of 1917* (Boston, 1923), 120–121; Massachusetts Constitutional Convention, *Journal of the Constitutional Convention of the Commonwealth of Massachusetts, 1917* (Boston, 1917), 789–801; Massachusetts, General Court, *House Journal, 1913*, 1332–1335; *1914*, 956–958, 1165; *1916*, 334–336; *1917*, 725–727.

46. Bridgman, *Constitutional Convention*, 120–121; *Journal of Constitutional Convention, 1917*, 789–801; Massachusetts, *House Journal, 1916*, 740–742, 842–846, 1381–1382; *1910*, 924–926; *1911*, 1219, 1276; *1913*, 1453; *1909*, 1036; *1910*, 988, 1355; *1914*, 1165–1168, 1262–1263, 1934–1941; *1917*, 392–393, 432–434, 470–471, 936–937, 1297; Massachusetts, General Court, *Senate Journal, 1913*, 923, 1105; *1910*, 789, 898; *1911*, 37, 100, 879, 983–994, 1040, 1102; Abrams, *Conservatism*, 233–234, 259–269. For Lomasney's role in reform generally see John D. Buenker, "The Mahatma and Progressive Reform: Martin Lomasney as Lawmaker, 1911–1917," *New England Quarterly* (September, 1971): 397–419.

47. Massachusetts, *Senate Journal, 1911*, 1552–1591, 1600–1601, 2051; *1914*, 1395; Massachusetts, *House Journal, 1913*, 1805, 2038, 2401; *1915*, 931–933, 994–995; Abrams, *Conservatism*, 260; D. G. Wayman, *David I. Walsh, Citizen Patriot* (Milwaukee, 1952), 60.

48. Massachusetts, *House Journal, 1911*, 1985–1987, 867–870, 73, 1408–1415; *1915*, 914–916, 1014–1016, 1047–1049; Massachusetts, *Senate Journal, 1915*, 749; Abrams, *Conservatism*, 259–260; Leslie Ainley, *Boston Mahatma: The Public Career of Martin Lomasney* (Boston, 1949), 139–142.

49. Massachusetts, *House Journal, 1916*, 464, 545–547; *1913*, 1329; *1917*, 1212–1217; *1911*, 80, 114, 134; *1915*, 663–665; *1917*, 1332; *1915*, 914–916, 964–966, 1014–1016, 1047–1049; *1911*, 409, 1278, 1438–1439, 1478, 1531; Massachusetts, *Senate Journal, 1915*, 749; *1911*, 1268, 1302.

50. Bridgman, *Constitutional Convention*, 78–79, 90–94, 125, 148–150; *Journal of Constitutional Convention, 1917*, 283, 774–775; Massachusetts Constitutional Convention, *Debates in the Massachusetts Constitutional Convention, 1917–1918* (Boston, 1919), 394–395, 441–444, 492–494, 521, 581–610, 637–795, 803–804; Ainley, *Boston Mahatma*, 139–142.

51. Rhode Island Bureau of Industrial Statistics, *Some Nativity and Race Factors in Rhode Island* (Providence, 1910), 220–350; Stedman and Stedman, "Rise of Democratic Party," 341; *Providence Journal*, February 10, 19, 25, March 17, 1910; February 11, March 8, 9, April 2, 1909; March 7, 1912; February 20, 1913. Portions of the material on Rhode Island in this book first appeared in John D. Buenker, "The Rise of Urban Liberalism in Rhode Island, 1909–1919," *Rhode Island History* (Spring, 1971): 35–52.

52. *Providence Journal*, February 17, 1910; *Providence Evening Bulletin*, January 20, March 23, 25, April 7, May 5, 1909; January 13, February 10, May 14, 1911; February 7, 21, April 10, 16, 1912; January 30, February 4, 12, March 4, 1913; January 21, February 26, 1915; April 6, 1917.

53. *Providence Journal*, March 24, 1910; *Providence Evening Bulletin*, January 6, 1911; February 16, 1912; February 25, 1913; February 16, 1915; April 6, 1916; March 15, April 27, 1909; May 4, 5, 1911; January 26, March 22, January 24, February 25, April 1, 2, 3, 1913; February 4, 9, March 24, 1915.

54. *Providence Journal*, March 23, 1910; *Providence Evening Bulletin*, January 24, May 11, 1911; February 19, March 16, April 6, 1909; February 13, April 17, 1912; January 12, 1915; April 20, 1918.

55. *Providence Journal*, February 15, 1910; *Providence Evening Bulletin*, February 14, 1911; January 3, March 20, 22, April 23, 1912; March 18, April 2, 8, 1913; January 14, April 8, 1915; April 18, 1917; Earl C. Tanner, *Introduction to the Economy of Rhode Island* (Providence, 1953), 106.

56. *Providence Evening Bulletin*, March 3, February 14, January 31, March 1, 1911; January 12, 1912; March 18, April 2, 1913; April 5, January 31, 1911; February 5, March 5, 1913; February 3, 1911; January 18, 1912; April 3, 1913; January 22, 1915; April 2, 1918; January 31, 1917; January 26, 1915; January 6, 1911; January 17, 1912; March 27, 1913; *Providence Journal*, February 18, March 24, 31, 1910.

57. Connecticut, General Assembly, *Senate Journal, 1909*, 1636–1637, 1684–1685, 1803–1805, 1857–1859; *1911*, 87, 182, 127–129, 1434, 1477, 1610–1620, 1903, 2032, 2068; *Hartford Courant*, April 13, July 12, July 20, August 2, 1911. Portions of the material on Connecticut in this book first appeared in John D. Buenker, "Progressivism in Connecticut: The Thrust of the Urban, New Stock Democrats," *The Connecticut Historical Society Bulletin* 35 (October, 1970): 97–109.

58. Connecticut, *Senate Journal, 1913*, 125, 148, 731, 946, 1119–1120;

1917, 193–197, 758–759; *1919*, 109; *1911*, 1538–1598, 1619–1620, 1835–1836; *Hartford Courant*, August 9, 30, 1911.

59. *Hartford Courant*, June 8, 1911; February 28, 1913; Connecticut, *Senate Journal, 1911*, 318, 959, 1240–1241; *1913*, 125, 169, 352, 428–429, 926, 1218, 1292, 1366–1367, 1477, 1524; *1915*, 1060; *1917*, 121, 153, 242, 248–249, 1078–1080, 1417–1419.

60. *Hartford Courant*, April 3, 1911; Connecticut, *Senate Journal, 1913*, 225, 1261–1263.

61. *Hartford Courant*, April 7, 1911; Connecticut, *Senate Journal, 1911*, 183, 317, 994, 1031, 1177, 1216, 1442, 1999; *1913*, 277, 1239, 1438, 1541.

62. Connecticut, *Senate Journal, 1913*, 276–277, 1264; *1917*, 154; *1913*, 149, 548–550.

63. *Hartford Courant*, May 4, 1911; Connecticut, *Senate Journal, 1911*, 143, 844, 957, 993, 1346–1352, 1402; *1913*, 277, 1439; *1913*, 1372; *1917*, 103; *1913*, 274–275, 909; *1917*, 157, 1401, 1294; *1913*, 229, 957; *1913*, 1372. See also *1917*, 197, 789; and *1913*, 273.

64. *Hartford Courant*, April 12, August 10, 1911; Connecticut, *Senate Journal, 1911*, 146, 814, 829, 848, 1163, 1566, 1700–1764, 1928–1960; *1913*, 279, 1170.

65. Connecticut, *Senate Journal, 1913*, 79–80, 144–149, 169; *1917*, 755, 185, 129; *1919*, 176.

CHAPTER 3

1. The biographies of these lawmakers are to be found in the same sources cited in Chapter 1, notes 30–32. Hughes defended strikers on trial for the Paterson mill disturbances and he himself had once worked in the same establishments. Spellacy later functioned as an attorney for Standard Oil, but began as counsel for the Hartford Central Labor Union. See *Hartford Courant*, July 26, 1911. Wagner's connection with labor is a recurrent theme in Huthmacher's biography of him.

2. Jones, *American Immigration*, 221–223; Karson, *Labor Unions and Politics*, 221–224; Brooks, *Toil and Trouble*, 119–125, 143–145.

3. Jones, *American Immigration*, 221–223; Karson, *Labor Unions and Politics*, 182–186; Brooks, *Toil and Trouble*, 119–125, 143–145.

4. Karson, *Labor Unions and Politics*, 29–42; Brooks, *Toil and Trouble*, 98–123.

5. Karson, *Labor Unions and Politics*, 125–143; Yellowitz, *Labor and Progressive Movement*, 130–138; Warner, *Progressivism in Ohio*, 335–336. The reader will recall from Chapter 2 the debate in both the Ohio and Massachusetts constitutional conventions concerning labor's position on wages, hours, and social insurance legislation. Karson on p. 129 notes the debate in the 1915 AFL convention over wages and hours legislation between Gompers's supporters and those of William Green of Ohio.

6. Karson, *Labor Unions and Politics*, 42–90; Brooks, *Toil and Trouble*, 98–114.

7. Yellowitz, *Labor and Progressive Movement*, 227–238.

8. Joseph Dineen, *The Purple Shamrock* (New York, 1949), 51–65; Sullivan, *Dunne*, 573–576; Staley, *Illinois Federation of Labor*, 418.

9. Yellowitz, *Labor and Progressive Movement*, 227–238; Huthmacher, *Senator Wagner*, 39; Weiss, *Charles Francis Murphy*, 87, 124, note 117; Garrett, *La Guardia Years*, 15; *New York Times*, May 7, 1915; January 19, 1917; February 14, 1918.

10. Massachusetts, *House Journal, 1909*, 780; *1910*, 867, 1103–1105, 1302–1313; *1911*, 1038–1045, 1080–1082, 1494, 1571–1573; *1913*, 1332–1335; Massachusetts, *Senate Journal, 1910*, 900, 971; *1911*, 1112; Abrams, *Conservatism*, 231–232, 258.

11. *Hartford Courant*, April 7, 28, May 12, July 20, 26, August 9, 1911; Connecticut, *Senate Journal, 1911*, 181, 217, 1413, 1443, 1493, 1507, 1613, 1708, 1829, 2001–2002; *1913*, 225–1520; *1917*, 153, 155, 196, 255, 593–595, 628–629, 743–744, 757.

12. Tanner, *Economy of Rhode Island*, 103; Massachusetts Institute of Technology, Division of Industrial and Municipal Research, *Industrial Survey of Metropolitan Providence for the Year 1926* (Cambridge, Mass., 1928), 75; *Providence Journal*, March 10, 24, 1910; *Providence Bulletin*,

January 17, 25, March 9, 11, 1909; January 31, February 10, 14, 1911;
February 16, 21, March 14, 1912; January 8, 24, February 7, 28, March 10,
1913; April 29, 1914; February 3, 1915.

13. Noble, *New Jersey Progressivism*, 127–128; New Jersey, *Assembly
Minutes, 1909*, 268–270; *1912*, 452, 891, 993, 1330, *1913*, 1003.

14. Illinois, *House Journal, 1909*, 235, 243, 258, 1092; *1915*, 1054; *Illinois
State Journal*, March 3, 1909; May 19, June 10, 11, 1915; *Illinois State
Register*, April 2, 1909; March 15, June 10, 1915; Staley, *Illinois Federation
of Labor*, 264, 544.

15. Warner, *Progressivism in Ohio*, 218, 335–349, 404; Ohio, *House
Journal, 1911*, 226, 794; *1919*, 953; Ohio, *Senate Journal, 1911*, 682, 737,
1919, 465.

16. For representative presentations of the above interpretations see
Fred A. Shannon, *The Farmer's Last Frontier, 1860–1897* (New York,
1945); George H. Miller, *Railroads and the Granger Laws* (Madison, 1971);
Stanley P. Caine, *The Myth of a Progressive Reform: Railroad Regulation in
Wisconsin, 1903–1910* (Madison, 1970); Lee Benson, *Merchants, Farmers
and Railroads: Railroad Regulation and New York Politics, 1850–1887*
(Cambridge, Mass., 1955); Gabriel Kolko, *The Triumph of Conservatism*
(New York, 1963), and *Railroads and Regulation, 1877–1916* (Princeton,
1965); Edwin Rozwenc, ed., *Roosevelt, Wilson, and the Trusts* (Boston,
1950).

17. Kolko, *Triumph of Conservatism*, 5–6, 120, 130, 161–163, 173, 178,
180, 283–285.

18. Huthmacher, *Senator Wagner*, 21, 28–29; *New York Times*, January
3, March 27, 1918. Weiss, *Charles Francis Murphy*, 82–88, also argues that
municipal ownership also had the advantage of increasing the number of
patronage jobs.

19. Noble, *New Jersey Progressivism*, 101–120; New Jersey, *Assembly
Minutes*, 1907, 620; *1909*, 732, 807; *1910*, 609–620; *1911*, 500–501; Link,
Road to the White House, 262–264.

20. Warner, *Progressivism in Ohio*, 278–280, 387–398; Ohio, *House
Journal, 1913*, 1061; *1914*, 130; *1915*, 603; *1917*, 858; Ohio, *Senate Journal,
1911*, 581; *1913*, 727; *1914*, 159–160; *1915*, 641; *1917*, 607.

21. Sullivan, *Dunne*, 437, 502, 524–529, 647; Dunne, *History*, 322–325,

477; Illinois, *House Journal, 1913*, 2109; *1915*, 210, 1016; *1917*, 17; Illinois, *Senate Journal, 1913*, 400, 647–648, 1136, 1418; *1915*, 147, 855; *Illinois State Journal*, June 26, 1913; June 9, 1915; *Illinois State Register*, March 4, 1911; June 4, 9, 1915; *Chicago Journal*, June 12, 1913.

22. Joseph B. Eastman, "The Public Service Commission of Massachusetts," *Quarterly Journal of Economics* 27 (August, 1913): 699; Abrams, *Conservatism*, 259; Massachusetts, *House Journal, 1911*, 1404, 1680–1682, 1714–1716, 1951–1952, 1968–1969.

23. *Providence Evening Bulletin*, January 4, February 24, 1911; February 27, March 20, 1912; January 9, 1913.

24. *Hartford Courant*, April 6, May 24, June 16, 27, 1911; Connecticut, *Senate Journal, 1909*, 1719; *1911*, 87, 313, 413, 1189–1195, 1261–1313, 1435; *1913*, 225, 272, 807; *1917*, 83, 103.

25. Huthmacher, *Senator Wagner*, 29–31; Weiss, *Charles Francis Murphy*, 84–89; *New York Times*, February 21, March 8, 26, May 3, 20, April 5, December 13, 1913; January 17, 30, February 28, March 9, 1918.

26. New Jersey, *Assembly Minutes, 1913*, 412–419, 858, 1240, 1255, 1426; *1911*, 990; *1912*, 133–136, 893, 1070, 1242; Link, *Road to the White House*, 266–267.

27. Warner, *Progressivism in Ohio*, 398–400; Ohio, *Senate Journal, 1913*, 766; Ohio, *House Journal, 1913*, 880, 1159.

28. Ohio, *Senate Journal, 1913*, 666; *1917*, 341; Ohio, *House Journal, 1913*, 713; *1917*, 669.

29. Ohio, *House Journal, 1911*, 1047; *1913*, 243, 293; *1914*, 192; *1915*, 781–819; *1913*, 163, 668, 168; *1911*, 760; *1915*, 1077; *1913*, 359–360, 545; *1911*, 408; *1917*, 539; Ohio, *Senate Journal, 1911*, 632; *1913*, 269, 714–715; *1914*, 191; *1915*, 266, 275; *1911*, 632; *1913*, 215–221; *1911*, 355; *1913*, 155, 496–497, 694; *1917*, 415–416.

30. Sullivan, *Dunne*, 648; *Illinois State Register*, June 10, 1915; Illinois, *House Journal, 1913*, 1896, 443; *1915*, 11, 726, 1180, 1096, 1164; *1909*, 236, 258, 508, 533, 1032–1034, 1320, 1225; *1911*, 202; *1915*, 726, 787, 101; *1913*, 1044; Illinois, *Senate Journal, 1913*, 1600, 1625, 1729; *1915*, 1180, 1479, 1534; *1909*, 297, 1191; *1911*, 348, 1174; *1913*, 2197; *1915*, 952.

31. Massachusetts, *House Journal, 1911*, 306–309; *1910*, 1361–1398,

1451–1453, 1008; *1914*, 2121–2130; *1915*, 263–265; Massachusetts, *Senate Journal, 1910*, 956, 973–977, 986, 1052, 1099; Wayman, *David I. Walsh*, 74; Abrams, *Conservatism*, 248–260; Bridgman, *Constitutional Convention*, 82, 110; *Debates of Constitutional Convention*, 778–779.

32. *Providence Journal*, January 20, February 3, 1910; *Providence Evening Bulletin*, January 12, 26, 28, April 14, 15, 20, 23, 29, May 5, 8, 1909; January 4, February 24, March 3, 1911; February 27, March 14, 20, 21, 26, April 27, 1912; January 9, February 4, March 4, April 2, 16, 1913; April 9, 1914; February 10, 16, 1915.

33. *Hartford Courant*, April 3, 6, 20, July 19, August 9, 1911. Connecticut, *Senate Journal, 1911*, 142–144, 159, 184, 207, 214, 450, 1628, 1671; *1913*, 59, 109, 223, 231–233, 263–264, 269–278, 447, 641, 647, 735, 807–808, 922, 923, 1001, 1168–1170, 1422–1423; *1917*, 151, 154, 185, 193–200, 240, 248–252, 598, 630, 635, 667, 785, 837–838, 1062, 1084–1085, 1424–1426; *1919*, 106, 176, 1067–1068; *1909*, 216.

34. See especially Sidney Ratner, *A Political and Social History of Federal Taxation* (New York, 1942), 65–315; and C. K. Yearley, *The Money Machines* (Albany, 1970), 3–137. Mathiez is quoted in Philip Stern, *The Great Treasury Raid* (New York, 1964), 14.

35. Sullivan, *Dunne*, 445; Dunne, *History*, 347; *Chicago Journal*, June 13, 1913; *Illinois State Journal*, February 23, 1913; Illinois, *House Journal, 1913*, 1034, 1465–1466; *1915*, 773; Illinois, *Senate Journal, 1913*, 53, 1201, 1289, 1770; *1915*, 673, 884; Gosnell, *Machine Politics,* 152; *Illinois Blue Book, 1917*, 388.

36. Warner, *Progressivism in Ohio*, 280–281, 396; Ohio, *Senate Journal, 1919*, 644; *1911*, 598; *1913*, 482; Ohio, *House Journal, 1919*, 969; *1911*, 436.

37. Warner, *Progressivism in Ohio*, 281, 397, 416–417, note 32; Ohio, *Senate Journal, 1919*, 350; Ohio, *House Journal, 1919*, 660.

38. Warner, *Progressivism in Ohio*, 429–430, 476; Ohio, *Senate Journal, 1913*, 710; *1917*, 39–40; Ohio, *House Journal, 1913*, 1031–1032; *1917*, 53–54.

39. *Providence Evening Bulletin*, April 25, 30, 1910; April 12, 21, May 2, 6, 11, 1911; January 30, February 2, 8, 9, 14, 15, 1912; March 18, 1913; April 14, 1915.

40. *Hartford Courant*, February 20, May 7, 1913; Connecticut, *Senate Journal, 1913*, 172, 232, 438–439, 479, 492–500; *1917*, 153, 235–236.

41. Ainley, *Boston Mahatma*, 143–146; Massachusetts, *Senate Journal, 1911*, 1565–1570, 1593; Massachusetts, *House Journal, 1911*, 1946–1948, 1995–1996, 2008–2020; *1913*, 1739–1741; *1915*, 1236–1238; *Journal of Constitutional Convention*, 675–677, 780–799, 832–837; *Debates of Constitutional Convention*, 841–843; Bridgman, *Constitutional Convention*, 127; *New York Times*, April 28, May 11, 1917; April 18, 20, 1919; Yearly, *Money Machines*, 244–245.

42. The quote is from George L. Mowry, *The Era of Theodore Roosevelt 1900–1912* (New York, 1958), 263–264. Ratner discusses the motives involved in the proposal of the income tax amendment. See his *Political and Social History*, 250–315; and also John D. Buenker, "Urban Liberalism and the Federal Income Tax Amendment," *Pennsylvania History* 36 (April, 1969): 192–215.

43. *Chicago Tribune*, February 3, 1910; Illinois, *Senate Journal, 1910*, 23, 129, 199; Illinois, *House Journal, 1910*, 76, 318; Sullivan, *Dunne*, 547.

44. Mowry, *Era of Theodore Roosevelt*, 236; *Ohio State Journal* (Columbus), January 20, 1911; *Cleveland Plain Dealer*, January 19, 1911; Ohio, *Senate Journal, 1911*, 48; Ohio, *House Journal, 1911*, 48.

45. *New York Times*, January 6, 1910; *New York World*, January 6, 1910; John D. Buenker, "Progressivism in Practice: New York State and the Federal Income Tax Amendment," *The New York Historical Society Quarterly* 52 (April, 1968): 139–160. See also Ratner, *Political and Social History*, 250–261.

46. *New York World*, January 6, 1910; Elihu Root, *The Proposed Income Tax Amendment*, U.S., 61st Cong., 2nd sess., 1910, Senate Document 398, 4–5; New York, *Assembly Journal, 1910*, 2: 1786; 3: 2392; New York, *Senate Journal, 1910*, 2: 1563.

47. Burns, *Lion and Fox*, 37; New York, *Senate Journal, 1911*, 1: 618; New York, *Assembly Journal, 1911*, 4: 3725; *Albany Evening Journal*, April 19, 1911.

48. Link, *Road to the White House*, 266–268; New Jersey, *Assembly Minutes, 1911*, 815; *1912*, 1407; *1913*, 93, 107; New Jersey, Legislature, *Senate Journal, 1911*, 401, 639–640; *1913*, 107; *Newark Evening News*, January 20, February 4, 1913.

49. Massachusetts, *House Journal, 1910*, 1115; *1911*, 1076, 1092; *1912*, 1365; *1913*, 740; Massachusetts, *Senate Journal, 1910*, 952; *1911*, 1001; *1912*, 1219; *1913*, 575.

50. *Providence Evening Bulletin*, April 29, 1910; February 2, March 22, 1912; March 26, April 9, 1913; *Providence Daily Journal*, January 7, 10, 1910; Ratner, *Political and Social History*, 305.

51. *Hartford Courant*, June 29, 1911, *Hartford Times*, June 28, 1911; Connecticut, *Senate Journal, 1911*, 55, 67–68, 1346–1347; Connecticut, General Assembly, *House Journal, 1911*, 225; *1913*, 965.

CHAPTER 4

1. Samuel P. Hays, "The Politics of Reform in Municipal Government in the Progressive Era," *Pacific Northwest Quarterly* 55 (October, 1964): 159–160.

2. Hays, "Politics of Reform," 160–169.

3. Hays, "Politics of Reform," 161–167; David M. Kennedy, ed., *Progressivism: The Critical Issues* (Boston, 1971), xi.

4. Hofstadter, *Age of Reform*, 262–265; Hays, "Politics of Reform," 157–169; James Weinstein, "Organized Business and the City Commissioner and Manager Movements," *Journal of Southern History* 28 (1962): 166–182; Holli, *Reform in Detroit*, 157–184.

5. Hays, "Politics of Reform," 157–169; Hofstadter, *Age of Reform*, 257–271; Holli, *Reform in Detroit*, 157–184.

6. Mark Foster, "Frank Hague of Jersey City: The Boss as Reformer," *New Jersey History* 85 (Summer, 1968): 106–117; Wayman, *David I. Walsh*, 60; Lane, *Political Life*, 95–102; Luthin, *American Demagogues*, 131–132.

7. Wayman, *David I. Walsh*, 60; Massachusetts, *House Journal, 1914*, 1744–1746, 1834; *1915*, 612.

8. Link, *Road to the White House*, 265–266; New Jersey, *Assembly Minutes, 1911*, 1066.

9. Link, *New Freedom*, 38–48; New Jersey, *Assembly Minutes, 1913*, 939–940, 1955–1965, 1976, 1990.

10. Handlin, *Al Smith*, 95–99; Ellis et al., *Short History*, 400–403.

11. Warner, *Progressivism in Ohio*, 269; Ohio, *Senate Journal, 1911*, 344; *1917*, 383–384, 396; *1913*, 87; 181, 331, 444, 480, 583; *1915*, 416; Ohio, *House Journal, 1911*, 203; *1917*, 482, 541; *1913*, 130–131, 745–746, 917, 1142, 1157, 1215; *1915*, 651.

12. Dunne, *History*, 371; Illinois, *House Journal, 1917*, 191; Illinois, *Senate Journal, 1917*, 389.

13. Riordon, *Plunkitt of Tammany*, 14–22; McKitrick, "Study of Corruption," 502–514; Huthmacher, *Senator Wagner*, 17; *Illinois State Journal*, May 8, 1913; May 5, 1915; *Illinois State Register*, March 15, April 23, 1913; Walter Townsend, *Illinois Democracy*, Vol. 1 (Springfield, 1935), 307.

14. Noble, *New Jersey Progressivism*, 143–148; New Jersey, *Assembly Minutes, 1907*, 474, 1015–1016, 1096; *1908*, 1016, 1246; Illinois, *House Journal, 1915*, 562–563, 1039; Illinois, *Senate Journal, 1915*, 120, 156; *Illinois State Journal*, March 10, 1911; May 8, 1913; May 5, 1915; *Illinois State Register*, March 26, 30, April 7, May 10, 17, 1911; March 15, April 23, 1913; *Chicago Daily News*, June 4, 1915.

15. Curley, *I'd Do It Again*, 26; Massachusetts, *House Journal, 1913*, 475–477, 559–561, 1571–1573, 1622–1624; *1916*, 1078–1105; Ainley, *Boston Mahatma*, 29–50, 189; Luthin, *American Demagogues*, 16–19; *Hartford Courant*, March 26, 1913; Connecticut, *Senate Journal, 1911*, 1627, 1670; *1913*, 273; *1915*, 60–62, 414–416; *1917*, 155, 1328–1329, 1348–1349; *1919*, 313, 1199–1201.

16. Warner, *Progressivism in Ohio*, 423–436; Ohio, *Senate Journal, 1913*, 367; Ohio, *House Journal, 1913*, 1257; *New York Times*, April 23, May 4, 1913.

17. Ohio, *Senate Journal, 1913*, 58; *1919*, 264; Ohio, *House Journal, 1913*, 79; *1919*, 465–466; Warner, *Progressivism in Ohio*, 276.

18. Ohio, *Senate Journal, 1911*, 511, 745; *1913*, 86, 621; *1915*, 769; *1917*, 373, 451; Ohio, *House Journal, 1911*, 497, 977; *1913*, 295, 762; *1915*, 882–883; *1917*, 791–792, 844.

19. Link, *Road to the White House*, 256–262; New Jersey, *Assembly Minutes, 1911*, 1308; Dunne, *History*, 340–341, 348; Sullivan, *Dunne*, 688–689, 728–730; Illinois, *House Journal, 1915*, 135; *1917*, 52; Illinois, *Senate Journal, 1911*, 1086; *1913*, 1004; *1915*, 74; *Illinois State Journal*, May 3, 1911; May 21, June 19, 1913; May 22, 1915; *Illinois State Register*, April 22, May 3, 16, 1911; March 24, May 20, June 3, 1915; *New York Times*, January 11, 1918.

20. *Hartford Courant*, July 27, August 11, 1911; February 20, 1913; Connecticut, *Senate Journal, 1911*, 1811, 315, 1555–1567, 1659; *1917*, 198, 243, 598–599; *1913*, 485–486, 729–730, 1475–1476; *Providence Journal*, January 4, 21, 25, February 3, 1910; *Providence Bulletin*, January 6, February 8, May 10, 1911; January 11, 24, February 1, 14, 20, March 1, 1912; January 15, 24, April 2, 1913; April 1, 7, 16, 1914; January 6, February 25, 1915; April 12, 18, 1917; Levine, *Theodore Francis Green*, 23.

21. Hays, "The Politics of Reform," 166–169; Kennedy, *Progressivism*, xi; Weinstein, "Organized Business," 166–182; Holli, *Reform in Detroit*, 157–184.

22. Hofstadter, *Age of Reform*, 257–261; Mowry, *Era of Theodore Roosevelt*, 78.

23. *New York Times*, December 9, 1913; Henry Jones Ford, "The Direct Primary," *North American Review* 190 (1909): 1–14.

24. Abrams, *Conservatism*, 293; Stedman and Stedman, "Rise of Democratic Party," 337–341; Cornwell, "Party Absorption," 206.

25. *New York Times*, April 7, 10, May 4, 1913; July 3, 9, 23, August 5, 9, September 5, 10, 1915; Weiss, *Charles Francis Murphy*, 84–85.

26. Tarr, *Boss Politics*, 185–187; Warner, *Progressivism in Ohio*, 17–87, *Providence Journal*, March 9, 12, 1910; *Providence Bulletin*, March 16, April 24, 1911; January 17, April 17, 1912; April 23, 1913; April 13, 1915; Connecticut, *Senate Journal, 1911*, 1020–1024; *1913*, 59–60, 143–144, 211–212, 292, 678, 940–942, 1001, 1129–1130; *1917*, 233, 955–957.

27. Handlin, *Al Smith*, 44–45, 61–64; *New York Times*, April 28, May 7, 13, 27, June 8, 18, 19, 25, July 1, 2, 1915; *Illinois State Register*, May 15, 1901; May 11, 1911; *Illinois State Journal*, May 14, 19, 22, 23, 1901; May 11, 1911; Illinois, *House Journal, 1911*, 39; Illinois, *Senate Journal, 1915*, 262.

28. *Hartford Courant*, August 16, September 15, 1911; March 7, April 30, 1913; Connecticut, *Senate Journal*, *1911*, 40, 1174–1175, 1878–1880, 1950–2014, 2095–2096; *1913*, 99, 1439, 1174–1175; Levine, *Theodore Francis Green*, 45; *Providence Journal*, January 5, February 11, 1910; *Providence Bulletin*, March 26, 29, 30, April 2, 1907; January 13, 21, 1910; January 31, 1911; January 25, 1912.

29. Hofstadter, *Age of Reform*, 257–261.

30. Dunne, *History*, 345; *Illinois State Journal*, March 9, May 2, 4, 1911; April 17, 28, May 7, 14, 1913; *Illinois State Register*, April 19, 21, 1911; May 6, 13, 1913; May 26, 1915; Illinois, *House Journal*, *1911*, 941; *1913*, 1016, 2117; Illinois, *Senate Journal*, *1911*, 397, 789, 924; *1913*, 397, 818–819.

31. Warner, *Progressivism in Ohio*, 281–282, 294, note 80, 392–394; Ohio, *Senate Journal*, *1913*, 348, 689; *1914*, 82, 151; *1915*, 864; *1911*, 734; *1913*, 650; Ohio, *House Journal*, *1913*, 841–842; *1914*, 120–121, 169–170; *1915*, 958–959; *1911*, 443; *1913*, 953.

32. *Hartford Courant*, June 22, August 9, 1911; Connecticut, *Senate Journal*, *1911*, 101, 220, 1216, 1293–1400; *Providence Journal*, March 23, 1910; *Providence Bulletin*, February 18, March 5, 1913.

33. Massachusetts, *House Journal*, *1910*, 429–431; *1911*, 1195–1197, 1955–1959; *1913*, 465–467, 1609–1611, 1710–1712; *Debates of Constitutional Convention*, 7–15; Bridgman, *Constitutional Convention*, 42–65; *Journal of Constitutional Convention*, 600–602; Michael E. Hennessy, *Four Decades of Massachusetts Politics, 1890–1935* (Norwood, Mass., 1935), 252–258; Huthmacher, *Massachusetts People*, 64.

34. Handlin, *Al Smith*, 44–45; *New York Times*, April 23, May 11, December 9, 10, 11, 12, 13, 1913; July 16, 1915; May 3, 10, 1917; Weiss, *Charles Francis Murphy*, 88.

35. Noble, *New Jersey Progressivism*, 134–135; Link, *Road to the White House*, 247–258; New Jersey, *Assembly Minutes*, *1909*, 1155–1156; *1911*, 663; Ohio, *Senate Journal*, *1911*, 700; Ohio, *House Journal*, *1913*, 1098.

36. Tarr, *Boss Politics*, 182; Illinois, *House Journal, 1910*, 298–299; *1912*, 23; *1913*, 1899; Illinois, *Senate Journal*, *1910*, 161, 248; *1912*, 22; *Illinois State Register*, February 2, 1910; May 9, 1912; January 27, 1915; *Chicago Journal*, June 20, 1913; *Illinois State Journal*, March 19, 1915.

37. Massachusetts, *House Journal, 1912*, 640–641; *1910*, 429–431; *1912*, 716; *1913*, 188–191, 972, 1217–1219, 1481–1533; *1916*, 744–775, 947–948; Abrams, *Conservatism*, 241; *Providence Bulletin*, March 8, 1911; March 1, April 18, 1912; March 26, 1913.

38. *Hartford Courant*, June 15, July 28, August 9, 1911; Connecticut, *Senate Journal, 1911*, 1501–1513, 1574; *1913*, 173, 273, 611, 709–710.

39. Ohio, *Senate Journal, 1911*, 697; *1913*, 109, 140; *1917*, 160; Ohio, *House Journal, 1911*, 232–233; *1913*, 161, 498; *1917*, 379–380; Connecticut, *Senate Journal, 1913*, 273; *1917*, 242; Massachusetts, *House Journal, 1913*, 1217–1219, 1481–1482, 1533; *1916*, 774–775, 947–948; *New York Times*, December 13, 1913; July 1, 15, August 20, 1915; January 11, 1917; *Providence Bulletin*, February 28, March 2, 25, 1910; January 20, February 23, March 2, April 4, 20, 21, 1911; January 12, April 26, 1912; January 30, 1913; February 18, 1915; April 9, 1918.

40. Lockard, *New England Politics*, 190–191; Cornwell, "Party Absorption," 206; *Providence Journal*, February 18, 1910; March 12, 1913; *Providence Bulletin*, February 7, March 2, 14, April 1, 4, 19, May 3, 1911; January 3, February 22, 24, March 7, 21, 22, April 2, 3, 10, 16, 18, 23, 26, 27, 1912; January 8, February 10, 28, March 11, 12, 26, April 25, 1913; April 1, 1914; April 4, 1916; Stedman and Stedman, "Rise of Democratic Party," 337–341.

41. *Hartford Courant*, June 15, July 6, 26, August 23, 1911; March 6, April 3, 16, May 15, 32, 28, 1913; Connecticut, *Senate Journal, 1913*, 226–228, 679, 1282–1283, 1429–1439; *1917*, 154, 593–595; *1909*, 93.

42. Massachusetts, *House Journal, 1915*, 802; *Journal of Constitutional Convention*, 689–690, 802–822; Bridgman, *Constitutional Convention*, 82, 116. The so-called Brayton's Law virtually turned the governor's appointment power over to the senate; the Republicans had used it to hamstring the last Democratic governor. *Providence Journal*, February 19, 1910; *Providence Bulletin*, January 6, 18, 20, 1909; January 13, 1911; January 11, 1912; January 30, 1913; April 15, 1914; *Hartford Courant*, May 3, 1911; *Providence Bulletin*, April 11, 1911.

43. *Providence Journal*, January 11, 12, 1910; *Providence Bulletin*, January 2, 4, March 21, 1912; January 7, 14, 1913; April 14, 1914; January 7, 13, 1915.

44. *New York Times*, December 9, 10, 11, 12, 13, 1913; October 6–31, November 1–3, 1915; Yellowitz, *Labor and Progressive Movement*, 239–

244; Handlin, *Al Smith*, 60–68, 95–99; Warner, *Progressivism in Ohio*, 312–343; Ohio, *Senate Journal, 1911*, 383; Ohio, *House Journal, 1911*, 1072–1073.

45. New Jersey, *Assembly Minutes, 1911*, 781; *1913*, 353; Link, *New Freedom*, 37–38; *Hartford Courant*, March 26, 1913; *Providence Bulletin*, January 18, March 19, April 17, 1912; April 8, 1913; April 1, 29, 1914; January 19, 25, February 17, 1915; April 7, 1916; April 6, 1917.

46. *Illinois State Journal*, May 11, 1911; March 12, 1915; *Illinois State Register*, May 11, 1911; March 23, 25, April 1, 14, 15, May 6, 1915; Illinois, *House Journal, 1911*, 1047; *1912*, 71, 83; *1913*, 297, 2116; *1915*, 112, 329; Illinois, *Senate Journal, 1911*, 924; *1912*, 19; *1913*, 1640; *1915*, 111, 140, 260; Bridgman, *Constitutional Convention*, 509, 145; Wayman, *David I. Walsh*, 44–70; Massachusetts, *House Journal, 1914*, 817–819, 1834–1836; *1915*, 326–362; *1916*, 715–717.

47. U.S. Congress, 62nd Cong., 2nd sess., *Congressional Record*, Appendix 161. For a complete discussion of urban lawmakers and the Seventeenth Amendment see John D. Buenker, "The Urban Political Machine and the Seventeenth Amendment," *Journal of American History* 56 (September, 1969): 305–322.

48. Dunne, *History*, 365; *Congressional Record*, 62nd Cong., 2nd sess., Appendix 161; *Providence Journal*, March 14, 1913; *Boston Daily Globe*, March 28, 1912.

49. New York, *Senate Journal*, 1:58; New York, *Assembly Journal*, 50, 74–75; *New York Times*, January 16, 1913.

50. *Providence Journal*, March 14, 1913.

51. Connecticut, *House Journal, 1913*, 97–98, 727–730; Connecticut, *Senate Journal, 1913*, 648.

52. *Boston Daily Globe*, March 28, April 17, 1912; Massachusetts, *Senate Journal, 1912*, 1149, 1491; Massachusetts, *House Journal, 1912*, 1134–1136, 1717.

53. Tarr, *Boss Politics*, 199–308; Dunne, *History*, 181–187; Illinois, *Senate Journal, 1913*, 383–385, 440; Illinois, *House Journal, 1913*, 232.

54. Ohio, *Senate Journal, 1913*, 228; Ohio, *House Journal, 1913*, 54.

55. New Jersey, *Assembly Minutes, 1913,* 335; New Jersey, *Senate Journal, 1913,* 595.

56. For a full discussion of the subject see John D. Buenker, "The Urban Political Machine and Woman Suffrage: A Study in Political Adaptability," *The Historian* 33 (February, 1971): 264–279. See also Andrew Sinclair, *The Better Half* (New York, 1965); Eleanor Flexner, *Century of Struggle* (Cambridge, Mass., 1959); Alan P. Grimes, *The Puritan Ethic and Woman Suffrage* (Princeton, 1967); Aileen S. Kraditor, *The Ideas of the Woman Suffrage Movement* (New York, 1965); Carrie Chapman Catt and Nettie Rogers Shuler, *Woman Suffrage and Politics: The Inner Story of the Suffrage Movement* (Seattle, 1969), 161; and Viorst, *Fall from Grace,* 128–130.

57. Flexner, *Century of Struggle,* 270–276; *New York Times,* November 3, 1915; Handlin, *Al Smith,* 52; *Chicago Daily News,* June 5, 1913; Curley, *I'd Do It Again,* 26.

58. Perkins, *Roosevelt,* 24–26; Kraditor, *Ideas of Suffrage,* 263–265; *Chicago Journal,* June 12, 1913.

59. Kraditor, *Ideas of Suffrage,* 138–162; National American Woman Suffrage Association, ed., *Victory: How Women Won It, A Centennial Symposium, 1840–1940* (New York, 1940), 110–115; *Illinois State Register,* April 15, 1919; Cornwell, "Bosses, Machines and Ethnic Groups," 29; *Providence Journal,* March 3, 1910; James J. Kenneally, "Catholics and Woman Suffrage in Massachusetts," *Catholic Historical Review* 53 (April, 1967): 43–57; Sinclair, *Better Half,* 245–247, 300–315, 320–321, 335; Barbara Solomon, *Ancestors and Immigrants: A Changing New England Tradition* (Cambridge, Mass., 1956), 54.

60. Flexner, *Century of Struggle,* 290; Sinclair, *Better Half,* 331; *New York Times,* November 6, 1917; June 12, 1919; New York, *Assembly Journal,* 3:7–8, Appendix II, 3; New York, *Senate Journal,* 3: 15.

61. *Chicago Journal,* June 12, 1913; *Chicago Daily News,* June 5, 1913; Townsend, *Illinois Democracy,* Vol. 1, 291; Dunne, *History,* 335–337; *Illinois State Journal,* May 23, 1915; Flexner, *Century of Struggle,* 276–277; Gosnell, *Machine Politics,* 148; Illinois, *House Journal, 1919,* 1020; Illinois, *Senate Journal, 1919,* 1260.

62. Ohio, *Senate Journal, 1917,* 169; *1919,* 105, 808; Ohio, *House Journal, 1917,* 133–134; *1919,* 174, 1141–1142.

63. Connecticut, *Senate Journal, 1913*, 920–921; *1917*, 1204–1206; *1920*, 15; Connecticut, *House Journal, 1920*, 16.

64. *Providence Journal*, January 7, April 21, 1920.

65. Flexner, *Century of Struggle*, 272–274, 288–289; Massachusetts, *House Journal, 1913*, 873–875, 1343–1349; *1919*, 1264–1266; Massachusetts, *Senate Journal, 1919*, 964–965; Ralph G. Martin, *The Bosses* (New York, 1964), 231.

66. Link, *New Freedom*, 53; Catt and Shuler, *Woman Suffrage*, 387; Flexner, *Century of Struggle*, 270–274, 292; New Jersey, *Assembly Minutes, 1920*, 110; New Jersey, *Senate Journal, 1920*, 236.

CHAPTER 5

1. Jones, *American Immigration*, 39–64; Baltzell, *Protestant Establishment*, 3–26, 46–86, 109–142; Viorst, *Fall from Grace*, 1–46.

2. Ray Allen Billington, *The Protestant Crusade, 1800–1860: A Study of the Origins of American Nativism* (Chicago, 1964), 1–32; Jones, *American Immigration*, 147–177.

3. Rischin, *Promised City*, 262–265; Handlin, *American People*, 104; Jones, *American Immigration*, 248–254; East, *Council-Manager Government*.

4. Anton Walburg, "The Question of Nationality," in *The Church and the City*, Robert Cross, ed. (Indianapolis, 1967), 114–126; Rischin, *Promised City*, 262–265; Higham, *Strangers in the Land*, 264–330; Handlin, *American People*, 47–164.

5. Higham, *Strangers in the Land*, 68–105; Solomon, *Ancestors and Immigrants*, 43–175; Handlin, *American People*, 98–99.

6. Lee Benson, *The Concept of Jacksonian Democracy: New York as a Test Case* (Princeton, 1961), 165–208; Kleppner, *Cross of Culture*, 75–95;

Tarr, *Boss Politics*, 19–21; Richard Jensen, "The Religious and Occupational Roots of Party Identification: Illinois and Indiana in the 1870's," *Civil War History* 16 (December, 1970): 325–343; Joseph R. Gusfield, *Symbolic Crusade: Status Politics and the American Temperance Movement* (Urbana, Ill., 1966), 6.

7. Benson, *Jacksonian Democracy*, 191–208; Jensen, "Religious and Occupational Roots," 325–333; Kleppner, *Cross of Culture*, 74; John A. Krout, *The Origins of Prohibition* (New York, 1967), 300.

8. Jensen, "Religious and Occupational Roots," 330–333; Tarr, *Boss Politics*, 174–175.

9. Will Herberg, *Protestant, Catholic, Jew: An Essay in American Religious Sociology* (Garden City, N.Y., 1960), 114–117; Viorst, *Fall from Grace*, 11–13.

10. Levine, *Irish Politicians*, 91–92; Greeley, *Catholic Experience*, 19–21; Herberg, *Protestant, Catholic, Jew*, 148–155.

11. Herberg, *Protestant, Catholic, Jew*, 117; Hofstadter, *Age of Reform*, 150–153; George E. Mowry, *The California Progressives* (Berkeley, 1951), 87; Morris Kertzer, *What Is a Jew?* (Cleveland, 1960), 41–46; Arthur Hertzberg, ed., *Judaism* (New York, 1962), 178; Glaab and Brown, *Urban America*, 236–237; Tarr, *Boss Politics*, 20–21.

12. Miller, *Boss Cox's Cincinnati*, 10–11, 177–178. See, for example, the referenda in Boston and San Francisco in Timberlake, *Prohibition*, 167–169.

13. Viorst, *Fall from Grace*, 17–40; Kleppner, *Cross of Culture*, 118–119; Jensen, "Religious and Occupational Roots," 325–343; Tarr, *Boss Politics*, 20–21; Reinhold H. Luthin, *The First Lincoln Campaign* (Cambridge, Mass., 1944), 3.

14. Benson, *Jacksonian Democracy*, 86–110, 165–191; Kleppner, *Cross of Culture*, 75, 169–170; Stedman and Stedman, "Rise of Democratic Party," 337; Jensen, "Religious and Occupational Roots," 325–343; *Racine Sunday Bulletin*, May 21, 1972.

15. George L. Mosse, *The Reformation* (New York, 1963), 57–80; Billington, *Protestant Crusade*, 1–48; Rischin, *Promised City*, 222.

16. *Hartford Courant*, July 21, August 2, 11, 17, 1911.

17. *Providence Bulletin*, January 29, 1912; *Hartford Courant*, January 22, March 1, 1913; Connecticut, *Senate Journal, 1913*, 59, 87–88, 276, 1375; *1917*, 154, 198, 233; *1919*, 134.

18. *Providence Bulletin*, April 18, 1910; February 29, March 13, 1912.

19. *Providence Bulletin*, January 28, February 25, April 2, 8, 1913; April 14, 1914; January 8, 1915; April 18, 1917; April 5, 20, 1918.

20. *Providence Bulletin*, March 7, 11, 20, 1913; April 9, 15, 1914; April 5, 1917.

21. *New York Times*, March 28, 31, May 4, 1913.

22. *New York Times*, January 21, 1916; March 20, 27, April 4, 5, 1918; January 15, 1920; Ohio, *House Journal, 1911*, 382; Ohio, *Senate Journal, 1911*, 184; Massachusetts, *House Journal, 1911*, 725–731; *1914*, 584–586, 945.

23. Handlin, *Uprooted*, 251; Zink, *City Bosses*, 11, 115, 129, 147–148.

24. Illinois, *House Journal, 1909*, 831; Illinois, *Senate Journal, 1909*, 1127; *Illinois State Journal*, January 7, 1919; Ohio, *Senate Journal, 1911*, 385; Connecticut, *Senate Journal, 1913*, 147, 979; *1917*, 198; *Providence Bulletin*, January 11, March 22, 1912; February 5, April 15, 1913; February 11, 1915; *New York Times*, January 15, 1913; March 26, 1914; February 2, 3, 5, 6, 8, March 21, 28, April 19, May 2, 11, 1917; March 25, 1920.

25. Kleppner, *Cross of Culture* 77–79, 167–172; *Providence Bulletin*, January 13, 1909; April 4, 1913; Handlin, *American People*, 121. Jonathan Kozol, *Death at an Early Age* (Boston, 1967), makes the same point about the present school crisis.

26. Handlin, *Uprooted*, 246–247.

27. Billington, *Protestant Crusade*, 289–321; *New York Times*, March 15, 22, 1916; January 29, April 11, 1918; Charles Merriam, *Chicago: A More Intimate View of Urban Politics* (New York, 1929), 134–148.

28. *Illinois State Journal*, March 21, 1913; *Illinois State Register*, March 16, 1911; Illinois, *House Journal, 1909*, 677, 967, 1029, 1064; Wayman, *David I. Walsh*, 53–54; Massachusetts, *House Journal, 1914*, 104, 839, 934–936, 1369–1373.

29. A. D. Van Nostrand, "The Lomasney Legend," *New England Quarterly* 21 (December, 1948): 435–458; Wayman, *David I. Walsh*, 97; Bridgman, *Constitutional Convention*, 22–39; Hennessy, *Four Decades*, 357, 483.

30. Higham, *Strangers in the Land*, 131–263; Jones, *American Immigration*, 247–278; Perkins, *Roosevelt*, 13; Viorst, *Fall from Grace*, 132–133.

31. Massachusetts, *House Journal, 1914*, 584–586, 945; *Providence Bulletin*, March 8, 1912; February 3, 11, 1913; January 21, 1915.

32. Handlin, *American People*, 121–148; Robert K. Murray, *The Red Scare: A Study in National Hysteria, 1919–1920* (New York, 1964), passim.

33. *Providence Bulletin*, April 4, 1913; April 3, 19, 1917; April 5, 1918.

34. Ohio, *House Journal, 1919*, 99, 437, 456–457, 816, 854, 897, 1018; Ohio, *Senate Journal, 1919*, 47, 153, 332, 281, 418, 664.

35. Huthmacher, *Senator Wagner*, 40–44; Handlin, *Al Smith*, 110; Ellis et al., *Short History*, 398–399; Rischin, *Promised City*, 265; *New York Times*, March 11, 12, 1913; January 18, 21, March 8, 16, 1917; April 11, 1918.

36. Handlin, *Al Smith*, 82–83; Ellis et al., *Short History*, 393; *New York Times*, January 10, 11, 13, February 3, 13, 24, March 31, 1920.

37. Sullivan, *Dunne*, 533–534, 555, 563, 634, 717, 755.

38. Sullivan, *Dunne*, 477–480, 727.

39. Gusfield, *Symbolic Crusade*, 5–8.

40. Sinclair, *Era of Excess*, 65, 97; *Illinois State Journal*, April 5, 1909; April 11, 25, 1915. Timberlake, *Prohibition*, 4–124, provides an excellent summary of the arguments in favor of Prohibition.

41. Walburg, "Question of Nationality," 118; Dunne, *History*, 371; *Illinois State Journal*, January 9, 1919. Timberlake, *Prohibition*, 119–121, presents Prohibition convincingly as an anti-immigrant, anti-Negro movement.

42. Greeley, *Catholic Experience*, 233–234; Tarr, *Boss Politics*, 174–175; Jensen, "Religious and Occupational Roots," 331–333; Kertzer, *What Is a*

Jew? 38–40; *Illinois State Journal*, January 9, 1919; *New York Times*, January 24, 1919; Timberlake, *Prohibition*, 30–34.

43. Timberlake, *Prohibition*, 67–99.

44. Phillips, *Chicago and the Down State*, 45, 137; Merriam, *Chicago, More Intimate View*, 60; Gosnell, *Machine Politics*, 148; Allswang, *House for All Peoples*, 118–120.

45. Illinois, *Senate Journal, 1917*, 342; Illinois, *House Journal, 1917*, 462. For a fuller discussion see John D. Buenker, "The Illinois Legislature and Prohibition, 1907–1919," *Journal of the Illinois State Historical Society* 62 (Winter, 1969): 363–384.

46. Illinois, *Senate Journal, 1919*, 22; Illinois, *House Journal, 1919*, 30; *Illinois State Journal*, January 15, 1919.

47. *New York Times*, January 31, March 16, 23, 24, 1916; March 8, April 12, May 4, 8, 10, 1917; January 23, 24, 29, 30, 1919; March 31, 1920; New York, *Assembly Journal, 1919*, 122–123; New York, *Senate Journal, 1919*, 113; Peter H. Odegard, *Pressure Politics: The Story of the Anti-Saloon League* (New York, 1928), 122–123.

48. Hays, *Response to Industrialism*, 149; *Trenton Evening Times*, March 10, 1919; March 10, 1922; New Jersey, *Assembly Minutes, 1922*, 818; New Jersey, *Senate Journal, 1922*, 629.

49. Ohio, *Senate Journal, 1919*, 1016; Warner, *Progressivism in Ohio*, 11; Ohio, *House Journal, 1913*, 1142; *1915*, 1125; *1919*, 30, 476, 1082; Ohio, *Senate Journal, 1913*, 331; *1915*, 786; *1919*, 19, 529, 539.

50. Massachusetts, *House Journal, 1910*, 927–928, *1918*, 559–561; Timberlake, *Prohibition*, 167–169; *Boston Globe*, March 27, April 2, 1918; Massachusetts, *Senate Journal, 1918*, 511.

51. *Providence Bulletin*, March 31, 1910; April 9, 1913; January 14, February 26, April 23, 1915; February 22, March 13, 1918; February 2, April 4, 17, 23, 1919.

52. *Hartford Courant*, February 12, 1919; Connecticut, *Senate Journal, 1917*, 149–150, 1172–1174, 1294; *1919*, 326–327; Connecticut, *House Journal, 1919*, 341, 389, 1190.

53. Huthmacher, *Massachusetts People*, 142.

54. Hofstadter, *Age of Reform*, 289; Timberlake, *Prohibition*, 2.

55. Huthmacher, *Massachusetts People*, 65; Curley, *I'd Do It Again*, 147.

56. For the cultural struggles of the 1920s and their political significance see Huthmacher, *Massachusetts People*; Allswang, *House for All Nations*; and Burner, *Politics of Provincialism*.

CHAPTER 6

1. See, for example, the "debate" between John Higham and Oscar Handlin in *The Progressive Era: Liberal Renaissance or Liberal Failure?* Arthur Mann, ed. (New York, 1963), 48–57.

2. John D. Hicks, *The Populist Revolt: A History of the Farmers' Alliance and the People's Party* (Minneapolis, 1931), 404–432; Wayne E. Fuller, "The Rural Roots of the Progressive Leaders," *Agricultural History* 42 (1968): 1–13.

3. Mowry, *California Progressives*, 86–104; Alfred D. Chandler, Jr., "The Origins of Progressive Leadership," in *The Letters of Theodore Roosevelt*, Vol. 8, Appendix III, Elting E. Morison, ed. (Cambridge, Mass., 1954).

4. Arthur Mann, *Yankee Reformers in the Urban Age* (Cambridge, Mass., 1954), 242; Robert H. Wiebe, *The Search for Order, 1877–1920* (New York, 1967), 133–195; Mowry, *California Progressives*, 86–104; Hofstadter, *Age of Reform*, 131–173.

5. Hays, "Politics of Reform," 157–169; Robert H. Wiebe, *Businessmen and Reform* (Cambridge, Mass., 1962), 206–225; Kolko, *Triumph of Conservatism*, 1–6.

6. Hofstadter, *Age of Reform*, 174–186.

7. Hofstadter, *Age of Reform*, 184–186; Freidel, *Roosevelt*, 120; Abrams, *Conservatism*, 132–133; Hays, *Response to Industrialism*, 149. Compare Hofstadter's view with that of immigrant political attitudes found in Jones, *American Immigration*, 230–246.

8. Warner, *Progressivism in Ohio*, 9, 224–238, 265–284, 386–435; Link, *Road to the White House*, 287; Crooks, *Politics and Progress*, 77, 121.

9. J. Joseph Huthmacher, "Urban Liberalism and the Age of Reform," *Mississippi Valley Historical Review* 44 (September, 1962): 321–341.

10. Huthmacher, *Senator Wagner*, 3–37; "Hughes and Murphy," 25–40; Weiss, *Charles Francis Murphy*, 69–91; Holli, *Reform in Detroit*, 33–184; Glaab and Brown, *Urban America*, 201–229; Rogin and Shover, *Political Change in California*, 55–85; Blum, *Joe Tumulty*, 1–37; Vecoli, *People of New Jersey*, 168.

11. Huthmacher, "Urban Liberalism," 231–241.

12. Perkins, *Roosevelt*, 14; Handlin, *Uprooted*, 221–226.

13. The reference to Hughes is from the *New York Times*, June 4, 1913.

14. Handlin, *Al Smith*, 190.

15. Van Nostrand, "Lomasney Legend," 437; Rogin and Shover, *Political Change in California*, 55–85.

16. Robert S. Binkerd, "Reminiscences," *Oral History Research Office* (1949): 59; Perkins, *Roosevelt*, 9–26.

17. Howe, *Confessions of a Reformer*, 109–115; Whitlock, *Forty Years*, 202–205, 296–297.

18. John Bartlett, *The Shorter Bartlett's Familiar Quotations* (New York, 1953), 132; Marcus Lee Hansen, *The Immigrant in American History* (New York, 1964). The theme of the conflict between the ethic of the middle class American intellectual and that of the white ethnic working class is developed fully in Michael Novak, *The Rise of the Unmeltable Ethnics* (New York, 1972), especially pp. 35–115, 135–166, 196–236. See also Lucy Dawidowicz and Leon Goldstein, *Politics in a Pluralistic Society* (New York, 1963), 91–92; and Milton M. Gordon, *Assimilation in American Life: The Role of Race, Religion and National Origins* (New York, 1964), 224–232.

19. Edwin Rozwenc, "The Progressive Era," in *Main Problems in American History*, Vol. 2, Howard Quint, Dean Albertson, and Milton Cantor, eds. (Homewood, Ill., 1968), 175.

20. Novak, *Unmeltable Ethnics*, 72–115, 135–236; Baltzell, *Protestant Establishment*, 49–52.

21. Hofstadter, *Age of Reform*, 9, 178–185; Garrett, *La Guardia Years*, 3–44.

22. Hofstadter, *Age of Reform*, 12–22, 269–271; Garrett, *La Guardia Years*, 20; Novak, *Unmeltable Ethnics*, 7, 99–100.

23. The works of Hofstadter, Hays, Kolko, and others referred to above clearly call many of the results of the reform tradition into question.

24. Benjamin Parke De Witt, *The Progressive Movement* (New York, 1915), 4–5; Michael Paul Rogin, "Progressivism and the California Electorate," *Journal of American History* 55 (September, 1968): 308–310.

25. The best analysis of the inadequacy of the concept of a progressive movement is Peter Filene, "An Obituary for the 'Progressive Movement,' " *American Quarterly* 22 (1970): 20–34.

26. Richard B. Sherman, "The Status Revolution and Massachusetts Progressive Leadership," *Political Science Quarterly* 78 (March, 1963): 55–70; Jack Tager, "Progressives, Conservatives, and the Theory of the Status Revolution," *Mid-America* 48 (July, 1966): 162–173; E. Daniel Potts, "The Progressive Profile in Iowa," *Mid-America* 47 (1965): 257–268; David P. Thelen, "Social Tensions and the Origins of Progressivism," *The Journal of American History* 56 (September, 1969): 323–341; William T. Kerr, Jr., "The Progressives of Washington, 1910–1912," *Pacific Northwest Quarterly* 55 (1964): 16–27; Gleason, *Conservative Reformers*; Howard Quint, "Political Socialism: The Light That Failed," in *Main Problems*, Quint, Albertson, and Cantor, eds., 209; Yellowitz, *Labor and Progressive Movement*; Hays, "Politics of Reform"; Wiebe, *Businessmen and Reform*; Fuller, "Rural Roots."

27. Filene, "Obituary for the 'Progressive Movement,' " 32. The variations on the movement theme have been sounded by John Braeman, "Seven Progressives," *Business History Review* 35 (Winter, 1961): 581–592; Sheldon Hackney, *Populism to Progressivism in Alabama* (Princeton, 1969), xii–xiii; Yellowitz, *Labor and Progressive Movement*, 2, 78, 112.

28. Arthur S. Link, "What Happened to the Progressive Movement in the 1920's?" *American Historical Review* 64 (July, 1959): 833–851; Huthmacher, "Urban Liberalism," 231–241; Thelen, "Social Tensions," 341; Thelen, *New Citizenship*, 288; Hackney, *Populism to Progressivism*, passim;

Carl Chrislock, *The Progressive Era in Minnesota* (Minneapolis, 1972), passim.

29. The idea of progressive reform as a response to industrialism was first developed by Samuel Hays in the book of that title. For an elaboration of the argument presented in the next several paragraphs see John D. Buenker, "The Progressive Era: A Search for a Synthesis," *Mid-America* 51 (July, 1969): 175–193.

30. Hays, *Response to Industrialism*, 48–70.

31. Novak, *Unmeltable Ethnics*, 257; Filene, "Obituary for the 'Progressive Movement,' " 33.

32. Rogin and Shover, *Political Change in California*, 83.

33. Hays, *Response to Industrialism*, 149; Cortez Ewing, *Congressional Elections, 1896–1944* (Norman, Okla., 1947), 53–60; *New York Times*, November 6, 1912.

34. Hays, *Response to Industrialism*, 149.

35. On Wilson's difficulties with urban political machines see John M. Blum, *Woodrow Wilson and the Politics of Morality* (Boston, 1956), 48–52, 58–63, 114–118.

36. Jerome M. Clubb and Howard W. Allen, "The Cities and the Election of 1928: Partisan Realignment?" *American Historical Review* 74 (April, 1969): 1205–1220.

37. Hofstadter, *Age of Reform*, 12–16, 131–173. For an earlier, near utopian version of the era's success see Vernon L. Parrington, *Main Currents in American Thought*, Vol. 3 (New York, 1930); and William Allen White, *The Old Order Changeth* (New York, 1910).

38. Link, "What Happened to the Progressive Movement?" 833–851. The shift from middle class to working class electoral support is clearly noted by Holli in *Reform in Detroit*, 125–156; Rogin and Shover, *Political Change in California*, 55–85; and Howe, *Confessions of a Reformer*, 109–115. The split between middle class and working class reformers over Prohibition is, as discussed in the previous chapter, central to Timberlake's thesis in *Prohibition*, especially p. 167.

39. For a discussion of the disruptive effects of the treaty fight on the

progressive coalition in Massachusetts, see Huthmacher, *Massachusetts People*, 19–47. See also Burner, *Politics of Provincialism*, 57–73; and Handlin, *Al Smith*, 133.

40. The subject of the changing impressions of the urban political machine and its functions is presented by several selections in Bruce M. Stave, *Urban Bosses, Machines, and Progressive Reformers* (Boston, 1972); and Blaine E. Brownell and Warren E. Stickle, *Bosses and Reformers* (Boston, 1973).

41. The newer view presented here is a composite of those of Merton, *Social Theory*, 71–82; Cornwell, "Bosses, Machines, and Ethnic Groups," 24–30; McKitrick, "Study of Corruption," 502–514; Glaab and Brown, *Urban America*, 207–223; Mandelbaum, *Boss Tweed*, 46–58; Callow, *Tweed Ring*, 48–90; and Joel A. Tarr, "The Urban Politician as Entrepreneur," *Mid-America* 49 (January, 1967): 55–67. The observations about the boss as an "unspecialized professional" are those of Monte Calvert, "Technical Decision-making in a Political Context: The American City, 1880–1925," in a paper presented to the Conference on Social Science Concepts in American Political History held at the State University College at Brockport, New York, October 25, 1969, and reprinted in Stave, *Urban Bosses*, 45–55.

42. See especially Merton, *Social Theory*, 71–82; and Cornwell, "Bosses, Machines, and Ethnic Groups," 24–30.

43. Link, "What Happened to the Progressive Movement?" 841–851; Handlin, *Al Smith*, 90–111; Huthmacher, *Massachusetts People*; Stedman and Stedman, "Rise of Democratic Party," 329–339.

44. Rogin and Shover, *Political Change in California*, 75–120; Huthmacher, *Senator Wagner*, 38–106; Arthur Mann, *La Guardia: A Fighter against His Times* (Philadelphia, 1959), 181–231; William Leuchtenberg, *The Perils of Prosperity, 1914–32* (Chicago, 1958), 137.

45. Rogin and Shover, *Political Change in California*, 55–56.

46. Hofstadter, *Age of Reform*, 302–328.

47. Hofstadter, *Age of Reform*, 303; Otis L. Graham, Jr., *An Encore for Reform: The Old Progressives and the New Deal* (New York, 1968), 187–212.

48. Huthmacher, *Senator Wagner*, 107–280; Walter Townsend, *Illinois Democracy*, Vol. 2 (Springfield, 1935), 6–8.

49. Lubell, *Future of American Politics*, 43–68; Hofstadter, *Age of Reform*, 185; Rogin and Shover, *Political Change in California*, 55–145.

50. Hofstadter, *Age of Reform*, 302–318.

51. Phillips, *Emerging Republican Majority*, 43–187; Richard M. Scammon and Ben J. Wattenberg, *The Real Majority* (New York, 1970), 25–84; Frederick G. Dutton, *Changing Sources of Power: American Politics in the 1970's* (New York, 1971), 15–71; Novak, *Unmeltable Ethnics*, 237–291.

52. *Washington Post*, October 9, 10, 1972.

53. Darrett B. Rutman, *The Morning of America, 1603–1789* (Boston, 1971), 227.

BIBLIOGRAPHY

Documents and Official Publications

The Commonwealth of Massachusetts. *Manual for the Use of the General Court. 1910–1913.*

Connecticut, General Assembly. *House Journal. 1911, 1913, 1920.*

Connecticut, General Assembly. *Register and Manual. 1911, 1913, 1915.*

Connecticut, General Assembly. *Senate Journal. 1909, 1911, 1913, 1915, 1917, 1919, 1920.*

Ely, Richard T. "Report of the Organization of the American Economic Association." *Publications of the American Economic Association* 1 (1886).

Illinois, General Assembly. *House Journal. 1909–1913, 1915, 1917, 1919.*

Illinois, General Assembly. *Laws of the State of Illinois. 1913, 1915.*

Illinois, General Assembly. *Senate Journal. 1909–1913, 1915, 1917, 1919.*

Illinois, Secretary of State. *Blue Book of the State of Illinois.* Danville, Ill., 1911, 1913, 1917.

Massachusetts Constitutional Convention. *Debates in the Massachusetts Constitutional Convention, 1917–1918.* Boston, 1919.

Massachusetts Constitutional Convention. *Journal of the Constitutional Convention of the Commonwealth of Massachusetts, 1917.* Boston, 1917.

Massachusetts, General Court. *House Journal. 1909–1918.*

Massachusetts, General Court. *Senate Journal. 1910–1912, 1914, 1915, 1918, 1919.*

Massachusetts Institute of Technology, Division of Industrial and Municipal Research. *Industrial Survey of Metropolitan Providence for the Year 1926.* Cambridge, Mass., 1928.

Mercer, James K. *Ohio Legislative History, 1909–1913, 1913–1917.* Columbus, 1913, 1917.

Murlin, Edgar J. *The New York Red Book*. Albany, 1913.

National American Woman Suffrage Assocation, ed. *Victory: How Women Won It, A Centennial Symposium, 1840–1940*. New York, 1940.

New Jersey, Legislature. *Assembly Minutes. 1907–1913, 1920, 1922*.

New Jersey, Legislature, *Legislative Manual of New Jersey, 1913*. Trenton, 1913.

New Jersey, Senate. *Senate Journal. 1913, 1920, 1922*.

New York, Legislature, *Assembly Journal. 1910, 1911, 1913*.

New York, Legislature, *Senate Journal. 1910, 1911, 1913*.

Ohio, General Assembly. *House Journal. 1911, 1913–1915, 1917, 1919*.

Ohio, General Assembly. *Senate Journal. 1911, 1913–1915, 1917, 1919*.

Parker, J. Fred, comp. *Manual with Rules and Orders, for the Use of the General Assembly of the State of Rhode Island*. Providence, 1913.

Rhode Island Bureau of Industrial Statistics. *Some Nativity and Race Factors in Rhode Island*. Providence, 1910.

Root, Elihu. *The Proposed Income Tax Amendment*. U.S. Congress, 61st Cong., 2nd sess., 1910. Senate Document 398.

U.S. Bureau of the Census, *Abstract of the Thirteenth Census of the United States, 1910*.

U.S. Congress, *Congressional Record*, 62nd Cong., 2nd sess., 1911, Appendix 161.

Newspapers

Albany Evening Journal. 1910, 1911, 1913, 1914.

Boston Daily Globe. 1912, 1918.

Chicago Daily News. 1913, 1915.

Chicago Journal. 1913.

Chicago Tribune. 1910, 1912, 1914.

Harrisburg Patriot. 1913, 1915.

Hartford Courant. 1911, 1913, 1919.

Hartford Times. 1911.

Illinois State Journal (Springfield). 1909, 1911, 1913–1915, 1919.

Illinois State Register (Springfield). 1909–1913, 1915.

New York Times. 1910, 1913–1920.

New York World. 1910.
Newark Evening News. 1913.
Ohio State Journal (Columbus). 1911.
Providence Evening Bulletin. 1909–1919.
Providence Daily Journal. 1909–1920.
Racine Sunday Bulletin. 1972.
Trenton Evening/Times. 1919, 1922.
Washington Post, 1972.

Articles and Periodicals

Abrams, Richard. "Paradox of Progressivism: Massachusetts on the Eve of Insurgency." *Political Science Quarterly*, September, 1960. pp. 378–392.

Addams, Jane. "Why the Ward Boss Rules." *The Outlook* 58 (April 2, 1898): 879–882.

Binkerd, Robert S. "Reminiscences." *Oral History Research Office.* 1949.

Braeman, John. "Seven Progressives." *Business History Review* 35 (Winter, 1961): 581–592.

Brown, H. La Rue. "Massachusetts and the Minimum Wage." *Annals of the American Academy of Political and Social Science* 48 (July, 1913): 13–21.

Buenker, John D. "Cleveland's New Stock Lawmakers and Progressive Reform." *Ohio History* 78 (Spring, 1969): 116–137.

Buenker, John D. "Edward F. Dunne: The Urban New Stock Democrat as Progressive." *Mid-America* 50 (January, 1968): 3–21.

Buenker, John D. "The Illinois Legislature and Prohibition, 1907–1919." *Journal of the Illinois State Historical Society* 62 (Winter, 1969): 363–384.

Buenker, John D. "The Mahatma and Progressive Reform: Martin Lomasney as Lawmaker, 1911–1917." *New England Quarterly*, September, 1971. pp. 397–419.

Buenker, John D. "The Progressive Era: A Search for a Synthesis." *Mid-America* 51 (July, 1969): 175–193.

Buenker, John D. "Progressivism in Connecticut: The Thrust of the Urban, New Stock Democrats." *The Connecticut Historical Society Bulletin* 35 (October, 1970): 97–109.

Buenker, John D. "Progressivism in Practice: New York State and the Federal Income Tax Amendment." *The New York Historical Society Quarterly* 52 (April, 1968): 139–160.

Buenker, John D. "The Rise of Urban Liberalism in Rhode Island, 1909–1919." *Rhode Island History*, Spring, 1971. pp. 35–51.

Buenker, John D. "Urban Immigrant Lawmakers and Progressive Reform in Illinois." In *Essays in Illinois History*, edited by Donald F. Tingley. Carbondale, Ill., 1968. pp. 52–74.

Buenker, John D. "Urban Liberalism and the Federal Income Tax Amendment." *Pennsylvania History* 36 (April, 1969): 192–215.

Buenker, John D. "Urban, New Stock Liberalism and Progressive Reform in New Jersey." *New Jersey History* 87 (Summer, 1969): 79–104.

Buenker, John D. "The Urban Political Machine and the Seventeenth Amendment." *Journal of American History* 56 (September, 1969): 305–322.

Buenker, John D. "The Urban Political Machine and Woman Suffrage: A Study in Political Adaptability." *The Historian* 33 (February, 1971): 264–279.

Clubb, Jerome M., and Allen, Howard W. "The Cities and the Election of 1928: Partisan Realignment?" *American Historical Review* 74 (April, 1969): 1205–1220.

Cornwell, Elmer E. "Bosses, Machines and Ethnic Groups." *Annals of the American Academy of Political and Social Science* 353 (May, 1964): 27–39.

Cornwell, Elmer E. "Party Absorption of Ethnic Groups: The Case of Providence, Rhode Island." *Social Forces* 38 (March, 1960): 205–210.

Cornwell, Elmer E. "A Note on Providence Politics in the Age of Bryan." *Rhode Island History* 19 (April, 1960): 33–40.

Eastman, Joseph B. "The Public Service Commission of Massachusetts." *Quarterly Journal of Economics* 27 (August, 1913): 699–707.

Filene, Peter. "An Obituary for the 'Progressive Movement.'" *American Quarterly* 22 (1970): 20–34.

Ford, Henry Jones. "The Direct Primary." *North American Review* 190 (1909): 1–14.

Fordyce, Wellington G. "Nationality Groups in Cleveland Politics." *The Ohio State Archaeological and Historical Quarterly* 46 (1937): 120–131.

Foster, Mark. "Frank Hague of Jersey City: The Boss as Reformer." *New Jersey History* 85 (Summer, 1968): 106–117.

Fuller, Wayne E. "The Rural Roots of the Progressive Leaders." *Agricultural History* 42 (1968): 1–13.

Hays, Samuel P. "The Politics of Reform in Municipal Government in the Progressive Era." *Pacific Northwest Quarterly* 55 (October, 1964): 157–169.

Huthmacher, J. Joseph. "Charles Evans Hughes and Charles Francis Murphy: The Metamorphosis of Progressivism." *New York History* 46 (January, 1965): 25–40.

Huthmacher, J. Joseph. "Urban Liberalism and the Age of Reform." *Mississippi Valley Historical Review* 44 (September, 1962): 231–241.

Jensen, Richard. "The Religious and Occupational Roots of Party Identification: Illinois and Indiana in the 1870's." *Civil War History* 16 (December, 1970): 325–343.

Jones, Chester. "The Rotten Boroughs of New England." *North American Review* 97 (April, 1913): 485–497.

Kenneally, James J. "Catholics and Woman Suffrage in Massachusetts." *Catholic Historical Review* 53 (April, 1967): 43–57.

Kerr, William T., Jr. "The Progressives of Washington, 1910–1912." *Pacific Northwest Quarterly* 55 (1964): 16–27.

Link, Arthur S. "What Happened to the Progressive Movement in the 1920's?" *American Historical Review* 64 (July, 1959): 833–851.

McKitrick, Eric. "The Study of Corruption." *Political Science Quarterly* 72 (December, 1957): 502–514.

McSeveney, Samuel T. "Voting in the Northeastern States during the Late Nineteenth Century." A paper read before the University of Wisconsin Political and Social History Conference, 1968.

Potts, E. Daniel. "The Progressive Profile in Iowa." *Mid-America* 47 (1965): 257–268.

Rogin, Michael Paul. "Progressivism and the California Electorate." *Journal of American History* 55 (September, 1968): 297–314.

Schaeffer, Joseph. "Who Elected Lincoln?" *The American Historical Review* 47 (October, 1941): 51–63.

Scott, James. "Corruption, Machine Politics and Political Change." *American Political Science Review*, December, 1969. pp. 1142–1158.

Sherman, Richard B. "Charles Sumner Bird and the Progressive Party in Massachusetts." *New England Quarterly* 33 (September, 1960): 325–340.

Sherman, Richard B. "Foss of Massachusetts: Demagogue vs. Progressive." *Mid-America* 43 (April, 1961): 75–94.

Sherman, Richard B. "The Status Revolution and Massachusetts Progressive Leadership." *Political Science Quarterly* 78 (March, 1963): 59–65.

Stedman, Murray S., and Stedman, Susan W. "The Rise of the Democratic Party of Rhode Island." *New England Quarterly* 24 (September, 1951): 329–341.

Tager, Jack. "Progressives, Conservatives, and the Theory of the Status Revolution." *Mid-America* 48 (July, 1966): 162–173.

Tarr, Joel A. "The Urban Politician as Entrepreneur." *Mid-America* 49 (January, 1967): 55–67.

Thelen, David P. "Social Tensions and the Origins of Progressivism." *The Journal of American History* 56 (September, 1969): 323–341.

Van Nostrand, A. D. "The Lomasney Legend." *New England Quarterly* 21 (December, 1948): 435–458.

Walburg, Anton. "The Question of Nationality." In *The Church and the City*, edited by Robert Cross. Indianapolis, 1967.

Walsh, David I. "Labor in Politics: Its Political Influence in New England." *Forum*, August, 1915. pp. 210–218.

Weinstein, James. "Organized Business and the City Commissioner and Manager Movements." *Journal of Southern History* 28 (1962): 166–182.

Wolfinger, Raymond. "The Development and Persistence of Ethnic Voting." In *American Ethnic Politics*, edited by Lawrence H. Fuchs. New York, 1968. pp. 165–193.

Books

Abell, Aaron I., ed. *American Catholic Thought on Social Questions.* Indianapolis, 1968.

Abrams, Richard M. *Conservatism in a Progressive Era.* Cambridge, Mass., 1964.

Ainley, Leslie. *Boston Mahatma: The Public Career of Martin Lomasney.* Boston, 1949.

Allswang, John M. *A House for All Peoples: Chicago's Ethnic Groups and Their Politics, 1890–1936.* Lexington, Ky., 1971.

Baltzell, E. Digby. *The Protestant Establishment.* New York, 1964.

Barron, Milton, ed. *Minorities in a Changing World.* New York, 1967.

Bartlett, John. *The Shorter Bartlett's Familiar Quotations.* New York, 1953.

Bean, Walton. *Boss Ruef's San Francisco.* Berkeley, 1952.

Beckner, Earl. *A History of Illinois Labor Legislation.* Chicago, 1929.

Benson, Lee. *The Concept of Jacksonian Democracy: New York as a Test Case.* Princeton, 1961.

Benson, Lee. *Merchants, Farmers, and Railroads: Railroad Regulation and New York Politics, 1850–1887.* Cambridge, Mass., 1955.

Billington, Ray Allen. *The Protestant Crusade, 1800–1860: A Study of the Origins of American Nativism.* Chicago, 1964.

Blum John M. *Joe Tumulty and the Wilson Era.* Boston, 1951.

Blum, John M. *Woodrow Wilson and the Poltics of Morality.* Boston, 1956.

Bowden, Robert. *Boies Penrose.* New York, 1937.

Bridgman, Raymond L. *The Massachusetts Constitutional Convention of 1917.* Boston, 1923.

Brinton, Crane. *Anatomy of a Revolution.* New York, 1965.

Brooks, Thomas R. *Toil and Trouble.* New York, 1964.

Brownell, Blaine A., and Stickle, Warren E. *Bosses and Reformers.* Boston, 1973.

Burner, David, *The Politics of Provincialism: The Democratic Party in Transition, 1918–1932.* New York, 1968.

Burns, James MacGregor. *Roosevelt: The Lion and the Fox.* New York, 1956.

Caine, Stanley P. *The Myth of a Progressive Reform: Railroad Regulation in Wisconsin, 1903–1910.* Madison, 1970.

Callow, Alexander B., Jr. *The Tweed Ring.* New York, 1966.

Catt, Carrie Chapman, and Shuler, Nettie Rogers. *Woman Suffrage and Politics: The Inner Story of the Suffrage Movement.* Seattle, 1969.

Chambers, Clarke A., *Seedtime of Reform: American Social Service and Social Action, 1918–1933.* Minneapolis, 1963.

Chrislock, Carl. *The Progressive Era in Minnesota.* Minneapolis, 1972.

Cooke, Edward F., and Janosik, G. Edward. *Guide to Pennsylvania Politics.* New York, 1957.

Crooks, James L. *Politics and Progress: The Rise of Urban Progressivism in Baltimore, 1895–1911.* Baton Rouge, 1968.

Cross, Robert D. *The Emergence of Liberal Catholicism in America.* Cambridge, Mass., 1967.

Curley, James Michael. *I'd Do It Again*. Englewood Cliffs, N.J., 1957.

Dahl, Robert A. *Who Governs? Democracy and Power in an American City*. New Haven, 1961.

Dawidowicz, Lucy, and Goldstein, Leon. *Politics in a Pluralistic Society*. New York, 1963.

De Witt, Benjamin Parke. *The Progressive Movement*. New York, 1915.

Dineen, Joseph. *The Purple Shamrock*. New York, 1949.

Dorsett, Lyle. *The Pendergast Machine*. New York, 1968.

Dunaway, Wayland. *History of Pennsylvania*. Englewood Cliffs, N.J., 1945.

Dunbar, Willis Frederick. *Michigan: A History of the Wolverine State*. Grand Rapids, 1965.

Dunne, Edward F. *History of Illinois*. Chicago, 1933.

Dutton, Frederick G. *Changing Sources of Power: American Politics in the 1970's*. New York, 1971.

East, John Porter. *Council-Manager Government: The Political Thought of Its Founder, Richard Childs*. Chapel Hill, N.C., 1965.

Eisenstein, Louis, and Rosenberg, Elliott. *A Stripe of Tammany's Tiger*. New York, 1966.

Ellis, David M.; Frost, James A.; Syrett, Harold C.; and Carman, Harry J. *A Short History of New York State*. Ithaca, 1957.

Ellis, John Tracy. *American Catholicism*. Chicago, 1969.

Ewing, Cortez. *Congressional Elections, 1896–1944*. Norman, Okla., 1947.

Fenton, John H. *Politics in the Border States*. New Orleans, 1957.

Fine, Sidney. *Laissez-Faire and the General-Welfare State: A Study of Conflict in American Thought*. Ann Arbor, 1966.

Finkelstein, Louis, ed. *The Jews: Their Religion and Culture*. New York, 1971.

Flexner, Eleanor. *Century of Struggle*. Cambridge, Mass., 1959.

Flynn, Edward. *You're the Boss*. New York, 1947.

Ford, Henry Jones. *Rise and Growth of American Politics*. New York, 1911.

Forthal, Sonya. *Cogwheels of Democracy: A Study of the Precinct Captain*. New York, 1946.

Freidel, Frank. *Franklin D. Roosevelt: The Apprenticeship*. Boston, 1952.

Gargan, Edward T. *Leo XIII and the Modern World*. New York, 1961.

Garrett, Charles. *The La Guardia Years*. New Brunswick, N.J., 1961.

Glaab, Charles, and Brown, A. Theordore. *A History of Urban America*. New York, 1967.

Glazer, Nathan. *American Judaism*. Chicago, 1957.

Glazer, Nathan, and Moynihan, Daniel P. *Beyond the Melting Pot*. Cambridge, Mass., 1970.

Gleason, Philip. *The Conservative Reformers: German-American Catholics and the Social Order*. South Bend, Ind., 1968.

Gleason, Philip. *Catholicism in America*. New York, 1970.

Gordon, Milton M. *Assimilation in American Life: The Role of Race, Religion and National Origins*. New York, 1964.

Gosnell, Harold F. *Boss Platt and His New York Machine*. New York, 1933.

Gosnell, Harold F. *Machine Politics: Chicago Model*. Chicago, 1968.

Gottfried, Alex. *Boss Cermak of Chicago: A Study of Political Leadership*. Seattle, 1962.

Graham, Otis L., Jr. *An Encore for Reform: The Old Progressives and the New Deal*. New York, 1968.

Greeley, Andrew. *The Catholic Experience: An Interpretation of the History of American Catholicism*. New York, 1969.

Green, R. W., ed. *Protestantism and Capitalism: The Weber Thesis and Its Critics*. New York, 1959.

Grimes, Alan P. *The Puritan Ethic and Woman Suffrage*. Princeton, 1967.

Gusfield, Joseph R. *Symbolic Crusade: Status Politics and the American Temperance Movement*. Urbana, Ill., 1966.

Hackney, Sheldon. *Populism to Progressivism in Alabama*. Princeton, 1969.

Handlin, Oscar. *Al Smith and His America*. Boston, 1958.

Handlin, Oscar. *The American People in the Twentieth Century*. Cambridge, Mass., 1966.

Handlin, Oscar. *The Uprooted*. New York, 1951.

Handlin, Oscar, ed. *Immigration as a Factor in American History*. Englewood Cliffs, N.J., 1959.

Hansen, Marcus Lee. *The Atlantic Migration, 1607–1860*. New York, 1961.

Hansen, Marcus Lee. *The Immigrant in American History*. New York, 1964.

Harrison, Carter, Jr. *Stormy Years*. Indianapolis, 1935.

Hays, Samuel P. *Response to Industrialism, 1885–1914*. Chicago, 1957.

Hennessy, Michael E. *Four Decades of Massachusetts Politics, 1890–1935*. Norwood, Mass., 1935.

Herberg, Will. *Protestant, Catholic, Jew: An Essay in American Religious Sociology*. Garden City, N.Y., 1960.

Hertzberg, Arthur, ed. *Judaism*. New York, 1962.

Hicks, John D. *The Populist Revolt: A History of the Farmers' Alliance and the People's Party*. Minneapolis, 1931.

Higham, John. *Strangers in the Land: Patterns of American Nativism, 1860–1925*. New York, 1955.

Hofstadter, Richard. *The Age of Reform*. New York, 1955.

Holli, Melvin G. *Reform in Detroit*. New York, 1969.

Hollingshead, August, and Redlich, Frederich C. *Social Class and Mental Illness*. New York, 1958.

Howe, Frederic C. *Confessions of a Reformer*. New York, 1925.

Huthmacher, J. Joseph. *Massachusetts People and Politics, 1919–1933*. New York, 1969.

Huthmacher, J. Joseph. *Senator Robert F. Wagner and the Rise of Urban Liberalism*. New York, 1968.

Huthmacher, J. Joseph. *Twentieth Century America*. Boston, 1966.

Jones, Maldwyn A. *American Immigration*. Chicago, 1965.

Kaplan, Mordecai M. *Judaism as a Civilization: Toward a Reconstruction of American Jewish Life*. New York, 1967.

Karson, Marc. *American Labor Unions and Politics, 1900–1918*. Carbondale, Ill., 1958.

Kennedy, David M., ed. *Progressivism: The Critical Issues*. Boston, 1971.

Kertzer, Morris. *What Is a Jew?* Cleveland, 1960.

Kleppner, Paul. *The Cross of Culture*. New York, 1970.

Krout, John A. *The Origins of Prohibition*. New York, 1967.

Kolko, Gabriel. *Railroads and Regulation, 1877–1916*. Princeton, 1965.

Kolko, Gabriel. *The Triumph of Conservatism*. New York, 1963.

Kozol, Jonathan. *Death at an Early Age*. Boston, 1967.

Kraditor, Aileen S. *The Ideas of the Woman Suffrage Movement*. New York, 1965.

Lane, Robert E. *Political Life: Why People Get Involved in Politics*. New York, 1959.

Leuchtenberg, William. *The Perils of Prosperity, 1914–32*. Chicago, 1958.

Levin, Murray B., and Blackwood, G. *The Compleat Politician*. Indianapolis, 1962.

Levine, Edward M. *The Irish and Irish Politicians*. Notre Dame, Ind., 1966.

Levine, Erwin. *Theodore Francis Green: The Rhode Island Years, 1906–1936*. Providence, 1963.

Lieberman, Joseph L. *The Power Broker*. Boston, 1966.

Link, Arthur S. *Wilson: The New Freedom*. Princeton, 1956.

Link, Arthur S. *Wilson: The Road to the White House*. Princeton, 1947.

Lockard, Duane. *New England State Politics*. Princeton, 1959.

Lubell, Samuel. *The Future of American Politics*. New York, 1965.

Lubove, Roy. *The Struggle for Social Security, 1900–1935*. Cambridge, Mass., 1968.

Luthin, Reinhard H. *American Demagogues: Twentieth Century*. Gloucester, Mass., 1959.

Luthin, Reinhard H. *The First Lincoln Campaign*. Cambridge, Mass., 1944.

McWilliams, Carey. *Brothers under the Skin*. Boston, 1964.

Mandelbaum, Seymour. *Boss Tweed's New York*. New York, 1965.

Mann, Arthur. *La Guardia: A Fighter against His Times*. Philadelphia, 1959.

Mann, Arthur, ed. *The Progressive Era: Liberal Renaissance or Liberal Failure?* New York, 1963.

Mann, Arthur. *Yankee Reformers in the Urban Age*. Cambridge, Mass., 1954.

Martin, Ralph G. *The Bosses*. New York, 1964.

Maxwell, Robert. *La Follette and the Rise of Progressivism in Wisconsin*. Madison, 1956.

Merriam, Charles. *Chicago: A More Intimate View of Urban Politics*. New York, 1929.

Merton, Robert K. *Social Theory and Social Structure*. New York, 1967.

Miller, George H. *Railroads and the Granger Laws*. Madison, 1970.

Miller, Zane L. *Boss Cox's Cincinnati: Urban Politics in the Progressive Era*. New York, 1968.

Moody, Joseph N., ed. *Catholic Social and Political Thought and Movements, 1789–1950*. New York, 1953.

Morison, Elting E., ed. *The Letters of Theodore Roosevelt*, Vol. 8. Appendix III. Cambridge, Mass., 1954.

Moscow, Warren. *What Have You Done for Me Lately?* Englewood Cliffs, N.J., 1967.

Mosse, George L. *The Reformation*. New York, 1963.

Mowry, George L. *The California Progressives*. Berkeley, 1951.

Mowry, George L. *The Era of Theodore Roosevelt, 1900–1912*. New York, 1958.

Murray, Robert K. *The Red Scare: A Study in National Hysteria, 1919–1920*. New York, 1964.

Nelli, Humbert S. *The Italians in Chicago, 1880–1930*. New York, 1970.

Noble, Ransom E. *New Jersey Progressivism before Wilson*. Princeton, 1946.

Novak, Michael. *The Rise of the Unmeltable Ethnics*. New York, 1972.

Odegard, Peter H. *Pressure Politics: The Story of the Anti-Saloon League*. New York, 1928.

Orth, Samuel P. *The Boss and the Machine*. New York, 1919.

Parrington, Vernon L. *Main Currents in American Thought*, Vol. 3. New York, 1930.

Patton, Clifford. *The Battle for Municipal Reform*. Washington, D.C., 1940.

Perkins, Frances. *The Roosevelt I Knew*. New York, 1946.

Phillips, Kevin. *The Emerging Republican Majority*. New Rochelle, N.Y., 1969.

Phillips, W. B. *Chicago and the Down State, 1870–1927*. New York, 1929.

Porter, Kirk H., and Johnson, Donald Bruce, eds. *National Party Platforms, 1840–1960*. Urbana, Ill., 1961.

Quaife, M. M., and Glazer, Sidney. *Michigan*. New York, 1948.

Quint, Howard; Alberton, Dean; and Cantor, Milton. *Main Problems in American History*, Vol. 2. Homewood, Ill., 1968.

Ratner, Sidney. *A Political and Social History of Federal Taxation*. New York, 1942.

Riordan, William. *Plunkitt of Tammany Hall*. New York, 1948.

Rischin, Moses. *The Promised City: New York's Jews, 1870–1914*. Cambridge, Mass., 1962.

Rogin, Michael P., and Shover, John L. *Political Change in California*. Westport, Conn., 1969.

Rozwenc, Edwin, ed. *Roosevelt, Wilson, and the Trusts*. Boston, 1950.

Rutman, Darret B. *The Morning of America, 1603–1789*. Boston, 1971.

Salter, John T. *The American Politician*. Chapel Hill, N.C., 1938.

Salter, John T. *Boss Rule: Portraits in City Politics*. New York, 1935.

Sarasohn, Stephen B., and Sarasohn, Vera H. *Political Party Patterns in Michigan*. Detroit, 1957.

Scammon, Richard M., and Wattenberg, Ben J. *The Real Majority*. New York, 1970.

Shannon, Fred A. *The Farmer's Last Frontier, 1860–1897*. New York, 1945.

Sinclair, Andrew. *The Better Half*. New York, 1965.

Sinclair, Andrew. *The Era of Excess: A Social History of the Prohibition Movement*. Boston, 1962.

Solomon, Barbara. *Ancestors and Immigrants: A Changing New England Tradition*. Cambridge, Mass., 1956.

Staley, Eugene. *History of the Illinois State Federation of Labor*. Chicago, 1930.

Stave, Bruce M. *Urban Bosses, Machines, and Progressive Reformers*. Boston, 1972.

Steffens, Lincoln. *The Autobiography of Lincoln Steffens*. New York, 1931.

Steffens, Lincoln. *The Upbuilders*. New York, 1909.

Stern, Philip. *The Great Treasury Raid*. New York, 1964.

Stinchcombe, Jean L. *Reform and Reaction: City Politics in Toledo*. Belmont, Calif., 1968.

Sullivan, William. *Dunne: Judge, Mayor, Governor*. Chicago, 1916.

Tager, Jack. *The Intellectual as Urban Reformer: Brand Whitlock and the Progressive Movement*. Cleveland, 1968.

Tanner, Earl C. *Introduction to the Economy of Rhode Island*. Providence, 1953.

Tarr, Joel A. *A Study in Boss Politics: William Lorimer of Chicago*. Urbana, Ill., 1971.

Thelen, David P. *The New Citizenship: Origins of Progressivism in Wisconsin, 1885–1900*. Columbia, Mo., 1972.

Thompson, Warren, and Whelpton, P. K. *Population Trends in the United States*. New York, 1933.

Timberlake, James H. *Prohibition and the Progressive Movement, 1900–1920*. New York, 1970.

Townsend, Walter. *Illinois Democracy*, Vol. 2. Springfield, Ill., 1935.

Vare, William S. *My Forty Years in Politics*. Philadelphia, 1933.

Vecoli, Rudolph. *The People of New Jersey*. Princeton, 1965.

Viorst, Milton. *Fall from Grace: The Republican Party and the Puritan Ethic*. New York, 1968.

Wallace, Lillian Parker. *Leo XIII and the Rise of Socialism.* Durham, N.C., 1966.

Warner, Hoyt L. *Progressivism in Ohio, 1897–1917.* Columbus, Ohio, 1964.

Wayman, D. G. *David I. Walsh, Citizen Patriot.* Milwaukee, 1952.

Weiss, Nancy Joan. *Charles Francis Murphy, 1858–1924: Respectability and Responsibility in Tammany Politics.* Northampton, Mass., 1968.

White, William Allen. *The Old Order Changeth.* New York, 1910.

Whitlock, Brand. *Forty Years of It.* New York, 1968.

Wiebe, Robert H. *Businessmen and Reform.* Cambridge, Mass., 1962.

Wiebe, Robert H. *The Search for Order, 1877–1920.* New York, 1967.

Wike, J. Roffe. *The Pennsylvania Manufacturers' Association.* Philadelphia, 1960.

Yearley, C. K. *The Money Machines.* Albany, 1970.

Yellowitz, Irwin. *Labor and the Progressive Movement in New York State, 1897–1916.* Ithaca, 1968.

Zink, Harold. *City Bosses in the United States.* Durham, N.C., 1931.

Index

Abolitionism, 168

Accidents, 72–73

Addams, Jane, 63, 157

Aldrich, Nelson, 16, 22, 102, 115, 153

Amelioration, politics of, 80–117

American Federation of Labor, 56, 59, 82, 83, 84, 89

Americanization, 198, 206, 227

Anti-Saloon League, 20, 26, 171–72, 186, 191, 192

Apportionment, 15, 137, 138, 151

Arbitration, compulsory, 88

Athletics, 177, 194

Baldwin, Simeon, 38, 116, 138

Ballot, Massachusetts, 146

Banking, laws, 98; regulation, 100

Barnes, William, 18, 51, 112, 142

Baseball, 175, 177

Bible, 179, 188

Blacklisting, 88, 90

Blue laws, 26, 28, 38, 172–78, 206

"Blue sky" law, 99

Bohemians, 9, 10

Bosses, 122, 156, 232; characters, 5; Democratic, 31; methods, 133; offended by Wilson, 223; old-line, 33; and reform, 29, 202; ward, 171, 211

Boss-machine-immigrant complex, 4, 201, 202

Boxing, 177, 178, 194

Brayton, Charles R., 16, 71, 102, 107, 110, 115, 132, 138, 141, 150, 153, 158

British, 6, 7, 163–64

Bryan, William Jennings, 7, 25, 84, 121, 231, 237

Business, 12–13; and competition, 214; and Democrats, 102–3; leaders, 27; public control, 99; regulation, 91–103, 201, 205, 226; rise of big, 200; small-town coalition, 134–35, 161; tactics, 91–92

California, 30, 199, 204, 216, 221, 234

Campaigns, contributions, 132

Catholics, 6, 7, 9, 10, 20, 30, 35, 45, 82, 164, 165, 169, 171, 172, 175, 179, 217, 237

Censorship, 180

Cermak, Anton, 10–11, 111, 143

Children, dependent, 76

Church, 46; hierarchy, 166

Cities, 2, 3, 21, 26, 69, 70; home rule, 135–39

City management system, 27

Civil service, 122, 126–27, 128

Classes, 27; and religion, 170; wage-earning, 135

Coalitions, 218–21, 226, 227

Codes, safety and health, 77

Commissioners, county, 147

Commissions, government by, 93, 94, 123, 124, 147; tax, 106

Compensation, workmen's, 51, 57, 68, 73

Conformity, 182–83

Connecticut, 13–14, 21, 38, 74–77, 81, 88, 97, 102–3, 108, 115–16, 128, 131–32, 137, 138, 140–41, 144–45, 150, 153, 159, 173–74, 178, 194

Conservatives, 236

Constitution, revision, 150–51

Constitutional convention, 149–51

Corporations, 98

Corruption, 27, 120, 133

Corrupt Practices Act (1911), 130

Coughlin, John, 157, 211

Cox, James M., 34, 56, 57, 59, 61, 90, 106

Curley, James M., 11, 85, 122, 123, 128, 160

Davis, Robert, 127, 143

Democracy, 215; social, 60–61

Democrats, Boston, 66–70; and boxing, 177–78; centrist, 236; Chicago, 60–61, 63–64, 96, 100–101, 105, 150–51; city organizations, 230; and civil service, 126; Cleveland, 58, 106; coalition, 37; composition, 236;

Connecticut, 38, 77, 147; and corrupt practices, 129; and cultural reform, 195; and direct election, 154–56; discredit of, 184; election, 23–24; ethnic party, 236; and government responsibility, 79; growth of party, 222; as hedonists, 171; Irish, 7, 21, 36; and labor, 22, 52–54, 84–91; 1910 landslide, 112–13, 114–15; liberalism and resurgence, 222; and machines, 223; minority party, 171; new stock, 1, 11–12, 24, 50, 77, 79, 81, 116–17, 166; New York, 145, 109; opponents of moralistic reform, 172; party of poor, 238; and Prohibition, 186; pro-union, 88; and reform and crime, 238; and regulatory measures, 93–103; revival, 202; Rhode Island, 146; ritualist, 171; and secession, 7; and Seventeenth Amendment, 156; and social legislation, 74, 77; success, 224; and tax, 109; upsurge in Northeast, 223; urban, 35, 138, 153, 155; and welfare, 50, 51; and woman suffrage, 158–61; and working conditions, 51, 67–70, 72–73; and workman's compensation, 73; and work week, 71–72

Deneen, Charles, 37, 65, 110, 143
Depression, 74
Dillon, Patrick, 39, 152, 153
Disadvantaged, 77–78
Disease, 72–73, 76
Dix, John, 37, 113
Donahue, Charles, 93, 98
Dunne, Edward F., 11, 32, 37, 60, 61, 62, 63, 64, 85, 86, 95, 96, 100, 105, 111, 126, 131, 140, 144, 150, 152, 155, 159, 185, 186, 187, 195, 233

Economy, and the states, 103
Education, 28, 69; and Protestant *Weltanschauung*, 212
Eighteenth Amendment, 13, 188, 189, 190, 191, 193, 194

Elections, 22, 23, 224; abuses, 130; alterations, 145; biennial, 148; city-wide, 120, 122; direct, 120, 152, 154; national, 146–47; 1914, 149; popular, 135; primary, 120; by ward, 123
Elective office, 120
Employment, 3, 4; agencies, 49; minimum age, 55
Enterprise, large-scale, 219
Ethnic groups, 5, 6, 82, 190, 236; and history, 212; and public schools, 194; unpopularity, 185

Fagan, Mark, 28, 30, 31, 35
Farmers, 21
Federations of labor, local, 85, 141, 149
Fielder, James F., 35, 114
Fifteenth Amendment, 156
Fitzgerald, Davey, 38, 145
Fitzgerald, John F., 7, 11, 36, 68, 69, 123, 152, 195
Fitzsimmons, Frank, 39, 139
Flinn, William S., 9, 19, 22
Flynn, Ed, 33, 38, 47, 233
Foley, James, 33, 50, 94
Foraker, Joseph B., 19, 20, 21
Ford, Cornelius, 52, 54, 55, 81, 89
Foreign stock, 71
Foss, Eugene, 36, 66, 69, 87, 96, 128, 148
French Canadians, 8, 10, 17

Gainer, Joseph, 39, 183
Gateway amendment, 150
Geran Bill, 143
Germans, 43, 164, 182, 183–84, 185, 217
Ghetto, American, 46
Glynn, Martin, 37, 93, 142, 146, 149
Gompers, Samuel, 48, 50, 59, 66, 83, 84, 85, 89, 149
Gospel, Social, 42–43, 168, 170
Government intervention by, 83; and redress, 215; regulation by, 92
Governor, power of, 149, 206
Grange, 198

Great Depression, 12, 197, 228, 233; federal action, 231
Green, Theodore Francis, 39, 132
Green, William, 56, 59, 129, 130
Greenlund, Carl, 34, 56, 106, 125, 192

Hague, Frank, 122, 124
Harmon, Judson, 34, 56, 111, 125
Harrison, Carter, 28, 30–31, 95, 159
Hatters case, 81, 88
Hearst, William Randolph, 31, 93
Historians, interpretations and evaluations, 209, 211, 213, 215; liberal, 212
Holidays, religious, 175
Home rule, 135–39
Homesteading, 70
Hoover, Herbert, 98
Housing, 3, 28, 69, 70
Howe, Frederic C., 25, 210
Hughes, Billy, 81, 207
Hughes, Charles Evans, 37, 50, 93, 111, 112, 116, 125

Igoe, Michael, 37, 105
Illinois, 15, 20–21, 37, 60–65, 85–86, 89–90, 95–96, 100–101, 104–5, 111, 121, 124, 126–27, 136, 137–38, 139–40, 155, 159, 180, 185–86; and Prohibition, 189–91
Immigrants, 1–6, 23–24, 35, 44, 46, 71, 181, 218; female, 158; influx, 47; Jewish, 46; and reform, 195, 201–2; restriction, 196, 198, 227; self-improvement, 196; superpatriotism, 183
Independents, 25
Industrial code, 58
Industrialization, 218
Industry, problems of urban, 186
Initiative, 139, 142
Injunctions, 88, 90
Insurance, 100; fire, 98, 100; old-age, 55; regulation, 100, 102; social, 70
Integration, social, 6
Intellectuals, 213, 236
International Workers of the World, 83, 182

Irish, 2, 6–7, 8, 9, 10, 21, 25, 30, 36, 37, 39, 52, 65, 68, 69, 101, 123, 144, 164; and labor, 87; and woman suffrage, 160
Italians, 39

Jews, 45, 46, 165, 169
Johnson, Hiram, 28, 30, 204, 227, 231, 234
Johnson, Thomas L., 28, 29, 32, 34, 43, 56, 90, 204, 210, 227
Jones, Samuel, 21, 28, 29, 32, 204
Judges, election, 148
Judson, Stiles, 116, 141, 174
Juries, reform of, 123
Justice, social and industrial, 43

Knights of Labor, 82
Know-Nothings, 7, 180
Kopplemann, Herman, 39, 103
Ku Klux Klan, 224, 227
Kulturkampf, American, 163–97

Labor, 22; boards, 58; child and female, 55, 56, 57–58, 62, 68, 71, 72, 75, 77–78; conditions, 28, 49, 63, 91, 97; and elections, 84–85; hours, 52–53, 57–58, 62, 67, 70, 71–72, 76; local federations, 64, 65; and management, 80; as political cipher, 83; radical groups, 84; as real ruling class, 61; rights of, 86, 91; and welfare, 56–57
Labor movement, 60
La Follette, Robert, 121, 223, 231
La Guardia, Fiorello, 184, 231
Laissez-faire, 92
Laws, employers' liability, 52; primary, 143; radical, 142
Legislation, ameliorative, 74, 210; antidiscriminatory, 184; antitrust, 98; class, 51; direct, 134, 139, 140–42; health and safety, 49; reform, 37, 125, 149–50; regulatory, 99–103; socioeconomic, 56, 60–61; unemployment, 64; welfare, 42, 47, 65–66, 70, 71, 202, 205, 231
Legislatures, 38
Levy, Aaron J., 98, 184

Liability, employers', 65
Liberalism, 213; bread and butter, 42–79; Democratic, 35; dimensions, 198–239; discovery, 236; elitism and radicalism, 236; emergence, 1–41; leaders' accounts, 208; middle class, 238; national, 207; negative, 171; parameters, 205; persistence of, 231; perspective, 225; and Progressive Era, 215–16, 230–31, 235; rise of, 228–31; role, 225–27; roots, 206; urban new stock, 54–55, 56, 221, 222; and working class, 239
Liberty, personal, 31, 171
Liquor, licensing, 193
Literacy tests, 181–82, 184
Lobbying, 131–32
Lodge, Henry Cabot, 21, 160
Lomasney, Martin, 4, 5, 7, 36, 69, 70, 87, 96, 101, 108–9, 123, 128, 145, 148, 151, 157, 160, 180, 181, 182, 196, 208, 233
Lorimer, William, 37, 143, 155
Lower class, 28, 203; voting, 120
Loyalty issue, 184
Lusk Committee, 184

Machines, 5, 18, 19, 30, 122, 209; and Democrats, 223; and direct primary, 142–44; European traditions, 213; evaluation, 209; and immigrants, 4, 5; and liberals, 214; origin and purpose, 228–30; and patricians, 132; and patronage, 126; politicians, 32; and reform, 29, 121, 133, 135, 204, 215; Republican, 30; and social aid, 47; success, 133; urban, 228–30; and woman suffrage, 156–57, 161; and working class, 229
Magee, Christopher Lyman, 9, 19
Mahan, Bryan, 39, 75
Mahon, John J., 33, 203
Management, 83
Markets, 174; bureau of, 100
Massachusetts, 15, 17, 36, 65–70, 81, 87–88, 96–97, 108–9, 114–15, 135, 138, 141, 144, 145, 148, 151, 154, 180–81, 182, 193; and reform, 230
Masses, 134, 209; goals, 215; new stock, 40; and reform, 203, 204–5
McCue, Martin, 188, 191
McDonough, John, 39, 75, 128, 138
McMillan, James, 20, 21
McNeil, Arch, 39, 88, 141
Mellon tax proposals, 231
Michigan, 20, 121; age of reform in, 29
Middle class, 27, 43, 104, 119, 204, 212, 218, 227, 236; leadership, 129; motivation, 200; and New Deal, 234; and new stock lawmakers, 209; old stock, 195, 216; Protestant, 169–70; reformist, 135; as uplifting, 196
Migrations, mass, 164–65
Miners, 56, 60, 63, 82
Monopoly, 101
Morality, 168
Mortality rate, 71
Mother's Pension Law, 56
Mugwumps, 25, 33
Murphy, Charles Francis, 7, 11, 27, 31, 38, 47, 86, 113, 157, 158, 204, 210

Nativism, 163, 164–65
Neebe, Frederick, 39, 88
New Deal, 12, 38, 42, 197, 231; goals, 235; and Progressive Era, 230, 233; status revolution, 235; support for, 232
New England, 8, 13–17, 36, 38–39
New Freedom, 92, 208, 217
New Immigrants, 2, 8, 10–11, 25, 165, 169, 173, 189; votes, 172
New Jersey, 15, 19, 23, 31, 35, 51–56, 81, 89, 94, 98–99, 113, 122, 123–24, 127, 130–31, 143, 150, 160–61; and Prohibition, 192
New Nationalism, 92, 217
New Nativism, 165–66
New stock lawmakers, 40, 52, 70, 78, 80, 91, 98, 135, 205, 221,

226, 231; and cultural and moral reform, 163–65; and democratic government, 149; and Democrats, 1; and direct legislation, 139–42; and immigration restriction, 181; and political reform, 151; and Prohibition, 194–95; and social conditions, 206; and woman suffrage, 156, 157, 161

New York (state), 15, 16, 18, 37–38, 81, 85, 93, 98, 111, 124–25, 129, 131, 136, 137, 149, 152, 158, 176–77, 184–85, 204; and Prohibition, 191–92; and reform, 230

New York State Factory Investigation Committee, 48

Nineteenth Amendment, 151, 156, 157–58, 205

Norris, George W., 121, 223

Nugent, James R., 33, 35, 94, 123, 124, 143, 160

O'Connell, William, 179, 181

Officeholding, 184; dual, 150

O'Gorman, James, 113, 207

O'Hara, Barratt, 37, 61, 208

Ohio, 15, 19–20, 21, 30, 34, 56, 81, 90–91, 94–95, 105–6, 111, 124, 125–26, 129–30, 136–37, 140, 143, 149, 155–56, 178, 210; and Prohibition, 192–93; welfare in, 56–58

Old Immigrants, 2, 8, 82, 165, 189

Old stock lawmakers, 39

Old World, 44, 45

Orientals, 165

Orphans, 78

O'Sullivan, Patrick, 88, 129, 132

Parochial schools, 179, 196, 227; state aid, 180

Patricians, 26–27, 28, 119–20, 121

Patronage, 120, 122

Pennsylvania, 21–22

Penrose, Boies, 10, 19, 22

Pensions, 51, 55, 59, 61, 69, 76, 78

Perkins, Frances, 31, 48, 85, 157, 207, 210

Pietism, 166, 167–68, 197; militant, 172; mores and values, 178; personal, 178; rural, 170

Pingree, Hazen, 9, 21, 27–28, 29, 43, 121, 204, 227

Plunkitt, George Washington, 16, 32, 126

Pluralism, cultural, 163–97

Political system, revamping, 118–62

Politicians, urban, 122

Politics, 4–6; and compromise, 220; free enterprise, 32; innovation in, 118; and native reformer, 214

Population, 2, 13–14

Populists, 121, 198

Pothier, Aram, 10, 17, 107

Power, political, 162

Prices, discrimination, 101; regulation, 98

Primary, direct, 133, 135, 142–46, 161

Private schools, 180

Progressives (party), 22, 36, 43, 61, 86, 110, 141, 216; life of, 222; officials, 199–200; profiles, 216

Progressivism, 30; achievements, 217; agrarian interpretation, 198–99; anxieties and prejudices, 212; coalitions, 220, 235, 238; and cultural issues, 163–97; and cultural reform, 195–96; defining values, 216; and Democrats, 34, 38–40; fate of, 218; goals, 235; government intervention, 92–103; in industrial states, 42; key to impulse, 196; and liberalism, 215–16, 230–31; local, 207; and machines, 34; and manners and morals, 171, 195, 197; motivation, 200; multiple movement, 216–17, 218; and New Deal, 231; new style, 231; in New York, 37–38, 48–52; objectives, 218; in Ohio, 99; record of, 209; and reform, 47, 118–19,

161; second decade, 91; on state level, 34; and taxation, 103–17; and unionism, 91; urban roots, 199, 207, 235; and welfare, 66, 78–79

Prohibition, 20, 26, 28, 38, 40, 140, 186–97, 206, 224, 227; and business, 188; enforcement, 196; as ethnic issue, 189; repeal, 197

Property qualifications, 16, 146–47, 150, 160

Protestantism, 1, 3, 20, 25, 43, 162, 164, 212; and Prohibition, 186; and Republicans, 8

Provincialism, politics of, 199

Public schools, 178, 196; and immigrants, 179; and minorities, 194

Public service commissions, 97

Public utilities, 93; municipal ownership, 95; regulation, 93–97; state commissions, 93–97

Public works, 74; superintendent, 100

Purchase and distribution, public, 98

Puritans, 45, 164, 167, 172, 211

Quay, Matthew, 9, 19
Quinn, Arthur, 35, 81
Quota system, 196

Railroads, 54, 60, 63, 76, 90, 95, 97, 101; commissions, 96; rates, 101

Ratification, 151–56, 193, 194

Reapportionment, 13, 15, 137–39, 150

Recall, 142

Recreation, 173, 177

Red Scare, 182, 183, 184, 227

Referendum, 139, 142, 150, 151

Reform, 40; and big business, 201; Democratic, 18; electoral, 35; impulse, 25, 91; leaders, 199; in Massachusetts, 36, 65–70; middle class, 221; most profound, 109; in Ohio, 57–60; organization and technique, 162; patrician, 26–27, 47, 121; po-

litical, 119; power, 214; and professionals and intellectuals, 200; and progressivism, 78–79, 161; shift of middle class from, 227; socioeconomic, 28, 33; urban, 123

Reformer-individualist-Anglo-Saxon complex, 201

Registration, 135; voting, 145

Religions, 164, 166–71; denominations, 168; and Prohibition, 187

Rent, 76

Reorganization, governmental, 124

Representation, 132

Republicans, 7; alliance with Democrats, 19; and apportionment, 15; and Catholic voters, 236; coalition, 12–13; complexity of party, 171; conservatism, 151; and handling of issues, 238; jamming new bills, 149; and labor, 21, 22, 36, 67, 69, 89; leaders, 9–10; liberals, 25; and minorities, 11; and moralistic reform, 172; "New Idea," 31, 94, 192; new stock, 24; in Northeast, 16; orientation, 19; as party of morality and temperance, 171; party of wealthy, 238; and popular elections, 152, 154; and power companies, 93; probusiness, 30, 74, 78, 132; and Progressive Era, 12, 20; and Prohibition, 172, 186; and property qualifications, 16; Protestant, 8, 171; and reform, 66; and small towns, 152, 153; and tax, 106, 109–10; and vested interests, 107; and voting qualifications, 147; working class members, 236; and workman's compensation, 73; and work week, 71–72

Responsibility, social, 210

Retirement, 59, 61

Revenue, 105

Revisionists, 79

Rhode Island, 14, 16, 39, 71–74,

88–89, 97, 102, 107–8, 115, 131, 132, 135, 137, 138–39, 144, 148, 150, 153, 158, 159–60, 174–76, 178, 182, 183, 193–94

Ritualism, 166–67, 197

Roosevelt, Franklin D., 38, 113, 176, 181, 202, 210, 232, 234

Roosevelt, Theodore, 18, 22, 84, 85, 92, 110, 182

Roraback, J. Henry, 17, 74, 75, 110, 116, 128, 138, 140, 147, 153, 173

Ruef, Abe, 9, 30

Sabbatarianism, 20

Saloons, 187

Secret ballot, 120

Securities, commissioner, 100; regulation, 103; tax, 109

Senate, as bastion of privilege and reaction, 152

Senators, direct election, 120, 135, 151; selection, 155

"Seven Sisters" laws, 98

Seventeenth Amendment, 151, 156, 205

Short ballot, 120

Slavery, 164

Small towns, 134–35, 152

Smith, Al, 11, 12, 15, 32, 33, 38, 47, 48, 86, 93, 109, 112, 113, 124, 125, 137, 149, 157, 158, 184, 185, 195, 203, 208, 210, 222, 223, 224, 227, 233

Smith, James, 7, 33, 35, 127, 143, 223

Socialists, 61, 79, 103, 180, 217

Spellacy, Thomas J., 38, 39, 76, 81, 88, 116, 131, 138, 141, 147, 173

States, industrial, 222; positive action by, 103

Status revolution, 121, 225, 235

Street railways, 99

Strikebreaking, 88, 90

Strikes, 82, 87, 88, 90

Suffrage, 3–4, 119, 158–61; males, 146, 147; reasons behind, 161; restricted, 146; woman, 120, 135, 156–61

Suffragettes, 156

Sullivan, Mark, 52, 127

Sullivan, Roger, 7, 33–34, 37, 95, 105, 143, 152, 159

Sullivan, Tim, 142, 181, 207

Sulzer, William, 37, 38, 51, 85, 142, 151

Sunday, 194, 206; observance, 172; work, 174

Taft, William Howard, 84, 111, 182

Taggart, Thomas, 7, 152

Tammany, 5, 16, 18, 26, 31–32, 34, 37, 47, 48, 85, 86, 93, 113, 126, 129, 136, 149, 158, 181, 184, 191, 202, 204, 210

Tariff, 74

Taxation, 103–17; corporate, 107, 109; general property, 109; income, 108, 109, 116, 205; in Massachusetts, 108; personal, 108; reform, 106

Teachers, 59, 61, 69

Temperance, 165

Textbooks, free, 180

Triangle factory legislation, 226

Triangle Shirtwaist Factory fire, 48, 49

Trusts, 92, 98

Truth in advertising, 100

Tumulty, Joe, 32, 33, 35, 52, 127, 207

Two-traditions argument, 214

Underprivileged, 30, 42

Unemployment, 28, 54

Unionism, 46, 78, 80–91, 204, 227; arbitration and conciliation, 91; bargaining, 90; and Democrats, 84, 87–91; immigrant members, 81–82; and Irish, 85; leaders, 66; and management, 91; organization, 90; and political action, 83–91; strengthening, 80

Upper class, 119; and cities, 170–71; and reform, 201

Urbanites, new stock, 46

Urbanization, 218

Urban lawmakers, 91

Vare, Edwin, 9, 19, 22

Vice and gambling, 26, 28, 168

Voting, 5, 6, 16, 135; Catholic, 237; female, 160; foreign, 159; urban, 134; waiting period, 184; working class, 134

Wages, 54, 58, 66, 97; minimum, 50, 54, 59, 61, 66, 70, 72

Wagner, Robert F., 32, 33, 38, 48, 81, 86, 93, 98, 112, 113, 131, 152, 176, 184, 203, 208, 210, 222, 231, 233, 234

Walker, Jimmy, 33, 50, 98, 108, 129, 178

Walsh, Allan, 35, 81, 123

Walsh, David I., 32, 36, 66, 68, 69, 97, 101, 123, 148, 151, 152, 195, 203, 207, 208, 222, 231

Welfare, 22, 56–57, 66, 109; major issues, 78; state, 42–79; worker support, 47

West, Albert, 39, 107, 149, 175

Whigs, 7

White, William Allen, 224, 228

Whitlock, Brand, 19–20, 25, 28, 29, 211

Whitman, Charles, 18, 20, 86, 178, 191

Widows, 78

Willis, Frank, 20, 106

Wilson, Charles, 102, 146

Wilson, Woodrow, 35, 52, 53, 55, 85, 92, 98, 113, 123, 130, 143, 160, 182, 203, 223, 224, 237; betrayal, 227

Women's Christian Temperance Union, 172, 186, 189, 191

Women's rights movement, 156

Working class, 22–23, 31, 44, 45, 82, 90, 103, 121, 227, 236; Catholics and Jews, 170; and machines, 229; and middle class liberals, 239; and New Deal, 234; numbers, 205; and Prohibition, 187; and religion, 170; and Republicans, 12; skilled, 71; as social problem, 198; views, 211; voting, 147, 223; and woman suffrage, 157–58

Workman's compensation, 50, 74, 77, 202

Work week, 71–72

World War I, 182, 187

Yankees, 38, 135; ethnic split, 193; reformers, 200

"Yellow dog" contracts, 88